7/08

Best Day Trips from London

25 Great Escapes by Train, Bus or Car

3rd Edition

by Stephen Brewer & Donald Olson

WILEY

Wiley Publishing, Inc.

Published by:

Wiley Publishing, Inc.

111 River St.
Hoboken, NJ 07030-5774

ISBN 978-0-470-18195-9
Editor: Ian Skinnari
Production Editor: Suzanna R. Thompson
Cartographer: Andrew Murphy
Photo Editor: Richard Fox
Production by Wiley Indianapolis Composition Services

Front cover photo: The Long Walk and Windsor Castle.
Front and back cover inset photo: Cotswolds cottage exterior.

For information on our other products and services or to obtain technical support, please contact our Customer Care Department within the U.S. at 800/762-2974, outside the U.S. at 317/572-3993 or fax 317/572-4002.

Wiley also publishes its books in a variety of electronic formats. Some content that appears in print may not be available in electronic formats.

Manufactured in the United States of America

5 4 3 2 1

Contents

Appendix A: England in Depth 205

by Darwin Porter & Danforth Prince

Appendix B: England's Art & Architecture 216

by Reid Bramblett

Appendix C: Useful Toll-Free Numbers & Websites 227

Index 232

List of Maps

An Invitation to the Reader

In researching this book, we discovered many wonderful places—hotels, restaurants, shops, and more. We're sure you'll find others. Please tell us about them, so we can share the information with your fellow travelers in upcoming editions. If you were disappointed with a recommendation, we'd love to know that, too. Please write to:

Frommer's Best Day Trips from London, 3rd Edition
Wiley Publishing, Inc. • 111 River St. • Hoboken, NJ 07030-5774

An Additional Note

Please be advised that travel information is subject to change at any time—and this is especially true of prices. We therefore suggest that you write or call ahead for confirmation when making your travel plans. The authors, editors, and publisher cannot be held responsible for the experiences of readers while traveling. Your safety is important to us, however, so we encourage you to stay alert and be aware of your surroundings. Keep a close eye on cameras, purses, and wallets, all favorite targets of thieves and pickpockets.

About the Authors

Stephen Brewer writes about England, Ireland, Italy, Greece, and other parts of the world for Frommer's and many other guidebooks and magazines. He is the author of *The Unofficial Guide to England* and *The Unofficial Guide to Ireland,* both published by Wiley. He is also the author of *Frommer's Venice Day by Day,* and was pleased to be a contributor to Wiley's recent *Dream Vacations.* Even though he would join Samuel Johnson in the belief that only someone suffering from general existential angst could ever grow tired of London, he never fails to be amazed by all the fascinating places to be enjoyed on easy day trips from the capital.

Donald Olson is a novelist, playwright, and travel writer. His seventh novel, *Memoirs Are Made of This* (written under the nom de plume Swan Adamson), was published in 2007 by Hodder Headline in the U.K. His plays have been produced in London, New York, Amsterdam, and Rotterdam. Donald Olson's travel stories have appeared in the *New York Times* and many other national publications. He is the author of *Frommer's Vancouver & Victoria, London For Dummies, Germany For Dummies,* and *England For Dummies,* which won the 2002 Lowell Thomas Travel Writing Award for "Best Guidebook."

Other Great Guides for Your Trip:

Frommer's London

Frommer's Portable London

London For Dummies

Frommer's England

England For Dummies

The Unofficial Guide to England

Frommer's Star Ratings, Icons & Abbreviations

Every hotel, restaurant, and attraction listing in this guide has been ranked for quality, value, service, amenities, and special features using a **star-rating system.** In country, state, and regional guides, we also rate towns and regions to help you narrow down your choices and budget your time accordingly. Hotels and restaurants are rated on a scale of zero (recommended) to three stars (exceptional). Attractions, shopping, nightlife, towns, and regions are rated according to the following scale: zero stars (recommended), one star (highly recommended), two stars (very highly recommended), and three stars (must-see).

In addition to the star-rating system, we also use **five feature icons** that point you to the great deals, in-the-know advice, and unique experiences that separate travelers from tourists. Throughout the book, look for:

Finds	Special finds—those places only insiders know about
Fun Fact	Fun facts—details that make travelers more informed and their trips more fun
Kids	Best bets for kids and advice for the whole family
Moments	Special moments—those experiences that memories are made of
Tips	Insider tips—great ways to save time and money

The following **abbreviations** are used for credit cards:

AE American Express	DISC Discover	V Visa
DC Diners Club	MC MasterCard	

Frommers.com

Now that you have this guidebook to help you plan a great trip, visit our website at **www. frommers.com** for additional travel information on more than 3,600 destinations. We update features regularly to give you instant access to the most current trip-planning information available. At Frommers.com, you'll find scoops on the best airfares, lodging rates, and car rental bargains. You can even book your travel online through our reliable travel booking partners. Other popular features include:

- Online updates of our most popular guidebooks
- Vacation sweepstakes and contest giveaways
- Newsletters highlighting the hottest travel trends
- Online travel message boards with featured travel discussions

The Best Day-Trip Experiences

*E*xcuse us while we drag out those wise and oft-quoted words from Samuel Johnson yet again: When you grow tired of London you've grown tired of life. Well, they're true. In all our years of traveling, we've never grown tired of London, and we doubt that you will, either. On the contrary, London rewards the repeat visitor with an inexhaustible array of things to see and do.

The countless treasures in its museums, the centuries of history in its landmarks, the energy and innovativeness of its arts and culture scene, and the slices of British life glimpsed on the streets all increase your yearning to return and explore more of this fascinating city.

But a trip to London can include more diverse sights and scenery than you ever thought possible. In a small country such as England, historic castles, picture-perfect villages, ancient cathedrals, and unforgettable landscapes are often no more than an hour away—close enough for you to easily visit as part of your London itinerary.

You may be surprised to discover just how much of England you can explore using London as a base. That is what this book is all about. We've rounded up our 25 favorite places in England that you can visit on easy day trips from London. You can reach all of them by train, bus, or car; enjoy a day's outing in a fascinating place; and be back in the capital in time for dinner and a play. Some of our day trips are only 20 minutes away from central London and can be reached by the London Underground. The farthest, York, is 195 miles (314km) to the north but you can get there in 2 hours on a fast intercity train.

DAY TRIPS MADE EASY

For each day-trip destination, we tell you how to get there, how long the journey takes, and what it costs. We provide you with all the practical information you need to know, such as admission fees and opening hours. We suggest a day's itinerary and plot it all out on a map for you. In addition, we give you tips on dining and shopping and other details to help you get the most out of your day away from London. We want to make sure that you don't miss the Tiepolo painting in Leeds Castle, that you visit Sissinghurst Gardens at a time when you can enjoy them without a crowd, that you follow the best walking route when exploring the ancient town of Rye.

England

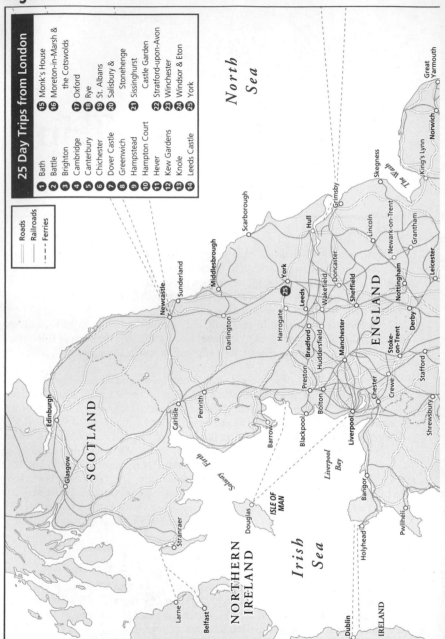

25 Day Trips from London

1. Bath
2. Battle
3. Brighton
4. Cambridge
5. Canterbury
6. Chichester
7. Dover Castle
8. Greenwich
9. Hampstead
10. Hampton Court
11. Hever
12. Kew Gardens
13. Knole
14. Leeds Castle
15. Monk's House
16. Moreton-in-Marsh & the Cotswolds
17. Oxford
18. Rye
19. St. Albans
20. Salisbury & Stonehenge
21. Sissinghurst Castle Garden
22. Stratford-upon-Avon
23. Winchester
24. Windsor & Eton
25. York

Roads
Railroads
Ferries

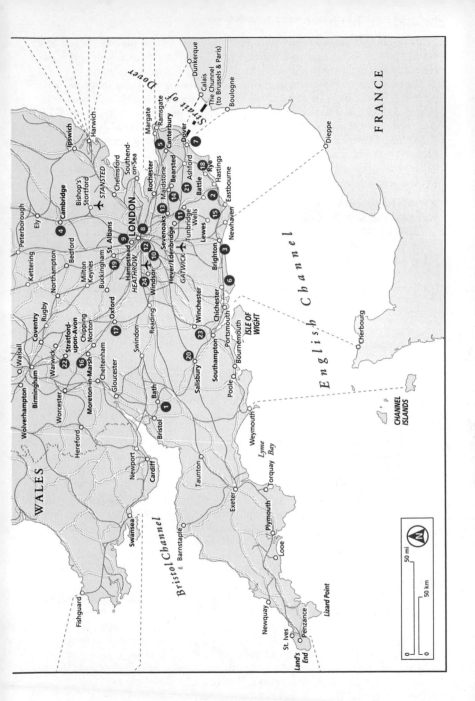

In "Planning Your Day Trips," you'll find general information on traveling in and out of London, including special passes that will bring down the cost of your trips. Following that, we devote a chapter to each of our 25 day-trip destinations.

There are a lot of trips to choose from, and each one is intriguing in its own way. All of them are worth a day of your time. What are your interests? Would you like to visit Monk's House, Virginia Woolf's country retreat near the Sussex Downs? Walk down the time-hallowed nave of 800-year-old Canterbury Cathedral? Stroll through a charming Cotswolds village where the cottages are built of honey-colored stone? Explore enormous Windsor Castle, the queen's favorite royal residence?

There are trips for every interest in this book. To help you narrow down your choices, here are some of our favorites, organized by category.

1 The Best Castles & Palaces

- **Brighton Royal Pavilion** ✸✸✸   The Royal Pavilion in Brighton is one of the most flamboyant royal residences you'll ever see. Designed for the fun-loving prince regent (later George IV), who lived here with his mistress until 1827, it's an extravagant fantasy of turrets, minarets, and Chinese motifs. See p. 45.

- **Dover Castle** ✸✸✸   The so-called "Key to England" has stood guard over the English Channel since Roman times. The sprawling fortification atop the famous White Cliffs has an ancient lighthouse, medieval tunnels, and even a secret underground compound. See trip 7.

- **Hampton Court** ✸✸✸   Henry VIII nabbed Hampton Court from its builder, Cardinal Wolsey, and turned it into a royal residence, which it remained until 1737. This enormous palace is glorious fun to explore, with rooms and kitchens dating back to Henry's Tudor times and separate suites designed by Christopher Wren for William and Mary in the early 18th century. See trip 10.

- **Hever Castle** ✸✸   This vision of crenellations and turrets, surrounded by a moat, fits anyone's notion of what a medieval castle should look like. The fact that Anne Boleyn, wife of Henry VIII, grew up at Hever gives the place historical clout, and former tenant William Waldorf Astor, the American millionaire, added acres of luxurious gardens. See trip 11.

- **Knole** ✸✸   Knole is officially a "house" rather than a "palace," but with 365 rooms and a courtyard for every day of the week, we think this 15th-century treasure qualifies as the latter. As you explore rooms filled with rare furnishings, textiles, and fine paintings, you'll see why Virginia Woolf, who set her novel *Orlando* here, described Knole as a "town rather than a house." See trip 13.

- **Warwick Castle** ✸✸✸   Thousand-year-old Warwick Castle, easily accessible from Stratford-upon-Avon (and described in our Stratford day trip), is one of the most popular tourist attractions in England. It features lavishly furnished rooms peopled with historic figures created by the wax experts at Madame Tussaud's, plus a real dungeon and lots of side attractions. See p. 178.

- **Windsor Castle** ✸✸✸   You've no doubt heard of Windsor Castle—it's one of the queen's royal residences. Now about 900 years old, Windsor is the largest inhabited castle in the world and has its own Changing of the Guard ceremony. On a self-guided tour of the State Apartments, you can visit the intimate chambers of Charles II and the enormous Waterloo Chamber, built to commemorate the victory over Napoleon in 1815. See p. 192.

2 The Best Cathedrals & Churches

- **Canterbury** 🕈🕈🕈 The first Gothic cathedral in England, Canterbury traces its history back to the arrival of St. Augustine in the 6th century. It became such a famous place of pilgrimage in the Middle Ages that it inspired Geoffrey Chaucer to write *The Canterbury Tales* about a group of Canterbury-bound pilgrims. It's an awe-inspiring sight inside and out. See p. 64.

- **Chichester** 🕈🕈 One of England's finest Norman structures is a magnificent expanse of light-colored stone, stained glass, arches, and vaulting. Exquisite Romanesque statues and a 20th-century window by Marc Chagall are among this mighty cathedral's treasures. See p. 72.

- **King's College Chapel, Cambridge** 🕈🕈🕈 When you visit the most beautiful of the university's many churches and chapels, you may be lucky enough to hear the acclaimed choir in a stunning setting embellished with a magnificent ceiling of carved stone and an altarpiece by Peter Paul Rubens. See p. 55.

- **St. Albans** 🕈🕈 St. Albans wasn't officially made a cathedral until 1877, but it had been in existence hundreds of years before that. This venerable church has its roots in Anglo-Roman history, for it was built near the site where Roman soldiers executed Alban, considered the first English martyr. Like Canterbury, St. Albans was a medieval mecca, drawing pilgrims to the shrine of St. Alban, which you can still see today. See p. 156.

- **Salisbury** 🕈🕈🕈 Built in the 13th century in record time, just 38 years (hundreds of years shorter than the construction time of most other cathedrals), Salisbury Cathedral is a soaring masterpiece of Gothic style and has an architectural integrity you won't find in many other churches. The edifice is topped by England's tallest spire. In the Chapter House are two national treasures: a copy of the Magna Carta and a beautifully preserved medieval stone frieze depicting stories from the Old Testament. See p. 164.

- **Winchester** 🕈🕈🕈 Before the Norman Conquest of 1066, Winchester was the capital of Anglo-Saxon Wessex and was more important than London. That importance is reflected in mighty Winchester Cathedral, a Norman-influenced structure that is the final resting place of 12 English kings (including William II, son of William the Conqueror). Begun in 1079, it has the longest nave in Europe and is the repository of many historic treasures. See p. 184.

- **York** 🕈🕈🕈 York Minster is the largest Gothic structure north of the Alps, and one of the most beautiful cathedrals in the world. Over half of all the medieval stained glass in England is found in this cathedral, built between 1220 and 1472. Beneath the cathedral is a fascinating archaeological excavation of 2,000-year-old Roman remains. See p. 199.

3 The Best Literary Sites

- **Hampstead** The poet John Keats lived for 2 years of his short life in a charming house in Hampstead, where he wrote "Ode to a Nightingale" and fell in love with his neighbor's daughter. Open to the public, the Keats House is one of several fascinating homes you can visit in Hampstead. See trip 9.

- **Monk's House** 🕈🕈🕈 The novelist Virginia Woolf and her husband Leonard Woolf often retreated from their home in London's Bloomsbury to this simple house and garden in Sussex, near the town of Lewes. Here they entertained the writers, artists, and intellectuals who formed the "Bloomsbury Group." Virginia drowned herself in the nearby River Ouse in 1941. See trip 15.

- **Rye** ✦✦✦   The charms of Rye, with its ancient cobbled streets, have seduced many a writer. The great American writer Henry James became a British citizen and moved to Lamb House in Rye. After his death, Lamb House became the home of E. F. Benson, author of the brilliantly funny *Mapp and Lucia* novels. The house is now a National Trust property. See trip 18.

- **Stratford-upon-Avon** ✦✦✦   England's greatest playwright was born, lived much of his life, and died in this Warwickshire village. William Shakespeare is a hot commodity in Stratford, but even the commercialization doesn't diminish the awe of visiting the house where he was born and other places associated with his Stratford life. See trip 22.

- **Winchester** ✦✦   The ever-popular author, Jane Austen, died in Winchester and is buried in Winchester Cathedral. Her house in the nearby village of Chawton, 17 miles (27km) from Winchester, is filled with Austen memorabilia. See trip 23.

4 The Best Day Trips for Families

- **Dover Castle** ✦✦✦   England's mightiest fortress has just about anything a connoisseur of castles can dream of—a ring of walkable walls, a huge keep (complete with multimedia shows), dank dungeons, miles of secret tunnels, great views over the English Channel, and even a Roman lighthouse. See trip 7.

- **Hampton Court** ✦✦✦   Hampton Court is huge, and the littlest kids won't be much interested, but older kids (ages 10 and up) may get a kick out of the costumed guides who lead tours of the staterooms. Little ones may find the famous maze more frightening than fun, but kids 8 and older will probably love it. And have your children take a look at the Tudor Kitchens, set up in preparation for a 16th-century feast. There's nary a microwave in sight. See trip 10.

- **Leeds Castle** ✦✦   An incredible maze of 2,400 yew trees, a creepy grotto, a well-stocked aviary, beautiful grounds and gardens, and, oh yes, a castle to tour will make Leeds a big hit with all members of the family. See trip 14.

- **Windsor** ✦✦✦   The castle itself will probably be of less interest to kids than Queen Mary's dollhouse, an enchanting miniature palace complete down to the tiniest detail. But kids will have a blast at nearby Legoland, a huge adventure park with lots and lots of rides. See trip 24.

- **York** ✦✦✦   There's something Harry Potter–magical about York, with its medieval walls and ancient streets and snickelways (alleys). The kids will love Jorvik Viking Centre, an attraction where you sit in "time capsules" and ride back to the Viking age. The scenes of village life are based on archaeological research, and even the faces of the animatronic inhabitants are modeled on Viking skulls. Kids also love the National Railway Museum, filled with historic trains and climb-aboard locomotives. See trip 25.

5 The Best Historic Sites

- **Bath** ✦✦✦   British history comes alive in this elegant city, which traces its origins to the Romans and became a fashionable watering hole in the 18th century. The Roman baths are remarkably intact, and lining leafy squares and crescents are Georgian town houses of golden stone that are so well preserved that UNESCO has designated the entire city a World Heritage Site. See trip 1.

- **Battle** ⚜⚜⚜   Battle was the site of a battle that changed the course of English history. It was here, in 1066, that William of Normandy defeated King Harold of England and became the new king of England. Today you can walk on the very battlefield and hear the story of what happened—it's a real thrill for history lovers. See trip 2.
- **Canterbury** ⚜⚜⚜   Canterbury Cathedral is one of the most venerable and venerated buildings in England. Throughout the Middle Ages pilgrims flocked to the cathedral to pray at the shrine of Thomas Becket, archbishop of Canterbury, who was slain by henchmen of King Henry II. Becket's shrine is gone, but the cathedral and its medieval atmosphere remain. St. Augustine's Abbey, a short walk from the cathedral, is one of the oldest monastic sites in England, set up by Augustine in A.D. 598 when he was sent from Rome to convert the natives. Today these ancient, evocative ruins have been designated a World Heritage Site by UNESCO, as has Canterbury Cathedral. See trip 5.
- **St. Albans** ⚜   Back in the 1st century A.D., the town that is now St. Albans was a thriving Roman community called Verulamium. Within the walled city were temples, official buildings, town houses, even an amphitheatre. On a day trip to St. Albans, you can visit the excavated remains of the amphitheatre, the largest such structure from Roman Britain, and see an array of Roman mosaics and implements in the Verulamium Museum. See trip 19.
- **Stonehenge** ⚜⚜⚜   This circle of monolithic stones erected more than 4,000 years ago is one of the world's most alluring ancient sites. The purpose this massive landmark might have once served has been argued over for generations, but the efforts taken to build it, the obvious importance of the place, its evocation of societies long vanished, and its eerie beauty make it one of the world's most important archaeological sights. See p. 166.
- **Winchester** ⚜⚜⚜   In post-Roman, pre-Conquest England, this lovely Hampshire town was the capital of the kingdom of Wessex. The remains of a dozen Anglo-Saxon kings rest in mighty Winchester Cathedral. The town has associations with the mysterious King Arthur, too: Arthur's "Round Table" (likely a fake, but most visitors aren't deterred by that fact) has been displayed in the Great Hall of Winchester Castle for some 600 years. See trip 23.
- **Runnymede** ⚜   In this meadow 3 miles (4.8km) from Windsor (described in our Windsor day trip), King John was forced by his own feudal lords in 1215 to affix his seal to a document called the Magna Carta. The Magna Carta established the principle of the constitutional monarchy and affirmed the individual's right to justice and liberty. The American Constitution is based on it. See p. 195.
- **York** ⚜⚜⚜   This beautiful Yorkshire city, the best-preserved medieval city in England, is girded by high walls. On a visit to York, you can walk along the circuit of walls where sentries once stood watch and traitors' heads were placed on spikes. Going back further in time, you can discover the Viking side of York at Jorvik Viking Centre, an attraction that re-creates the city's Viking past. Stepping back even further, in the Yorkshire Museum you can see a wealth of artifacts from York's Roman period, dating back almost 2,000 years. See trip 25.

6 The Best Gardens

- **Hampton Court** ⚜⚜⚜   Hampton Court is a wonderland both inside and out. The gardens that surround the palace are a delightful mix of 500 years of royal gardening history. Marvel at the formal gardens with their symmetrically clipped trees, get lost in the famous Maze, and have a look at the Great Vine, the oldest grape-producing vine in the world. See trip 10.

- **Hidcote Manor Garden** &&&&& This series of outdoor rooms created by a wealthy American has influenced garden design for generations and remains one of the most enchanting corners of the Cotswolds. See trip 16.
- **Kew Gardens** &&&&& The official name is the Royal Botanic Gardens, but everyone calls them Kew Gardens. These 300 acres (120 hectares) of superbly landscaped grounds are within Greater London and can be reached on the Underground. Visiting Kew is like escaping into a gardener's dream. You'll find rare plants and gorgeous landscaping in dozens of separate garden areas and in the giant glasshouse conservatories. See trip 12.
- **Sissinghurst Castle Garden** &&&&& Now among the most famous gardens in the world, this evocative series of "outdoor rooms" planted amid the partially restored remains of a medieval castle and manor house are the creation of the poet and novelist Vita Sackville-West and her husband, the diplomat and writer Harold Nicolson. See trip 21.

7 The Best Trips for Museum-Lovers

- **Cambridge** &&& The **Fitzwilliam Museum** (p. 57), one of Britain's most important art collections, includes stunning collections of antiquities, medieval illuminated manuscripts, and a surprisingly large number of masterworks by artists ranging from van Dyck to Picasso. **Kettle's Yard** (p. 57), meanwhile, is a showcase of 20th-century art and design.
- **Chichester** &&& The **Pallant House Gallery** (p. 72), one of many notable attractions in this charming town, is one of the country's finest showplaces for modern British art, and works by Barbara Hepworth, Ben Nicholson, and Henry Moore hang in stunning galleries.
- **Greenwich** &&& Greenwich, designated a World Heritage Site by UNESCO, is awash in architecturally significant buildings and unusual museums. Explore the 19th-century clipper ship *Cutty Sark,* then step into the **National Maritime Museum** (p. 85) for a look at England's seafaring past. Next door you can enjoy the architectural and artistic delights of the **Queen's House** (p. 85), the first neoclassical building in England and used as a model for the White House. Afterward, climb the hill in Greenwich Great Park to the **Old Royal Observatory** (p. 85), where you can see the collection of gleaming chronometers that helped mariners establish longitude at sea; right outside the observatory is the Prime Meridian Line (longitude 0°), from which all time is measured.
- **Hampstead** &&& Palatial **Kenwood House** (p. 89) on Hampstead Heath contains a marvelous collection of paintings, including a Rembrandt self-portrait and Vermeer's *The Guitar Player.* **Fenton House** (p. 88), another Hampstead treasure-trove, contains a priceless collection of early keyboard instruments. Built in 1939 by the architect Erno Goldfinger as his home and office, 2 Willow Road is a rare example of the International Style. The Freud Museum, home of famed psychoanalyst Sigmund Freud from the late 1930s until his death, contains a collection of his books, letters, and antiquities.
- **Hampton Court** &&&&& The palace is filled with artwork, but our favorite paintings are on view in the **Lower Orangery** (p. 98). This is where you'll find a series

called *The Triumphs of Caesar* painted by Andrea Mantegna and completed in 1505. The series is considered one of the most important works of the Italian Renaissance. Hampton Court's **Renaissance Picture Gallery** (p. 96) contains 16th- and early-17th-century works by Lucas Cranach, Pieter Bruegel, Correggio, Bronzino, Titian, and others.

- **Kew** 𝕲𝕲𝕲   The Royal Botanic Gardens at Kew (called Kew Gardens) is a living museum of plants from around the world. Now over 250 years old, this 300-acre (120-hectare) site is so botanically important that UNESCO designated it a World Heritage Site. Wander the beautifully landscaped grounds and visit the extraordinary Victorian glasshouse conservatories. See trip 12.
- **Oxford** 𝕲𝕲𝕲   A visit to the world-class **Ashmolean Museum** (p. 143) is a highlight of a visit to one of the world's most famous universities. Casts of the Parthenon frieze and other antiquities, Islamic pottery and Chinese ceramics, and such masterpieces as Paolo Uccello's *Hunt in the Forest* are among the treasures.
- **York** 𝕲𝕲𝕲   York is filled with museums, but pride of place goes to the **National Railway Museum** (p. 202), where you can view the private train cars used by Queen Victoria in the 19th century and Queen Elizabeth II in the 20th. The **York Castle Museum** (p. 201) uses a trove of now-vanished everyday objects to re-create slices of life over the past 4 centuries. **York Art Gallery** (p. 202) displays 7 centuries of western European painting. The **Yorkshire Museum** (p. 202) provides a solid overview of Yorkshire's history from the Roman era up to the 16th century.

8 The Best Restaurants

- **Terre à Terre** 𝕲𝕲 **(Brighton)**   For a new take on vegetarian cuisine, try Terre à Terre in Brighton. If you're curious about meatless cuisine but put off by the same old same old vegetarian choices, this hip and popular restaurant will awaken your taste buds to new possibilities. See p. 50.
- **The Wells** 𝕲 **(Hampstead)**   A new restaurant in an old Hampstead house, The Wells is a great place for lunch, dinner, or a drink. The decor is sleekly contemporary but very comfortable, and the food is simple and satisfying without a lot of culinary frills. You can eat in the restaurant or choose from a bar menu. See p. 92.
- **Shelleys** 𝕲𝕲 **(Lewes)**   At Shelleys you can enjoy a gracious meal after reliving the lives of the Bloomsbury Group at nearby Monk's House and Charleston. In a handsome old country-house hotel, you'll be served innovative dishes that use local lamb, fish, and produce. See p. 130.
- **The Monastery (Rye)**   One of Rye's best restaurants serves up delicious English and Italian dishes in friendly, informal surroundings that include a garden for summer dining. See p. 152.

9 The Most Charming Villages

- **Hampstead** 𝕲𝕲   Though it's now part of Greater London, Hampstead was once a separate village, and it retains a village character to this day. Its old leafy streets and quiet lanes are filled with charming nooks and crannies and a medley of Regency and Victorian homes. You can visit several historic Hampstead homes on your day trip. Walk into the adjacent parkland of Hampstead Heath and you're in the country. See trip 9.

- **Moreton-in-Marsh** 🐑🐑   If you've come to England with a preconceived notion that Brits wear tweeds and live in charming stone cottages surrounded by green meadows, you'll be pleased to find yourself in this typical Cotswolds village. Plus, other charming villages are nearby, and the beautiful countryside may well lure you out for a long ramble. See trip 16.
- **Rye** 🐑🐑🐑   The spell of Rye, with its cobblestone streets lined with Tudor and Elizabethan houses, is hard to resist—and its charms are not lost on legions of visitors. Even so, this ancient town in East Sussex perched on a hilltop near the sea is a delight to explore. See trip 18.

10 The Best Places to Spend More than a Day

- **Bath** 🐑🐑🐑   Let your imagination run wild in this well-preserved 18th-century city. Consider what it was like to be a Roman legionnaire soaking in the Roman Baths; pretend that Number 1, Royal Crescent, a Regency-era town house-cum-museum, is your address; picture yourself attending a ball in the Assembly Rooms. Come evening, you can dine well in any number of excellent restaurants and attend a performance at the 300-year-old Theatre Royal, one of Britain's oldest working stages. See trip 1.
- **Brighton** 🐑   If you fancy a short stay at the seaside, you might want to consider an overnight stay in Brighton on the Sussex coast. England's most popular seaside retreat is charming in parts (especially its medieval lanes) and tacky in others (its amusement pier) but pulses with a lively resort atmosphere and up-to-the-groove nightlife. See trip 3.
- **Moreton-in-Marsh** 🐑   If London life has you craving a bit of bucolic R&R, you can do no better than this typical Cotswolds village of honey-colored stone in one of the most picturesque corners of England. You'll enjoy Moreton and other nearby villages, quaint inns, and the atmospheric wolds, the highland pasturelands where the region's famous sheep graze. See trip 16.
- **Rye** 🐑🐑🐑   Once you see Rye, you'll probably want to extend your stay. There are plenty of hotels and B&Bs in historic buildings, including the Mermaid Inn, one of the oldest inns in England. The town is noted for its fine restaurants, many of which specialize in seafood. For some scary fun, you can rent a "Ghost Walk" audio tour and explore the ancient streets at night. See trip 18.
- **Salisbury** 🐑🐑🐑   In this prosperous British cathedral city, a lively market spreads over medieval streets. The cathedral spire, the tallest in England, may look familiar—the scene was a favorite subject of landscape painter John Constable. You can easily spend a day or more seeing such sights as 18th-century Mompesson House and nearby Stonehenge, and you can also nip over to nearby Winchester (trip 23) to experience another wonderful cathedral city. See trip 20.
- **York** 🐑🐑🐑   The Queen of the North, as the historic walled city of York is called, has so much to see and do that you may want to prolong your stay. York Minster is the largest cathedral north of the Alps, medieval and Georgian streets and houses are well preserved, and you'll find any number of fine hotels and excellent restaurants, plus good shopping and 2 days' worth of sightseeing. See trip 25.

Planning Your Day Trips

*T*he range of day-trip options out of London is considerable, and sorting out the places you want to go and the logistics of getting to them takes both planning and patience. That's why we've filled this chapter with things you need to know before you head out, and some tips that might help you save some money as you travel. First, to help you zone in on day trips that will appeal most to you, we've included a chart listing various attractions and activities available at each destination (see below).

Once you've chosen some trips you think you'd like to make, we strongly suggest that you go to the relevant day-trip chapters and do some homework. Pay special attention to how long it takes to reach the various destinations and our advice on the minimum time to allot to a place; some spots (Hampton Court and Greenwich, just to name a couple) can easily be tackled as half-day excursions, allowing you to work several day-trip outings into your London vacation itinerary. Look also at our sections on scheduling considerations, which take into account such factors as seasonal closings.

In each of our 25 day-trip chapters, we also give you specific information to help you get to your chosen destination by train, bus, or car. In this chapter, you'll find more general information about each of these transportation options, as well as info on how to get around London and reach the various stations from which you'll be departing. Don't feel daunted by the many options available to you as a day-tripper from London: Once you start planning, you'll discover that one of the great pleasures of being in the capital is the ease with which you can get out of town!

1 When to Go: Day Trips for All Seasons

SPRING

English gardens are at their peak in spring. This is the time to enjoy the world acclaimed plantings at **Sissinghurst Castle Garden** and **Hidcote Manor** (in the Cotswolds), as well as the gardens at **Hever Castle** and **Leeds Castle.**

The sky stays light well into the evening, so you'll have extra time to get the most out of any day trip you make.

Day Trips at a Glance	Biking	Boating/River Excursions	Country Walks	Castle or Palace	Church or Cathedral	Historical/Archaeological Sites	Gardens	Charming Town or Village	Families	Literary Sites	Museums	Overnight Options	See page
Bath	✓	✓			✓	✓	✓	✓	✓	✓	✓	✓	p. 30
Battle					✓	✓		✓			✓		p. 39
Brighton			✓		✓			✓	✓		✓	✓	p. 44
Cambridge	✓	✓			✓	✓		✓	✓		✓	✓	p. 52
Canterbury	✓	✓			✓	✓				✓	✓	✓	p. 61
Chichester	✓		✓		✓	✓		✓			✓		p. 70
Dover Castle		✓	✓		✓			✓					p. 75
Greenwich		✓			✓			✓			✓		p. 82
Hampstead			✓					✓		✓	✓		p. 87
Hampton Court	✓	✓	✓	✓			✓	✓			✓		p. 93
Hever Castle			✓	✓	✓	✓	✓						p. 99
Kew Gardens		✓					✓		✓				p. 105
Knole			✓	✓			✓		✓				p. 112
Leeds Castle				✓			✓	✓	✓				p. 118
Monk's House & Charleston							✓	✓		✓		✓	p. 124
Moreton-in-Marsh/ Cotswolds	✓		✓				✓	✓	✓			✓	p. 131
Oxford		✓	✓				✓	✓	✓	✓	✓	✓	p. 138
Rye	✓		✓	✓	✓			✓		✓		✓	p. 147
St. Albans	✓		✓	✓	✓	✓					✓		p. 154
Salisbury & Stonehenge			✓		✓	✓		✓	✓			✓	p. 160
Sissinghurst Castle Garden							✓			✓			p. 169
Stratford-upon-Avon		✓	✓		✓	✓				✓		✓	p. 174
Winchester					✓	✓		✓		✓	✓		p. 182
Windsor & Eton	✓	✓	✓	✓		✓	✓		✓				p. 190
York		✓	✓		✓	✓		✓	✓		✓	✓	p. 197

SUMMER

All of England seems to move outdoors in summer, and you can enjoy the grounds of such houses and castles as **Knole, Monk's House** and **Charleston,** and **Windsor.**

Summertime weather also enables you to get the most out of a visit to **Battle, St. Albans, Stonehenge,** and other places where you'll spend a good portion of your time out-of-doors. And many cities, **Winchester** and **Salisbury** among them, host lively summer festivals.

You can include a long walk and other outdoor activities on your day-trip schedules—walk along the White Cliffs after visiting **Dover Castle,** punt along the River Cam in **Cambridge,** or bicycle through **Oxford.**

Kew Gardens, Greenwich, Hampton Court, and **Hampstead** provide welcome and handy retreats from the London heat. A day trip to **Brighton** can include a dip in the sea.

AUTUMN

The **Cotswolds** are especially alluring in the fall, when the air is crisp and forested hillsides are a carpet of color.

Crowds thin out, so you'll find it easier to enjoy such popular spots as **Bath, Canterbury, Stratford-upon-Avon,** and **York.**

WINTER

English towns are especially welcoming in the winter. With its cobbled lanes and cozy inns, **Rye** is an appealing place to spend a winter's day or an overnight. Wherever you go—whether you enjoy a country lunch in a **Cotswolds** village or nip into a **York** pub for a pint—you're likely to find yourself sitting in front of a roaring fire.

Many day-trip destinations provide a wealth of indoor activities to get you out of the winter chill—the museums and chapels of **Cambridge** and **Oxford,** the medieval monuments of **York,** the staterooms of **Hampton Court** and **Windsor,** the tunnels of **Dover Castle.**

CALENDAR OF SPECIAL EVENTS

If your visit to London coincides with one of the following events in our day-trip destinations, you may well want to go out of your way to take part in the festivities. For more about events throughout England, go to www.visitbritain.com.

February

Jorvik Festival, York, 2 weeks from mid-February to late February (Day Trip 25). Vikings retake the city, with costumed parades, mock battles, storytelling, song fests, food fairs, and more. For more information, call ✆ **01904/ 643211** or e-mail jorvik@york archaeology.co.uk.

March

Bath Literature Festival, Bath, early March (Day Trip 1). Some of the world's most acclaimed authors are on hand for readings and discussions of their works (✆ **01225/463231;** www. bathfestivals.org.uk).

April

The Shakespeare Season, Stratford-upon-Avon, early April (Day Trip 22). The Royal Shakespeare Company (RSC) opens its season, which runs through October, presenting works by the Bard on the stages of the Swan Theatre, Royal Shakespeare Theatre, and Courtyard Theatre. Contact the RSC (✆ **01789/403444;** www.rsc. org.uk) for information and schedules.

May

Brighton Festival, Brighton, most of May (Day Trip 3). The largest performing arts festival in Britain stages more than 400 events, bringing theatre, dance, classical music, opera, film, and other programs to venues around the city (✆ **01273/709709;** www.brightonfestival.org).

Glyndebourne Festival, Lewes, May through August (Day Trip 15). One of the world's most acclaimed opera festivals stages six productions, attracting the world's leading voices and legions of ardent fans to a stunning hall (✆ **01273/813813;** www.glynde bourne.com).

Bath International Music Festival, Bath, mid-May to early June (Day Trip 1). Classical and popular musicians from around the world perform in theatres and churches throughout this elegant and historic city (℃ **01225/ 462231;** www.bathmusicfest.org.uk).

Salisbury Festival, Salisbury, late May, early June (Day Trip 20). Classical music, theatre, jazz, films, and other events enliven the city for 2 weeks each spring (℃ **01722/332977;** www.salisburyfestival.co.uk).

July

Hampton Court Flower Show, Hampton Court, early July (Day Trip 10). The world's largest horticultural show features magnificent floral displays and show gardens. For information, contact the Royal Horticultural Society (℃ **0870/9063791;** www.rhs. org.uk).

Winchester Festival, Winchester, early July (Day Trip 23). Choral concerts in the city's famous cathedral, plays at the Theatre Royal, and other musical and theatrical events are on tap the first 2 weeks of the month (℃ **01962/ 877977;** www.musicatwinchester.co. uk).

Southern Cathedrals Festival, Chichester, Salisbury, and Winchester, alternating years, second part of July (Day Trips 6, 20, and 23). Choirs from the cathedrals of these three cities gather for concerts, candlelight recitals, and other events; the locale alternates between the three cities every year. For an up-to-date schedule and festival information, call ℃ **01722/555125** or check www.southerncathedralsfestival. org.uk.

Cambridge Folk Festival, Cambridge, late July (Day Trip 4). One of Europe's largest and most acclaimed celebrations of folk music brings together performers from around the world (℃ **01223/357851;** www. cambridgefolkfestival.co.uk).

August

Pride in Brighton and Hove, Brighton, first week in August (Day Trip 3). Brighton and adjoining Hove are the settings for one of Europe's largest gay pride celebrations, with a big parade and lively street parties. For more information, call ℃ **01273/ 775939** or go to www.brightonpride. org.

September

Balloon Festival, Leeds Castle, September (Day Trip 14). Scores of hot-air balloons lift off from the castle grounds and fill the skies over Kent. For more information on this event, contact the castle (℃ **01622/871117;** www.leeds-castle.com).

Cambridge Film Festival, Cambridge, September (Day Trip 4). One of Britain's most prestigious film festivals screens new works from around the world as well as vintage celluloid. For advance information visit **www. cambridgefilmfestival.org.uk**.

November

Guy Fawkes Night, Lewes and other towns and cities throughout England, November 5 (Day Trip 15). On this evening in 1605, Guy Fawkes and members of the Gunpowder Plot attempted to blow up Parliament in retaliation for anti-Catholic legislation; Fawkes and others were apprehended and executed, and now all of England commemorates the anniversary with fireworks and huge bonfires. The festivities in Lewes are the most enthusiastic and are preceded by a lavish, costumed procession. For further details, contact the Lewes District Council (℃ **01273/ 483448;** www.lewes.gov.uk).

London-Brighton Veteran Car Run, Brighton, first Sunday in November (Day Trip 3). Brighton is the end of the 50-mile jaunt down from London, and the streets fill with the vintage entries (© **01580/893413;** www.vccofgb.co.uk/lontobri).

December

Christmas Concert, Oxford, shortly before Christmas (Day Trip 17). Christ Church Cathedral is the setting for a concert in which the Cathedral Singers are joined by singers from around the world (© **01865/305305;** www.cathedralsingers.org.uk).

Festival of Nine Lessons and Nine Carols, Cambridge, December 24 (Day Trip 4). England's most noted Christmas service, broadcast around the world, features the voices of the King's Chapel Choir. You can contact King's College (© **01223/331313;** www.kings.cam.ac.uk) for further details.

Ice-Skating at Hampton Court (Day Trip 10). From the beginning of December through mid-January, you can skate on the banks of the Thames in the shadow of England's greatest Tudor palace (**www.hamptoncourt palaceicerink.com**).

2 Getting Around London

This guidebook is not about London; it's about day trips from London. But because you may be traveling within London to get to a train or bus station for the start of your day trips, we've provided the basic information you need in order to get around London by subway (Underground), bus, and taxi.

For general London travel information, contact **Transport for London** (© **020/ 7222-1234;** www.tfl.gov.uk). You can get free bus and Underground maps and buy Travelcards and bus passes (explained below) at any major Underground station or at the London Travel Information Centres in the stations at Euston, Liverpool Street, Piccadilly Circus, Victoria, and Heathrow Terminals 1, 2, and 3.

THE LONDON UNDERGROUND

London has the oldest and most comprehensive subway system in the world, and all of the city's train stations can be reached by subway. So can three of our day trips: to Greenwich, Hampstead, and Kew Gardens.

The subway is called the Underground or the "Tube." Thirteen Underground lines crisscross the city and intersect at various stations where you can change from one train to the next. On Underground maps, every line is color-coded, which makes planning your route easy. All you need to know are the name of your stop, the Underground lines that go there, and the direction you're heading. After you figure out which line(s) to take, look on the Underground map for the name of the last stop in the direction you need to go. The name of that last stop on the line is marked on the front of the train and often on electronic signboards that display the name of the arriving train. The signage within the Underground system is clear and helpful.

Most of the Underground system operates with automated entry and exit gates. You feed your ticket into the slot, the ticket disappears and pops up again, the gate bangs open, and you remove your ticket and pass through. At the other end you do the same to get out, but the machine keeps the ticket (unless your ticket is good for more than one trip, in which case it is returned to you). If you are using a Travelcard, your ticket will be good for multiple journeys. For 7-day Travelcards, you will be issued one of the new hard-plastic "Oyster" cards; Oyster cards look much like a credit card and are incredibly easy to use: Just touch the card to the panel at the entry and exit gates.

Central London Train Stations

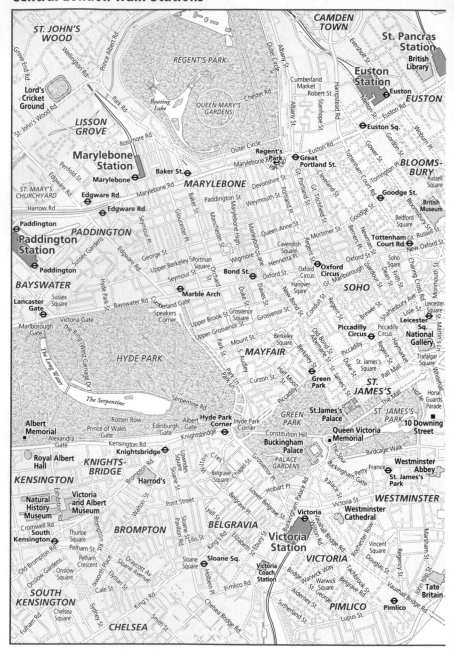

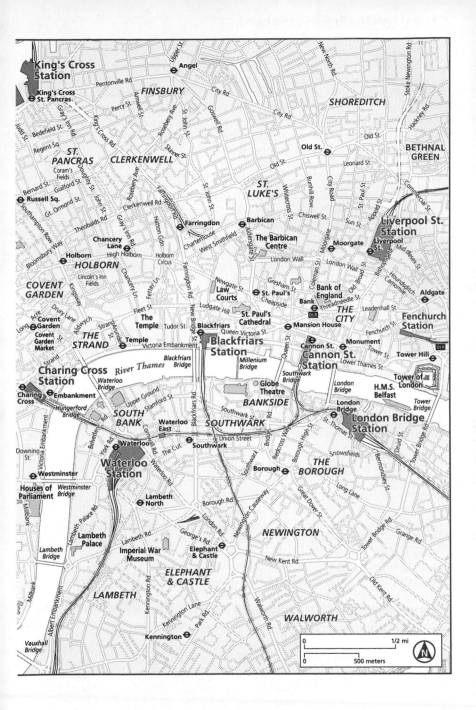

King's Cross Station
King's Cross
St. Pancras
Angel
FINSBURY
SHOREDITCH
BETHNAL GREEN
Old St.
ST. PANCRAS
CLERKENWELL
ST. LUKE'S
Russell Sq.
Moorgate
Liverpool St. Station
Liverpool St.
Farringdon
Barbican
The Barbican Centre
Holborn
Chancery Lane
HOLBORN
Aldgate
COVENT GARDEN
Law Courts
St. Paul's
Bank of England
THE CITY
Fenchurch Station
Covent Garden
Covent Garden Market
THE STRAND
The Temple
Temple
Blackfriars
St. Paul's Cathedral
Mansion House
Bank
Monument
Tower Hill
Cannon St.
Cannon St. Station
Charing Cross Station
Charing Cross
Embankment
River Thames
Blackfriars Station
Blackfriars Bridge
Millenium Bridge
Globe Theatre
Southwark Bridge
London Bridge
Tower of London
H.M.S. Belfast
Tower Bridge
Waterloo Bridge
Hungerford Bridge
SOUTH BANK
Waterloo East
BANKSIDE
SOUTHWARK
London Bridge
London Bridge Station
Waterloo
Southwark
Westminster
Waterloo Station
Waterloo North
THE BOROUGH
Houses of Parliament
Westminster Bridge
Borough
Lambeth Palace
Lambeth Bridge
Imperial War Museum
Elephant & Castle
NEWINGTON
ELEPHANT & CASTLE
LAMBETH
WALWORTH
Vauxhall Bridge
Kennington

0   1/2 mi
0   500 meters
N

Money in England

Britain's decimal monetary system is based on the pound (£), which is made up of 100 pence (written as "p"). The exchange rate used in this book is £1 = $2 (or $1 = 50p), though fluctuations are constant. Currency exchange services can be found in railway stations, at most post offices, and in many tourist information centers. Note, however, that you'll almost always get the best exchange rate by withdrawing funds from an ATM (automated teller machine) or using a credit card (though the latter may not be accepted in some stores and restaurants, so come prepared).

Traveling to your destination by Underground may require transferring from one Underground line to another. All Underground maps clearly show where various lines converge. Signs in the stations direct you from one line to another. To get from one line to another, you go through tunnels (which the Brits call "subways"), and you may have to go up or down a level or two. If, for instance, you are trying to get to Victoria Station from Russell Square, you'll need to take the Piccadilly Line toward Heathrow, then transfer at Green Park to the Victoria Line and travel in the direction of Brixton. The signage throughout the Underground system is clear, simple, and easy to follow.

Underground service stops around midnight (a little earlier on less-used lines); keep that in mind if you plan on arriving back in London on a late train.

Security throughout the Underground system increased dramatically following the terrorist attacks in July 2005. Please note that bags and backpacks may be subject to inspection by uniformed personnel and that unattended packages or suitcases are quickly reported and confiscated. You will also encounter many service disruptions and temporary closures, especially on weekends, as major improvements are made in preparation for the 2012 Olympics, to be held in London.

BUYING UNDERGROUND TICKETS

You can purchase Underground tickets at the ticket window in the station or from one of the automated machines found in most stations. (Machines can change £5, £10, and £20 notes, and some take credit and debit cards.) Tickets are valid for use on the day of issue only.

For fare purposes, the city is divided into six zones. **Zone 1** covers all of central London. **Zone 6** extends as far as Heathrow to the west and Upminster to the east. Make sure your ticket covers all the zones you're traveling through, or you may have to pay a £10 ($20) penalty fare.

At press time, a **single-fare one-way ticket** within one zone cost a whopping £4 ($8). Yes, that's exorbitant and no, you don't have to pay it every time you hop on the Underground. Instead, buy a multiuse Travelcard or Oyster card and save a bundle.

SAVING WITH TRAVELCARDS & THE OYSTER

Paying a full-price one-way fare every time you use the Underground is costly. To save money, consider buying a Travelcard, which allows unlimited travel by Underground and bus, or an Oyster, about the size of a credit card and easy to use—you just swipe it over an electronic pad when entering and leaving the Underground or a bus. Not only will you save money with either option, but you'll enjoy the freedom of nipping around London without worrying about paying each time you step onto a bus or the Underground.

You can purchase **Travelcards** at any Underground station ticket window, or from vending machines that take credit cards. At press time, the following Travelcards were available:

- A 1-Day Travelcard for **Zones 1 and 2** (everything in central London) costs £6.60 ($13) for an adult and £3.30 ($6.60) for children 5 to 15. A card valid only during **off-peak** hours (after 9:30am weekdays, all day Sat–Sun, and public holidays) costs £5.10 ($10) for adults.
- A 1-Day Travelcard for **all zones** costs £13.20 ($26) for adults and £6.60 ($13) for children. The **off-peak** versions cost £6.70 ($13) for adults and £2 ($4) for children.
- The 3-Day Travelcard for **Zones 1 and 2**, good for travel on any 3 consecutive days, costs £16.40 ($33) for adults and £8.20 ($16) for children.
- A 3-Day Travelcard for **all zones** costs £39.60 ($79) for adults and £19.80 ($40) for children. The **off-peak** version costs £20.10 ($40) for adults and £6 ($12) for children.
- The 7-Day Travelcard for **Zones 1 and 2**, which is issued as an Oyster, is valid at all times and costs £23.20 ($46) for adults and £11.60 ($23) for children.
- A 7-day Travelcard for travel in **all zones**, also issued in Oyster form, is £43 ($86) for adults and £21.50 ($43) for children.

While the **Oyster** entitles Londoners all sorts of discounts, travelers can benefit, too. When you buy an Oyster at any ticket window in any denomination, you automatically get substantial discounts every time you travel. The cost of a trip on the Underground, for instance, drops from £4 ($8) to £1.50 ($3), and bus fare from £2 ($4) to 90p ($1.80). What's more, the daily amount you spend is automatically capped at 50p ($1) less than what you'd pay with a Travelcard—that is, no matter how much you travel, you will spend less than you will with a Travelcard.

Using Your All-Zone London Travelcard for Day Trips

As a day-tripper, you might find the Travelcard more advantageous than the Oyster: We've discovered that it's often cheaper to buy an All-Zone London Travelcard and pay supplemental rail fares to day-trip destinations than it is to buy a multiday BritRail pass. The All-Zone card covers a very large area in and around London. You can use it to get to Greenwich, Hampstead, and Kew Gardens at no additional cost. For longer day trips, simply show your All-Zone Travel Card at the ticket window of a London train station and tell the clerk you want to pay the supplemental fare to your destination. This way, your fare does not begin until you reach the end of Zone 6. You can often get to places such as Knole, Hever Castle, Windsor, St. Albans, Dover, Lewes, and Brighton for less than £12 ($24) return, and the costs of some longer-distance day trips may also be reduced.

3 Day-Tripping by Train

The English still tour their country by train. We do, too, and we recommend the train over all other forms of transportation, especially if you're a first-time visitor to England. When all goes well, traveling by train is fun and convenient. In cities outside of London, the train stations are never more than a few minutes' walk or a simple bus ride from the town center.

That said, we feel obligated to tell you that the train system in the U.K. has seriously deteriorated since it was privatized in the 1980s. In fact, the British rail system is currently in something of a crisis and in the midst of a multibillion-pound, 5-year restoration plan scheduled for completion by the end of 2008. There have already been many improvements, but it's still true that trains are frequently canceled, departure tracks are changed without notice, service can be slow and sporadic (especially on Sun, a favorite day for day-trippers), and railway employees don't always have the correct information to help you on your journey (sometimes they barely speak English). Compartments in some of the commuter lines are full of litter, and on many local trains the windows are scratched so badly you can't see out.

All of our information, including fares, was correct at press time. But train information and fares in the U.K. change often, so we want to err on the side of caution and ask you to keep the following in mind:

- Always **call National Rail Enquiries** (© **08457/484950**) the night before your train trip to verify departure times and departure stations. Ask about any possible interruptions in service and how to avoid delays. For example, track work might delay trains to Dover from Victoria, though trains from Charing Cross might be running on time.
- Whenever possible, **choose a direct train** over one that requires a change along the way. In some cases, trains going to the same destination (such as Canterbury or Dover) depart from different London stations. From one station the train may go direct to your destination, but from the other it may not. It's always wise to ask National Rail Enquiries or information agents at the railway stations for the quickest and most direct routes to a destination.
- **Arrive at the station a few minutes early**—a half-hour early if you need to buy a ticket or have your BritRail pass (discussed below) validated.
- At the station, the departures board will tell you when your train is leaving (expect delays) and from what track. But **tracks can get switched without an announcement being made,** so always verify with a railway employee, before you board, that the train is going to your destination. Ask the employee at the gate or one of the conductors outside the train.
- When you reach your destination, **verify return times** to London. If there isn't a person at the ticket window, the departure times should be posted on a signboard outside or within the station.
- On some lines, Sunday is now one of the worst days to travel because there are fewer trains and they tend to be slow. Track work is often undertaken on Sunday, sometimes causing long delays or requiring that you complete part of the journey by bus. Be aware of these considerations and **try to leave London earlier in the morning** so you will have more time at your destination if you are delayed. We've been on trains where trips that should have taken 90 minutes turned into 3-hour marathons.

TRAIN TYPES

There is no longer one unified British Rail system. The system was privatized many years ago, and various train companies now service different routes and cities. The sleek, high-speed **intercity (IC) trains** that run along the heavily traveled, main-line routes out of London are the most dependable and the most comfortable trains you can take. You can ride these fast trains to York, Stratford-upon-Avon, and Bath. For shorter trips, such as to Brighton and Cambridge, you often take **commuter trains.**

In some cases you may need to transfer to an even smaller **local train** to reach your destination. The local trains connect larger towns to smaller ones and are very basic, without toilets or food service. These trains are sometimes not even staffed with ticket takers, so be sure you have all the information you need before you board. Smoking is not permitted on local trains, and is confined to strictly designated areas on commuter and intercity trains. To day-trip destinations such as Kew Gardens, Greenwich, or Hampstead, you can take the **London Underground.**

LOCAL STATIONS

At many of our day-trip destinations outside of London, the local train station is a small, one-person operation. Sometimes (particularly on Sun) no one is available to help with information or ticket sales, or the station closes down in the afternoon. You will always find train schedules posted in or just outside the station, but don't expect much in the way of services.

In these small local stations there are often only two tracks with an overpass to get from one side to the other. When you're returning to London, make sure you're on the correct side of the track. There is usually a sign telling you which side is for the London-bound train.

GETTING ON & OFF

Except on small local trains, an announcement is usually made before the train arrives at each station. Station stops are short, so be ready to disembark when the train comes to a halt. In newer trains, you push a well-marked button to open the door automatically. In older trains, you need to open the door yourself. It may open from the inside, or you may have to open the window and reach outside to turn the door handle. Remember, there might not be staff on board, so be sure you know exactly where to change and where to get off before you board your train in London.

SCHEDULING YOUR DAY TRIP

For the most current train schedules and fares, call **National Rail Enquiries** at ℰ **08457/484950** in the United Kingdom. You can also find timetable information and fare schedules online at **www.nationalrail.co.uk**. You can purchase tickets on this site, but you'll probably find it easier just to buy your tickets at the station. An exception, however, is in cases where a company that operates a long-distance route will offer a discount for online purchases on its site. This is where purchases get tricky, because operators and their rate structures change frequently; a call to National Rail Enquiries can usually help you sort out this complex system. Indeed, even if you find all the information you need online, you should also always call National Rail Enquiries before your journey to verify times and departure stations. Throughout this book we provide basic schedule information.

BUYING YOUR TRAIN TICKET

Before you board the train, purchase your ticket with cash or credit card at a ticket window or at one of the ticket machines in train stations (these take cash and credit/debit cards). If you have a BritRail pass (see "Using BritRail Passes," below), you must have it validated at a ticket window before your first journey. After that, you don't have to bother with buying tickets; just board the train. At the platform barrier you will have to feed your ticket through a turnstile or show your BritRail pass in order to enter. The same procedure applies at the end of the line, though very small stations have no turnstiles.

Different train lines use slightly different terminology and impose different restrictions, but generally speaking, in England a one-way train ticket is called a **"single"** and a round-trip ticket is a **"return."** If you go on a day trip, ask for a **day return.** After 9:30am you can often, but not always, get a **cheap day return;** you can also save money by buying your ticket in advance (these are usually called **"saver returns"**). In the chapters that follow, we list the cheapest fares available for same-day travel. When purchasing your tickets, be sure to ask if any time restrictions might affect your plans. Keep in mind, too, that sometimes the cheapest way to travel in a single day is to purchase two one-way (single) tickets.

When you buy your ticket, you must choose between **first** and **standard (second) class.** First-class tickets cost about one-third more than standard class. The first-class cars have roomier seats, but you can travel quite comfortably in standard class, and some commuter trains have no first-class cars. If you want a first-class ticket, you must request one—otherwise the agent will sell you a standard-class ticket.

First-class service on some intercity train routes includes free coffee, tea, beverages, and snacks served at your seat, plus a free newspaper and a higher standard of personal service. Standard-class passengers can buy sandwiches and drinks in a cafe car. On some lines an employee comes through with a food and beverage trolley.

Local trains do not offer first-class service or food service.

USING BRITRAIL PASSES

If you plan to travel around England extensively by train, consider purchasing a BritRail pass. These must be purchased before you arrive in England. BritRail passes are convenient because you don't have to stand in line to buy train tickets; if a train is in the station, you can just hop on. But if you're going to be in London for a week and making only one or two short day trips, it makes more sense to buy an All-Zone London Travel Card (see above) instead; this will provide unlimited transport within London and allow you to travel outside the capital for a relatively small supplemental fee. BritRail passes can be ordered through a travel agent or by contacting **Rail Europe** (© 877/272-RAIL [7245]; www.raileurope.com), or **BritRail** (© 866/BRIT-RAIL; www.britrail.com). Note that travelers from Australia, New Zealand, and Ireland cannot get passes through Rail Europe. The BritRail passes most pertinent to day-trippers are:

BritRail London Plus Pass   This pass is good for 2, 4, and 7 days of travel and covers a large area around London. It gets you to Cambridge, Oxford, Canterbury, Dover, Winchester, Salisbury, and everywhere in between—so, it will get you to many of the day trips in this book. But with costs, for example, of $113 for 2 days' first-class travel, you'll probably find it less expensive to buy individual tickets, depending on how many day trips you plan to take. If you're taking day trips to Hampton Court or Windsor, places closer to London, you'll be better off paying the regular train fares from London or getting a 7-Day All-Zone London Travel Card.

BritRail Flexipass   This pass allows you to travel any 4, 8, or 15 days within a 2-month time period. Dollarwise, it makes sense only if every one of your day-trip destinations is to a place some distance from London, such as Stratford-upon-Avon, Bath, York, or Moreton-in-Marsh. At press time, a 4-day, first-class Flexipass costs $436 for adults and $370 for seniors over 60; 4 days of second-class travel cost $293 for adults (no senior rate available). Children up to age 15 travel free with a ticketed adult. The Flexipass allows you to visit Wales and Scotland in addition to every place we list in this guide.

LONDON'S TRAIN STATIONS

London has 11 major train stations, so getting to the right station to catch your train is important. (Throughout this book, we always tell you which London station serves the particular destination we're describing.) The Underground (subway) serves all of London's train stations. In every station, a large overhead display, usually near the platforms, lists the departing trains and platforms.

Below we list our day-trip destinations after the stations from which you'll most likely be departing, but please note: It's sometimes possible to use more than one station, and service may change depending on day of the week, track work, and other considerations. It's always a good idea to check with **National Rail Enquiries** at © **08457/484950** before setting off.

If you're day-tripping from London, you'll depart from one of the following stations (you can locate each station on the "Central London Train Stations" map on p. 16):

Charing Cross Station   Trains from here travel southeast to Battle, Canterbury, Dover, Rye, Staplehurst (for Sissinghurst), and English Channel ports that connect with ferry service to the Continent.

Euston Station   Trains from this station head to St. Albans and north to the Lake District and up to Scotland.

King's Cross Station   Trains from here travel to St. Albans and destinations in the east of England, including Cambridge and York.

Paddington Station   Trains from Paddington travel southwest to Windsor and Bath and northwest to Moreton-in-Marsh, Oxford, and Stratford-upon-Avon.

Victoria Station   Head here for trains traveling to the south and southeast of England, including Bearsted (for Leeds Castle), Brighton, Canterbury, Hever, Lewes (for Monk's House and Charleston), and Sevenoaks (for Knole).

Waterloo Station   This station is primarily for trains going to the south of England, including Hampton Court, Salisbury, Winchester, and Windsor. Waterloo Station is connected to Waterloo International, the terminal at which Eurostar trains used to arrive from and depart for Paris and Brussels; the newly refurbished and reopened St. Pancras station now serves as the terminus for the Eurostar.

TRIPPING BY COACH (BUS)

A long-distance touring bus in England is a **coach.** Buses are what you take for local transportation. The main, long-distance coach company is **National Express** (© **0990/ 808080;** www.nationalexpress.com). Their bus routes cover the entire country, and their comfortable coaches are equipped with reclining seats, a toilet, and often a food and beverage service. Tickets usually cost half of what the train fare costs, and are even cheaper if you buy a return ticket. The one drawback, at least for the busy day-tripper without much time, is that coaches may take twice as long as the train—if the train is running on time, that is.

If you travel by coach from London, you'll depart from **Victoria Coach Station,** Buckingham Palace Road (© **020/7730-3466;** Tube: Victoria), located just 2 blocks from Victoria Station. Coach stations in cities outside of London are always close to the city center, often next to the train station.

National Express offers several **Brit Xplorer passes** for unlimited travel on their extensive network, which covers all of England. A 7-day pass costs £79 ($158); a 14-day pass costs £139 ($278), and a 28-day pass costs £219 ($438). The passes are a money-saving option if you plan to travel fairly extensively, and to venture far afield from London on your day trips (for example, to Moreton-in-Marsh, York, Bath, Salisbury, Stratford-upon-Avon, or Winchester).

4 Day-Tripping by Car

We strongly recommend that people making day trips from London, especially first-time travelers, travel by train or coach (bus) instead of by car. Much of a car trip can be spent on motorways without much scenery, so what's the point? Most of our day trips are localized adventures in one place or town and don't require any driving. Our subsidiary sights—Stonehenge, say, which is 9 miles (14km) from Salisbury—can easily be reached by bus or taxi from the primary day-trip destination.

But having a car does open up regions of the English countryside for deeper exploration. In areas such as the Cotswolds, where trains do not serve villages and where local bus service is sporadic or infrequent, having a car can be handy. And if you're exploring several of the houses, gardens, and castles of Kent and Sussex, you can reach them more easily by car than by train or coach.

However, in most instances, a car is only a cost-effective and reasonable alternative to public transportation if you plan to group several of our day trips into a road trip on which you visit multiple destinations and spend a night or two outside the capital. For instance, you might want to rent a car at Gatwick Airport, drive from there to Knole and Hever Castle, then spend the night in Rye, with a visit the next day to Sissinghurst and Battle. Or you may want to drive from Heathrow Airport to Salisbury (with a stop at Stonehenge en route), and use that city as an overnight base from which to visit Wilton House, as well as nearby Winchester and Chawton, before you return to London. Or you might want to rent a car at Heathrow and drive west to Oxford for the night, make a stop at Blenheim, then continue on to Bath the next day before settling for the night in the Cotswolds. While our focus in this book is on day trips, we do mention places that might warrant an overnight stay, and we recommend our favorite hotels in each.

Overall, though, for your single day-trip excursions outside of London, trains and buses are far better options than cars. Even if you plan on visiting two or more of our day-trip destinations in a single day—combining Sissinghurst and Rye, for instance—you'll still find it less expensive and just as quick to travel by train. Remember that you can always hire a taxi to meet you at a train station and take you to a great house or garden or castle in the country. In every day-trip chapter, we give you the local numbers for taxi companies.

BEFORE YOU RENT A CAR

Driving in England requires real skill and dexterity, and it's not for the faint of heart. If you are a nervous driver at home in your own car, do not put yourself through the ordeal of driving in England. Before you even consider renting a car, ask yourself if you'd be comfortable driving with a steering wheel on the right-hand side of the vehicle while shifting with your left hand. (You can get an automatic, but it costs considerably more.) Remember, you must drive on the left and pass on the right. Two essential rules for drivers are: Always look to the right, the direction from which oncoming traffic will approach; and, to ensure you're on the left side of the road, make certain that the center of the road is to your right.

RENTING A CAR

Do yourself a favor: Forget about renting a car in London. Driving in the city is an endurance test, and given the fact that drivers are now assessed a daily £8 ($16) "congestion charge" to use a car in central London, it can be incredibly expensive as well. Add, too, the hassle and cost of parking, which can be upwards of £30 ($60) a day. If you want to travel with Londoners on their own turf (or in their own tunnels), the Tube (Underground) is a great way to go. If you want a car to explore the countryside, you can rent one for the day, either at Heathrow or Gatwick airports, or in a hub city or town after you arrive. It's a good idea to reserve the car before you arrive.

Americans, Canadians, Australians, and New Zealanders renting a car in England need a valid driver's license from their home country that they've had for at least 1 year. In most cases, depending on the agency, you must be at least 23 years old (21 in some instances, 25 in others) and no older than 70. (Some companies have raised the maximum age to 75.)

RENTAL CAR COSTS

The price of renting a car depends on a host of factors, including the size of the car, the length of time you keep it, where and when you pick it up and drop it off, and how far you drive it. Asking a few key questions can save you money. Here are some factors to keep in mind when renting a car in England:

- You can often get a lower car-rental rate if you reserve 7 days in advance using a toll-free reservations number.
- Find out if the quoted price includes the 17.5% VAT (Value-Added Tax).
- A rental package with unlimited mileage is usually your best option.
- Weekend rates may be lower than weekday rates.
- Don't forget to mention membership in AAA, AARP, frequent-flier programs, and trade unions. These usually entitle you to discounts ranging from 5% to 30%. Ask your travel agent to check any and all of these rates.
- Most car rentals are worth at least 500 miles (800km) on your frequent-flier account.
- Some airlines offer package deals that include car rental.
- Be prepared for high petrol (gas) prices; you may be paying almost three times what you would in the U.S., for example.

INSURANCE FOR CAR RENTALS

On top of the standard rental prices, other optional charges apply to most car rentals. The **Collision Damage Waiver (CDW),** which limits your liability for damages caused by a collision, is covered by many credit card companies if you pay with their credit card. Check with your credit card company before you go so you can avoid paying this fee (as much as $15 per day).

The car rental companies also offer **additional liability insurance** (if you harm others in an accident), **personal accident insurance** (if you harm yourself or your passengers), and **personal effects insurance** (if your property is stolen from your car). If you have insurance on your car at home, you're probably covered for most of these unlikelihoods. If your own insurance doesn't cover you for rentals, or if you don't have auto insurance, you should consider these additional types of coverage.

Although not as common a practice as in the United States, some companies in the U.K. also offer **refueling packages,** in which you pay for an entire tank of gas upfront. The price is usually fairly competitive with local gas prices, but you don't get credit for any gas remaining in the tank. If you reject this option, you pay only for the gas you use, but you have to return the car with a full tank or face costly per-gallon charges for any shortfall. If you think that a stop at a gas station on the way back to the airport will make you miss your plane, then by all means take advantage of the fuel purchase option. Otherwise, skip it.

CAR RENTALS ON THE WEB

As with other aspects of planning your trip, using the Internet can make comparison-shopping for a car rental much easier. All the major booking websites—**Expedia** (www.expedia.com), **Frommer's** (www.frommers.com), **Travelocity** (www.travelocity.com), and **Yahoo! Travel** (http://travel.yahoo.com), for example—have search engines that can dig up discounted car rental rates. Just enter the size of the car you want, the pickup and return dates, and the city where you want to rent, and the site returns a price. You can even make the reservation through these sites.

WHERE TO RENT A CAR

Note: For contact details on major car rental agencies operating in Britain, see appendix C.

You'll save yourself time, bother, and expense if you rent a car at one of London's two major airports, Heathrow or Gatwick. Both are connected to the city by excellent public transportation: You can reach Heathrow on the Underground for a basic fare of £4 ($8); or you can reach it on the **Heathrow Express,** which makes the trip from Paddington Station in just 15 minutes for £13 ($26) standard class. The **Gatwick Express** connects Victoria Station with Gatwick Airport in a half-hour; the fare is £15.50 ($31) standard class.

From both airports you can easily get onto the M25, the ring road that encircles London, and from the M25 you can easily access the major roads leading to all parts of the country. When renting a car for airport pickup, be sure to ask where the facility is located and how you can reach it—some agencies are located far from the terminals and do not provide shuttle service, making them difficult and costly to reach.

Alternatively, you may want to take a train to a major city outside London and rent a car there. However, options can be limited in all but major cities.

MOTORWAYS, DUAL CARRIAGEWAYS & ROUNDABOUTS

What is commonly known as a freeway in some countries, the Brits call a **motorway** (indicated as "M" plus a number on maps). A two-way road is a **single carriageway,** and a four-lane divided highway (two lanes in each direction) is a **dual carriageway.** Country roads, some of them paved-over tracks dating back centuries, are full of twists and turns and are often barely wide enough for two cars to pass.

One element of British roads that invariably throws non-native drivers is the **roundabout**—a traffic junction where several roads meet at one traffic circle. On a roundabout, the cars to your right (that is, those already on the roundabout) always have the right of way.

On certain sections of the motorway, where speeding is especially dangerous, speed cameras have recently been installed. The cameras take a photograph of any car exceeding the speed limit so the police can trace the culprit. You will see a camera symbol upon entering these areas. Surveillance cameras have also been installed at some traffic lights to catch anyone who runs a red.

Before you arrive in England, or before you leave on your car journey, find and purchase a good-quality, large-scale road map with a scale of 3 miles to 1 inch or 2km to 1 centimeter.

RULES OF THE ROAD

You need to know some general facts if you're going to drive in England.

- In England, all distances and speed limits are shown in miles and miles per hour (mph). If you need to translate from the metric system, a kilometer is .62 of a mile, and a mile is 1.61km.
- Speed limits are usually:
  30 mph (48kmph) in towns
  40 mph (65kmph) on some town roads where posted
  60 mph (97kmph) on most single carriageway (two-way) roads
  70 mph (113kmph) on dual carriageways and motorways
- Road signs are usually the standard international signs. Buy a booklet (available at many shops and in airports) called Highway Code for about £1 ($2) before you set out, or visit **www.highwaycode.gov.uk**. The information in the booklet and on the website is essential for driving in England.
- The law requires you to wear a seat belt. If you have children, make sure that you ask the car rental agency about seat belts or car seats before you rent.
- At roundabouts, traffic coming from the right has the right of way.
- You can pass other vehicles only on the right.
- Parking in the center of most towns is difficult and expensive. Make sure you read all posted restrictions, or park in a lot.
- You must stop for pedestrians in cross walks marked by striped lines (called **zebra crossings**) on the road. Pedestrians have the right of way.

EMERGENCIES ON THE ROAD

All motorways have emergency telephones stationed about .6 miles (1km) apart. The phone operator will obtain emergency or automotive services if you require them. If you must pull over to the side of the motorway, park as close to the far edge of the shoulder as possible. Motorway service stations are usually about 25 miles (40km) apart and occasionally as far as 50 miles (81km) apart.

FILLING THE TANK

Petrol (gasoline) stations are self-service. The green filler pipe is for unleaded petrol, the red filler pipe is for leaded petrol, and the black filler pipe is for diesel fuel. Petrol is often cheapest at supermarkets, but going to a motorway service station is more convenient. Petrol is purchased by the liter (3.78 liters equals 1 gal.). Expect to pay about 95p ($1.90) per liter (more than $7 per gal.) for unleaded petrol.

5 Traveling Locally from Your Destination

USING LOCAL BUSES

In some of our day trips we list major attractions that are several miles from the principal day-trip destination. To reach these places—Jane Austen's House in Chawton, for instance, which is 17 miles (28km) from Winchester—your best bet is a taxi or a local bus. We provide current local bus information whenever possible, but it's important for you to double-check times and services at the local tourist information center (in Winchester, for example, if you're going to Chawton). Local bus service is reliable, but local timetables may not suit your schedule.

If your train station is a little way from the town center and you don't want to walk, there will almost always be a local bus that travels between the station and the center of town. Have some pound and smaller coins with you because drivers usually won't take bank notes.

TAKING A TAXI

To reach subsidiary sites from some of our primary day-trip destinations, you can save yourself a lot of time and bother by taking a taxi instead of waiting for a local bus or renting a car. But in only one of our day trips, to Monk's House (Virginia Woolf's country home in Rodmell, Sussex) and nearby Charleston (Vanessa Bell and Duncan Grant's house), is it necessary to take a taxi if you want to see both places in 1 day.

In the "Getting Around" section in every day trip, we provide the numbers for local taxi companies. Reserve a taxi in advance, or you may have to wait for an hour or more once you arrive at the train station. Our general experience with local taxis is that the fare usually falls between £8 ($16) and £15 ($30) per ride.

RENTING A BICYCLE

England is a wonderful country for cycling. Though it may be difficult to fit a bicycle journey into your day-trip itinerary, it's not impossible and it can add a lot to your enjoyment of a region. If there is a particularly charming, scenic, or interesting bike route in or around a day-trip destination, we tell you about it under "Outdoor Activities." These are not 20-mile (32km) rides suitable only for serious cyclists, but easygoing jaunts. We'll also tell you where you can rent a bike locally.

ESCORTED TOURS

Maybe you only have time for a trip or two outside of London and don't want to bother with train schedules, admission hours, and other details. If so, an escorted tour can be an easy and cost-effective alternative to making day trips on your own. Keep in mind, though, that the ease of an escorted tour comes at a price—a loss of flexibility. On an escorted tour you won't be able to linger on the lawns at Leeds Castle or dawdle in front of a painting at Hampton Court if the coach is ready to pull out of the car park. Prices usually include admission fees as well as pickup in central London and at some central London hotels.

Below is a sampling of recommended tour companies that offer half- and full-day tours from London. For a list of others, visit the **Britain & London Visitor Centre,** 1 Lower Regent St., Piccadilly Circus, London W1, and Tourist Information Centres elsewhere around the country (or check online: in the "Visitor Information" section of each day trip, we list the "official" website, if one is available, for each town or major attraction). **VisitBritain (www.visitbritain.com),** the country's official tourist agency, is another good source of information: The main VisitBritain office for **North America** is at 551 Fifth Ave., Suite 701, New York, NY 10176-0799 (© **800/462-2748**). In **Australia:** Level 2, 15 Blue St., North Sydney, NSW 2060 (© **02/9021-4400**). In **New Zealand,** call © **0800/700-741;** phone and Web inquiries only. In **Ireland,** call © **0845/644-3010;** phone and Web inquiries only.

- **Astral Travels,** 72 New Bond St. (© **0870/225-5303;** www.astraltravels.co.uk), offers a sights-filled full-day tour of Stratford-upon-Avon, the Cotswolds, and Oxford for £75 ($150), and a trip to Canterbury, the Kent countryside, and Leeds Castle for the same price.
- **Sightseeingtours.co.uk** (© **0870/745-1046;** www.21stcenturytravel.co.uk) offers tours that include a full day in Bath and the Cotswolds, with a cream tea, for £67 ($134) adults and £60 ($120) children, and a day at Leeds Castle and in Canterbury and Kent for £64 ($128) adults and £54 ($108) children.

Traveler's Checklist

When setting out on a day trip, be sure you have:

- Your passport
- Your health insurance card
- A credit card other than those issued by American Express; many establishments outside London don't accept Amex
- An extra set of camera batteries, and enough film or extra memory cards for digital cameras
- AAA and AARP cards, student IDs, and other cards that might entitle you to discounted admissions
- Called ahead to verify that the establishments you plan to visit will be open
- Checked with National Rail Enquiries (and/or the appropriate bus company) to make sure there are no delays, cancellations, or schedule changes that will affect your trip

6 Saving Money on Admissions

If you plan to make several day trips and visit a number of historic properties, consider arming yourself with the **Great British Heritage Pass.** The pass gives you free entry to hundreds of properties throughout the U.K. that are associated with the National Trust and English Heritage, including a number in London and many of those we visit on our day trips. A shortlist of the properties you might visit is Blenheim Palace, Dover Castle, Fenton House in Hampstead, Hampton Court, Hever Castle, Mompesson House in Salisbury, Rochester Castle, the Roman Baths and Pump Room in Bath, Shakespeare's Birthplace in Avon, Sissinghurst Castle Garden, Stonehenge, Warwick Castle, Winchester City Mill, and Windsor Castle.

Prices: Four days, £28 ($56); 7 days, £39 ($78); 15 days, £52 ($104); and 1 month, £70 ($140).

Before you jump in and purchase the pass, check admission fees for the properties you might want to visit and do a little math. Fees vary but usually run between £6 ($12) and £12 ($24) per property. If you plan to visit only one or two properties, the pass is not cost-effective. If, however, you plan to make several trips out of London and visit four or more properties, the pass may provide a substantial savings. Remember, too, that many National Trust properties are closed November through March, so if you are visiting during those months, the pass may be of little use to you.

The pass is only available to nonresidents of the U.K., but it can be purchased before or after your arrival in Britain. In the U.S. and Canada, you can purchase the pass from travel agents, or through **Rail Europe** (© 877/272-RAIL [7245]). In Britain, you can purchase the pass from the **Britain & London Visitor Centre,** 1 Lower Regent St., Piccadilly Circus, London W1 (Tube: Piccadilly); or from Tourist Information Centres at airports, ports, and major cities throughout England. For more information about the Great British Heritage Pass, including a full list of properties, visit **www.britishheritagepass.com**; you can also purchase the pass online through this site.

Trip 1

Bath

*T*he Romans channeled Bath's hot, sulfurous waters into elaborate thermal pools some 2,000 years ago, and legend has it that the healing effects of the local springs were known to Celtic tribes a millennium before that. But it was 18th-century ladies and dandies who created one of England's most elegant and beautiful cities when they began coming to Bath to take the waters and enjoy the season in terraced houses on elegant squares and curving crescents. Among those who found themselves amid the city's swirling social milieu was Jane Austen, who lived here in the early 19th century. In the end, she didn't care for the place, but in the salons and ballrooms she found plenty of fodder for her novels of manners. These days, millions of visitors come to this city of soft, mellow stone—designated by UNESCO as a World Heritage Site—not to take the waters (although that can be done) but simply to enjoy Bath's unique beauty. The Roman baths where legionnaires once enjoyed their R&R and well-preserved 18th-century landmarks such as the Royal Crescent, one of the most distinctive assemblages of residential architecture in the world, and the Assembly Rooms, once the social epicenter of Bath, reflect the city's storied history. Jane Austen, Bath's most famous resident, is remembered with a museum and study center devoted to her work.

Bath is an ideal choice for a full-day trip from London—the train journey is only about 90 minutes, there are plenty of sights to fill a day, many places to enjoy a good lunch and tea, and you can be back in London in time for the theatre. There's enough to do and see in Bath to make it a good place for an overnight stop, too, and you might want to consider combining an overnight trip to Bath with a visit to the **Cotswolds** and **Oxford** (trips 16 and 17); see the last section in this chapter for hotel recommendations.

1 Essentials

VISITOR INFORMATION

The **Bath Tourist Information Centre** (*©* 01225/477-101; www.visitbath.co.uk) is in the center of town, in Abbey Church Yard. The center is open Monday to Saturday from 9:30am to 5pm and Sunday from 10am to 4pm.

Bath

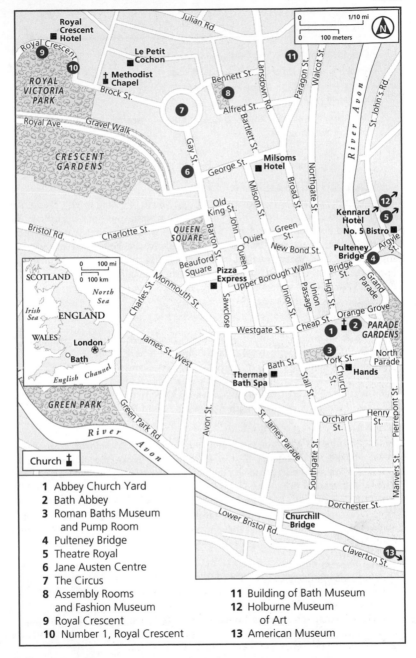

Church †

1 Abbey Church Yard
2 Bath Abbey
3 Roman Baths Museum and Pump Room
4 Pulteney Bridge
5 Theatre Royal
6 Jane Austen Centre
7 The Circus
8 Assembly Rooms and Fashion Museum
9 Royal Crescent
10 Number 1, Royal Crescent
11 Building of Bath Museum
12 Holburne Museum of Art
13 American Museum

Bath Highlights

- Exploring the ancient Roman baths.
- Strolling across shop-lined Pulteney Bridge.
- Visiting the Fashion Museum—one of the world's leading collections of historical couture.
- Admiring the elegant town houses of Royal Crescent, and touring Number 1, Royal Crescent.

SCHEDULING CONSIDERATIONS

Bath is a very popular weekend destination, so if you're planning to visit on a Friday or Saturday and spend the night, it's a good idea to reserve your hotel in advance. You might want to plan your visit to Bath to coincide with one of the many events the city hosts throughout the year. These include the **Bath Music Festival** in late May and early June, the **Jane Austen Festival** in September, and the **Mozartfest** in November. For information on these and other events in Bath, contact the **Bath Festivals Office** (© **01225/463-362**; www.bathfestivals.org.uk).

GETTING THERE

BY TRAIN

Trains run about every half-hour from London's Paddington Station to Bath Spa. The trip takes 90 minutes, with the first train departing at 6:30am and the last train returning to London at 10:52pm. The "Cheap Day Return" fare is £47 ($94). For information, call © **08457/484950** or go to www.nationalrail.co.uk. The Bath train station is at the south edge of the city center, off Dorchester Street, about a 5-minute walk down Manvers Street from Bath Abbey and Grand Parade.

BY CAR

Bath is 115 miles (185km) west of London. The M4 links London with Bath, and the trip usually takes about 2 hours. Most of the city center is closed to traffic, and much of the street parking is reserved for residents. It's easiest to use the city's Park and Ride facilities, well marked from entrance routes into the city; the most convenient when entering the city from the M4 from London is Lansdown, on the north side of the city. The facilities operate Monday through Saturday 7:15am to 7:30pm; parking is free. Buses to the city center leave about every 10 to 15 minutes and cost £1.50 ($3) return.

BY BUS

National Express buses leave London's Victoria Coach Station for Bath every hour, with some half-hourly departures. Travel times vary from 3 hours and 15 minutes for the direct trip to 4 or even close to 5 hours for trips that require a change. The day-return fare is £18 ($36). The bus station is on Manvers Street, near the train station. For more information, call © **08705/808080** or go to www.nationalexpress.com.

GETTING AROUND

City buses run from the train station to locations around town, but most places are within walking distance. There is a taxi rank outside the station, or you can call **AA Taxis** (© **01225/460-888**). The center is compact, and many streets are open only to pedestrian traffic, making it easy to get around Bath on foot. The easiest way to get from the south side of the city center (where Bath Abbey and the Roman Baths are located) to the north side (for the Assembly Rooms, Circus, and Royal Crescent) is to follow High Street north as it becomes Broad Street and Lansdown Road, then turn left (west) onto Bennett Street.

2 A Day in Bath

The lively center of the city is pedestrian-only. Start your tour at ❶ **Abbey Church Yard,** adjacent to ❷ **Bath Abbey** ✿ (✆ **01225/422-462;** www.bathabbey.org). This airy cathedral was established in the 8th century and was the site of the coronation of the first English king, Edgar, in 973. The Normans tore down the original and built their own massive cathedral here, but it was in ruins by 1499, when a new church was begun. That edifice succumbed to Henry VIII's dissolution of the monasteries in the mid–16th century, but Elizabeth I ordered it restored and the abbey was promptly rebuilt in the Gothic Perpendicular style, with a graceful fan-vaulted ceiling and large expanses of stained glass that fill the church with light; little wonder the cathedral is nicknamed the "Lantern of the West." Bath Abbey is open Monday to Saturday from 9am to 6pm (to 4:30pm in winter); on Sunday it's open from 1 to 2:30pm and 4:30 to 5:30pm. The suggested donation is £2.50 ($5).

Just across Abbey Church Yard is the ❸ **Roman Baths Museum and Pump Room** ✿✿✿ (✆ **01225/477-785;** www.romanbaths.co.uk), a bath complex built by the Romans that remains, in part, just as they left it. The springs in Bath were known and used by the Celts as long ago as 875 B.C. In A.D. 75 the Romans channeled the waters into a luxurious bathing complex that rivals any of the baths in Rome or elsewhere in Italy. A terrace overlooks the large pool where legionnaires once soaked in waters that continue to bubble forth at 116°F (47°C) at the rate of about 240,000 gallons a day. In a maze of subterranean chambers, which you navigate with the aid of excellent self-guided audio commentary, are the remains of steaming pools and saunas, surrounded by elaborate paving. Allow yourself at least an hour to see everything. The baths are open daily, but hours vary seasonally (Jan–Feb and Nov–Dec 9:30am–5:30pm; Mar–June and Sept–Oct 9am–6pm; July–Aug 9am–9pm; last admission is always 1 hr. before closing). Admission is £11.25 ($23) for adults, £8.70 ($17) for seniors and students, £6.50 ($13) for children 6 to 16, and £29 ($58) for families of up to two adults and two children. A combined ticket to the Roman Baths and the Fashion Museum (see below) costs £13.50 ($27) for adults, £11.50 ($23) for seniors and students, £8 ($16) for children 6 to 16, and £38 ($76) for families of up to two adults and four children. You can sample the famous waters in the adjacent 18th-century Pump Room (free with your admission ticket), though you may opt to sip coffee or tea to the musical accompaniment of a string trio instead.

The Grand Parade leads a few blocks north to ❹ **Pulteney Bridge** ✿✿, an 18th-century span over the Avon River modeled on the Ponte Vecchio in Florence—and like its Italian counterpart, lined with shops. Return to the west bank of the bridge and follow Upper Borough Walls Street through the city center to the ❺ **Theatre Royal** ✿✿ (✆ **01225/448-844;** www.theatreroyal.org.uk), one of Britain's oldest working stages. If you're unable to attend a performance, you might be around to join one of the tours on the first Wednesday of every month at 11am and every Saturday at noon; the fee is £3 ($6) for adults and £2 ($4) for children. The house next to the theatre was once the home of Beau Nash, an 18th-century arbiter of taste and a high-living gambler who is credited with putting Bath on the map as a fashionable watering hole (see "The Beau of Bath," below).

Gay Street leads north past Queen Square to the ❻ **Jane Austen Centre** ✿ (𝒞 **01225/443-000**; www.janeausten.co.uk), a rather dull but informative collection of text-heavy displays that honor the ever-popular novelist of late-18th- and early-19th-century manners. Jane visited Bath twice in the late 18th century and lived here from 1801 to 1806, drawing from her experiences for her novels; Bath figures prominently in *Persuasion* and *Northanger Abbey*. The most satisfying part of a visit is the gossipy introductory lecture; among the juicy information that you'll hear is how Jane came to loathe Bath, where she and her mother and sister fell upon hard times. The center is open daily 9:45am to 5:30pm in the summer (until 8:30pm Thurs–Sat July–Aug; Sun–Fri 11am–4:30pm and Sat 9:45am–5:30pm in the winter). Admission is £6.50 ($13) for adults, £4.95 ($10) for seniors and students, £3.50 ($7) for children 6 to 15, and £18 ($36) for families of up to two adults and four children. You'll need about 30 minutes to tour the entire museum.

From the Jane Austen Centre, Gay Street continues north to ❼ **The Circus** ✿, where three semicircular terraces of Regency town houses surround a circular park. The Circus was designed by noted architect John Wood the Elder (responsible for much of Bath's 18th-c. development) in the prevalent neoclassical style; note the symmetry and classical columns reminiscent of Imperial Rome. The ❽ **Assembly Rooms and Fashion Museum** ✿ (𝒞 **01225/477-789**; www.fashionmuseum.co.uk), just east of the Circus on Bennett Street, evoke a lifestyle in which balls, card-playing, and gossip ranked high among life's priorities. If the Assembly Rooms are not being used for a private function, you can stroll through the four elegant rooms that were the center of 18th-century Bath's social life. There's not much to see or do in the Assembly Rooms, but it's easy to imagine the twitter of gossip and laughter as the regulars of the Bath season kept tabs on one another. Downstairs, and open daily, is the Fashion Museum, where you can view the finery in which a lady or dandy of the time would have danced away an evening. This is one of the world's leading collections of fashion (about 2,000 pieces are on display at any one time) and takes about an hour to see. Just as intriguing as the historic fashions are creations by Versace, Armani, and other contemporary designers. Hours are daily from 10am to 5pm (until 4pm Nov–Feb). Admission to the Assembly Rooms is free (but please note you cannot see them if an event is taking place); the museum costs £6.75 ($14) for adults, £5.75 ($11) for seniors and students, £4.75 ($9.50) children 6 to 18, and £18 ($36) for families of up to two adults and four children. A combined ticket to the Museum of Costume and the Roman Baths Museum (see above) costs £13.50 ($27) for adults, £11.50 ($23) for seniors and students, £8 ($16) for children 6 to 16, and £38 ($76) for families of up to two adults and four children.

Brock Street leads west from The Circus to Royal Victoria Park and the amazing ❾ **Royal Crescent** ✿✿✿, an exclusive residential semicircle of elegant town houses built by John Wood the Younger from 1767 to 1774, and one of the most distinctive examples of Georgian architecture in the world. The focus of the design is on the classical face of the crescent; there's characteristic symmetry and proportion of the facades facing the arc, though the rear facades are far more individualistic. At ❿ **Number 1, Royal Crescent** ✿✿✿ (𝒞 **01225/428-126**; www.bath-preservation-trust.org.uk/museums/no1) you can step into one of the town houses, a spacious "corner" house whose tenants included, in 1776, the duke of York, second son of George III. The Bath Preservation Trust has restored the house using only paint, wallpapers, fabrics,

The Beau of Bath

Bath was a sleepy, inelegant little place when Beau Nash (1674–1761) arrived in 1705 to try his hand at some games of chance. Nash, then 31, had more or less given up law and made his living by gambling. He was well known in London social circles for his looks, charm, aplomb, and stylish attire. He was lucky in Bath, decided to stay on as assistant to the town's master of ceremonies, and soon made his mark by enforcing dress codes and rules of behavior at dances, installing streetlights, and improving lodgings. He put Bath on the map as one of Europe's fashionable spas, with a sparkling new Pump Room for taking the waters, Assembly Rooms for dances, terraces on handsome houses, and other improvements we still enjoy today. Bath staged a grand funeral ceremony when Nash died penniless in 1761 at age 87 (ironically, he was buried in an unmarked pauper's grave)—and the elegant town continues to pay tribute to Beau Nash with its perfectly preserved beauty.

and other materials available in the 18th century, and furnished the three floors with a superlative collection of period antiques. The attractive card table in the study would have been a handy piece of equipment, given the popularity of gambling in Georgian Bath. The house is open mid-February through November, Tuesday to Sunday from 10:30am to 5pm (until 4pm in Nov); last admission is half an hour before close. Admission is £5 ($10) for adults; £4 ($8) for seniors and students, £2.50 ($5) for children 6 to 18; and £12 ($24) for families of up to two adults and two children.

ORGANIZED TOURS

Among the many walking tours of Bath (the Tourist Information Centre has a complete list), you get the best overview on the free, 2-hour **Mayor of Bath's Honorary Civic Walking Tour,** with stops at the Pump Room, Pulteney Bridge, Royal Crescent, and other architectural gems. The tour departs from outside the Abbey Church Yard entrance to the Pump Room at 10:30am daily, with additional walks at 2pm every day except Saturday. From May through September, there are evening walks at 7pm on Tuesday, Friday, and Saturday.

City Sightseeing (© 01871/666-0000) offers a 1-hour open-top bus tour with audio commentary at a cost of £10 ($20) for adults, £8 ($16) for seniors and students, and £4.50 ($9) for children. Tours depart from the bus station every 15 minutes in summer, otherwise hourly. Tickets are valid all day, and you can get off and on to explore places along the route.

The 90-minute tours of **Bizarre Bath** (© 01225/335-124; www.bizarrebath.co.uk) use street theatre to amuse visitors with cleverly scripted dialogues and reenactments for a humorous look at the city. Tours leave from in front of the Huntsman Inn in North Parade Passage every evening at 8pm from March through September, and cost £7 ($14) for adults, £5 ($10) for students; purchase tickets, in cash, at the time of the walk.

On Saturday and Sunday at 11am throughout the year, the **Jane Austen Centre** (© 01225/443-000; www.janeausten.co.uk) sponsors **Jane Austen's Bath,** a walking tour that focuses on the novelist's residences and settings for her novels. Walks begin in Abbey Church Yard and cost £3.50 ($7).

MORE THINGS TO SEE & DO

⓫ Building of Bath Museum 𝒦   Exhibits in this museum, which examines the city's Georgian and Regency architecture and interiors, detail the crafts used in the course of construction and introduce the architects who contributed to Bath's remarkable development.

The Countess of Huntingdon's Chapel, The Vineyard (off Paragon St.). ℂ 01225/333-895. Admission £4 ($8) adults, £3.50 ($7) seniors and students, £2 ($4) children 5–15. Mid-Feb to Nov Tues–Sun 10:30am–5pm. To reach the museum from the Assembly Rooms, head east on Alfred St. and north on Paragon St.; the museum will be on your left.

⓬ Holburne Museum of Art 𝒦   When this mansion was Bath's finest hotel, Jane Austen kept an eye on the fashionable clientele from her house nearby. Now the elegant rooms house silver, glass, and other decorative objects, as well as paintings by Joseph Turner, Thomas Gainsborough, and other masters, collected by 19th-century Bath resident Sir William Holburne.

Great Pulteney St. ℂ 01225/466-669. www.bath.ac.uk/Holburne. Admission £4.50 ($9) adults, £3.50 ($7) seniors, free for children. Tues–Sat 10am–5pm; Sun 11am–5pm.

⓭ American Museum 𝒦𝒦   On display at 19th-century Claverton Manor are quilts, folk art, Shaker pieces, and the other holdings of Britain's only museum devoted to Americana. Nearly 125 acres (51 hectares) of gardens, including a replica of the one at Mount Vernon, spill down the hillside. The museum is closed most of the winter, except from mid-November to mid-December, when the rooms are decorated for Christmas.

Off The Avenue, Bathwick Hill. ℂ 01225/460-503. www.americanmuseum.org. Admission £7.50 ($15) adults, £6.50 ($13) seniors and students, £4 ($8) children. Mid-Mar to mid-Nov Tues–Sun 2–5pm; mid-Nov to mid-Dec Tues–Sun noon–4:30pm. Bus: 18 to the museum from the train station and other stops in the city center.

OUTDOOR ACTIVITIES

Skiffs, punts, and canoes are available for rental from the **Victorian Bath Boating Station,** on the River Avon beneath the Pulteney Bridge; a gambol in the waters provides nice views of this attractive city from a different perspective. (May–Sept daily 10am–6pm; ℂ **01225/466-407**). The nearby **Kennet and Avon Canal towpath** is one of many local places ideal for hiking, cycling, and boating. The **Bath and Dundas Canal Company** (ℂ **01225/722-292**) at the canal information office rents bikes

---

⌜Tips⌝ A New Royal Bath for Bath

Visitors to Bath can once again soak in the city's famous warm, mineral-laden waters. The newly opened **Thermae Bath Spa,** Hot Bath St. (ℂ **01225/33-5678**; www.thermaebathspa.com), offers spa sessions in the New Royal Bath, a striking mixture of historic architecture and contemporary design just a few steps from the ancient Roman Baths. You can soak and swim in the Minerva Bath, a large open-air pool on the roof with marvelous views over the city, or in the Cross Bath, a smaller open-air pool where a 1½-hour soak costs £12 ($24) and no reservation is required. All manner of other spa treatments are available, from Vichy showers to facials. Check the website for more information.

as well as canoes and other boats for a leisurely outing in the green pastoral country-side; if you've been feeling city-bound in London, this is a good way to get out into the fresh air. It's 5 miles (8km) south of Bath on the A36 at Monkton Combe. (Take bus no. 4, 5, or 6 from the train station.)

3 Shopping

One of Bath's liveliest shopping venues is the **Green Park Arts and Craft Market,** in the historic Green Park train station, north of the center off Charles Street; the market is open from 9am to 5pm Tuesday through Sunday and hosts vendors selling everything from antiques to crafts to farm produce. Vendors at the **Bartlett Street Antique Centre,** near the Assembly Rooms on Bartlett Street, open Monday to Saturday from 9am to 5pm, sell jewelry, silver, prints, and other easily portable items. Vendors in the **Bath Saturday Antiques Market,** in the Old Cattle Market on Bath Walcot Street, sell collectibles of an unusually high quality on Saturday from 6:30am to 2:30pm. Quill pens, needlepoint kits, and other items associated with Jane Austen are for sale in the gift shop of the **Jane Austen Centre** (✆ **01225/443-000**).

4 Where to Dine

Hands ✦ LIGHT FARE/TEA   These bright, airy rooms next to Bath Abbey are especially popular for morning coffee and afternoon tea. Breakfast and lunchtime sandwiches and salads are available, too. Lunch offerings include hearty portions of well-prepared traditional Cornish pasties, steak pie, and a ploughman's lunch.

Abbey St. ✆ **01225/463-928.** Lunch £4.50–£7 ($9–$14); cream teas £3.75–£7.75 ($7.50–$15). MC, V. Tues–Sat 9:30am–5:30pm; Sun 11am–4:30pm.

Le Petit Cochon ✦ MODERN FRENCH   Le Petit Cochon (The Little Pig) is Bath's only French brasserie and offers about a dozen dishes each day based on traditional French cafe cooking (steak and frites, coq au vin, and boeuf bourguignon). You can stop in for a morning espresso and croissant or drop by for a leisurely lunch or dinner with a glass of wine. The atmosphere is casual, the food great, and the fixed-price lunch a good value.

11 Margarets Buildings (off Brock St.). ✆ **01225/421-251.** Main courses £8–£13 ($16–$26); fixed-price lunch £10–£11 ($20–$22). MC, V. Mon–Sat 10:30am–10:30pm.

No. 5 Bistro ✦✦ FRENCH   A welcoming, casual air pervades this handsome restaurant at the east end of Pulteney Bridge. Typical offerings from the small but appealing menu of simple, excellent French bistro-style preparations include pan-fried pepper steak, Provençal fish soup, chargrilled loin of lamb, and vegetarian dishes such as roast stuffed peppers and vegetable gratin.

5 Argyle St. ✆ **01225/444-499.** Main courses £14–£17 ($28–$34); fixed-price lunch £7.95 ($16); fixed-price dinner £9.95 ($20). AE, MC, V. Daily noon–2:30pm and 6:30–10pm.

Pizza Express ✦ Kids PIZZA/PASTA   If you're looking for a kid-friendly restaurant in Bath, or just want a good, reasonably priced meal, try Pizza Express. The service is relaxed and friendly, kids are given crayons and paper, and the pizzas are great. There's nothing spectacular or showy on the menu, but the food is consistently good.

1–3 Barton St. ✆ **01225/420-119.** Main courses £7–£13 ($14–$26). AE, MC, V. Daily 11:30am–midnight.

5 Extending Your Trip

Bath is so engaging that you may want to spend the evening taking in a play at the Royal Theatre or enjoying a leisurely dinner, and continue your sightseeing the next day. Bath is also a handy stopover if you want to continue on to the nearby Cotswolds and Oxford.

Kennard Hotel 👁👁   Just across the Pulteney Bridge from the city center, this handsome town house was built as lodgings in 1794 and still treats guests to tidy and comfortable accommodations, an attractive breakfast room, and a gracious welcome.

11 Henrietta St. ℂ **01225/310-472.** www.kennard.co.uk. £98–£118 ($196–$236) double. MC, V.

Milsoms Hotel 👁👁   Milsoms offers a great location, good value, and a kind of unique charm. There are only nine rooms but each has been individually decorated in a fresh, contemporary look. Be aware that the reception area is up a fairly steep flight of stairs, and there is no elevator. The Loch Fyne restaurant, located below the hotel, is a nice choice for dinner, serving some of the city's freshest and most adeptly prepared fish.

24 Milsom St., Bath, Somerset BA1 1DG. ℂ **01225/750-128.** www.milsomshotel.co.uk. £85–£115 ($170–$230) double. AE, DC, MC, V.

Royal Crescent Hotel 👁👁👁   These elegant, interconnected town houses not only boast the best address in town (right in the center of the Royal Crescent) but provide elegant and lavishly appointed accommodations as well as a delightful garden and beautiful pool and spa. Check the website for special offers.

16 Royal Crescent, Bath, Somerset BA1 2LS. ℂ **01225/823-333.** www.royalcrescent.co.uk. From £290 ($580) double. AE, MC, V.

Trip 2

Battle

*I*n the annals of British history, the year 1066 looms large. In that year, in a battle that changed the course of English history, Duke William of Normandy defeated Harold, the Saxon king of England, at the Battle of Hastings. William planned the attack for months in advance and transported 7,000 troops across the Channel on 600 ships. Harold rode south from York, where he was trying to repel a Viking attack, to meet the new threat.

The armies were equal in number and well matched in strength, but Harold was killed, hit by an arrow and finished off by a sword, and the English troops retreated. After the battle, William became known as William the Conqueror. He had himself crowned king at Westminster Abbey on Christmas Day and again at Winchester, and then began construction of the Tower of London and other fortifications. In short, a new page in English history was turned.

Within 6 years William had consolidated his power throughout England. For taxation purposes, the new monarch compiled a list of every property and building in his newly conquered land. The list became the famous *Domesday Book,* which is today a unique record of England in the 11th century. But all this history started with a battle, and that's where Battle comes into the viewfinder. In the town, preserved behind high brick walls, is the battlefield where Saxon and Norman soldiers clashed on that fateful day in 1066. For anyone with an interest in history, Battle is a memorable spot to visit. Located 57 miles (92km) south of London and just 90 minutes away by train, Battle makes a memorable day trip, and one that needn't take an entire day. You may want to combine your visit to Battle with a trip to **Rye** (see trip 18). Trains depart Brighton hourly for the 45-minute journey to Rye.

1 Essentials

VISITOR INFORMATION

The **Battle Tourist Information Centre,** Battle Abbey Gatehouse, 88 High St. (© **01424/773-721;** www.visitsussex.org), has a free pamphlet that includes a town map. The center is open daily, from 9:30am to 5:30pm in summer and from 10am to 4pm in winter.

Battle Highlights

• Walking the battleground where King Harold of England fought Duke William of Normandy.

• Exploring the ruins of Battle Abbey.

SCHEDULING CONSIDERATIONS

The **battlefield site** is open daily until 6pm in summer, until 5pm in October, and until 4pm November through March. The last audio tours are issued 1 hour before closing. To enjoy this experience, give yourself at least 1 unhurried hour, preferably 2 hours. This is primarily an outdoor excursion and you'll probably enjoy it more on a warm, or at least rainless, day between April and October.

GETTING THERE
BY TRAIN

Battle is a stop on the London–Hastings line, and direct train service is available from London's Charing Cross Station. The trip takes about 90 minutes. A standard day return costs about £21 ($42). The first direct train from London departs at 8:15am; the last direct train to London departs Battle at 9:52pm. For train schedules and information, call **National Rail Enquiries** at $(\\!\mathcal{C})$ **08457/484950** or visit www.national rail.co.uk.

BY BUS

There is currently no daytime coach service from London to Battle.

BY CAR

Battle is about 6 miles (9.5km) north of Hastings on A2100. From London, head southeast toward the coast and Hastings on A21, cutting south at Sevenoaks and continuing along A21 to Battle via A2100. The trip takes about 1½ to 2 hours, depending on the traffic. Free parking lots are located near the entrance to the battlefield.

GETTING AROUND

To reach the battlefield from the train station, take Station Road to Lower Lake, and follow Lower Lake north as it becomes Upper Lake; the easy walk takes about 10 minutes. Taxis are usually available outside the station, or you can reserve one by calling **Town Country** $(\mathcal{C}$ **01424/772-222**) or **4167 Cars** $(\mathcal{C}$ **01424/774-167**). Walking is the only way to see the battlefield.

2 A Day in Battle

The **Battle of Hastings Abbey and Battlefield** *꽃꽃꽃* ($\mathcal{C}$ **01424/773-792**), hidden behind high walls on High Street, is the one site that you want to see in Battle. This ancient battleground offers a fascinating journey back in time, and you should give yourself at least 2 unhurried hours to take it all in. The preservationist organization English Heritage (**www.english-heritage.org.uk**), which owns the site, has done a clever job of making the experience both interesting and informative. With your ticket you're given an audio guide that is keyed to important spots along a pathway that runs

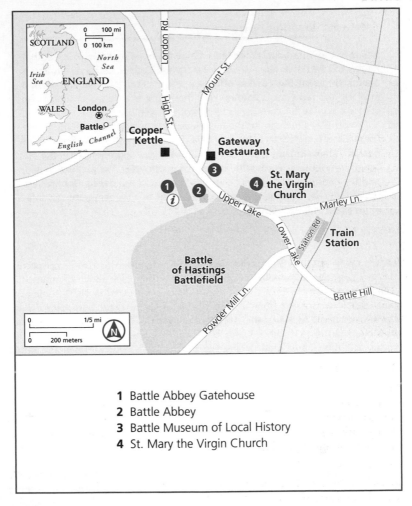

1 Battle Abbey Gatehouse
2 Battle Abbey
3 Battle Museum of Local History
4 St. Mary the Virgin Church

through the field. The site is open daily from 10am to 6pm (Oct–Mar until 4pm). Admission is £6.30 ($13) for adults, £4.70 ($10) for seniors, and £3.20 ($6.40) for children.

Enter through the ❶ **Abbey Gatehouse,** built in 1338. The tour starts with an outdoor video presentation that fills you in on the major events leading up to the battle. Next comes an exhibition, "Prelude to Battle," which uses text panels to draw you deeper into the story of the intrigues and the royal power struggle between King Harold and Duke William of Normandy. Finally, you walk onto the battlefield itself, where descriptive panels linked to the audio tour line the pathway. The battle's events unfold as seen through the eyes of three different narrators: Aelfric, a Saxon thane; Henri, a French knight; and Edith, the wife of King Harold. As you tour the battlefield,

Moments   **Incendiary Traditions**

Sitting in the front hallway of the Almonry, the building on High Street that houses the Battle Museum of Local History and Copper Kettle restaurant, is one of the oldest **Guy Fawkes effigies** in the country. Bearded and dressed in black and red with a pointed hat, the figure is paraded around town before a bonfire is lit on Guy Fawkes Night, November 5.

Fawkes was a member of the notorious Gunpowder Plot of 1605, whose members attempted to blow up Parliament to oppose the oppression of Roman Catholicism under King James I. Fawkes was apprehended in the cellars of the House of Lords with 36 kegs of gunpowder, the plot was foiled, and the conspirators were hung upside down and quartered. Bonfires are burned all over England on Guy Fawkes Night to commemorate this infamous event in British history.

you can follow the story and tactics used by both sides from these three perspectives. The complete tour takes about an hour; a shorter version takes about 45 minutes.

➋ **Battle Abbey,** the great church that William constructed in 1070 (some of the stone used was imported from William's lands in Caen, France) to mark the spot where King Harold was slain, was destroyed by Henry VIII during the Dissolution of the Monasteries in 1539, when Henry broke with the Church of Rome. Today it's an atmospheric ruin, whose most notable features include a medieval gatehouse and the ancient Dorter Range, where the abbey's monks once slept.

Leaving the Battle Abbey site, turn left and cross High Street to reach the small ➌ **Battle Museum of Local History** (✆ 01424/775-955; www.battlemuseum. org.uk). Among the artifacts on display are the only battle-axe discovered from the Battle of Hastings site, and early-19th-century engravings of the famous Bayeux Tapestry (which chronicled the battle). The museum is open April through October Monday to Saturday from 10:30am to 4:30pm, and Sunday 2 to 5pm. Admission is £1 ($2).

Heading back down High Street, you reach Upper Lake and ➍ **St. Mary the Virgin Church** ✦ (✆ 01424/773-649), originally built on the battlefield in 1115, though it now stands outside the abbey's walls. The church has a magnificent Romanesque nave, a Norman font with medieval cover, rare 14th-century wall paintings, and the gilded alabaster tomb of Sir Anthony Browne, to whom Henry VIII granted the Battle Abbey. The church is open Easter through September, Monday to Friday from 10:30am to 4:30pm, October through Easter, Wednesday to Friday from 10am to noon.

OUTDOOR ACTIVITIES

For a full day's outing, consider walking from Battle to **Rye** (p. 147) and returning to London from there. The walk, about 12 miles (19km), is lovely, passing through woods and fields along a well-tended route known as the "1066 Country Walk." The route is relatively flat and leads through several villages where you can stop for a cup of tea or something to eat. You might want to consider a morning visit to Battle and an afternoon walk to Rye, arriving there in time for a look around the town and perhaps an early dinner before boarding the train back to London.

3 Shopping

Friar House, High Street (© **01424/777100**), dates back to 1642 and sells pottery made in 17th-century style.

4 Where to Dine

Copper Kettle LIGHT FARE/TEAS   Located in the Almonry, a lovely, beamed medieval hall (where the Town Council meets) with a pretty walled garden, this is an atmospheric spot for a simple lunch or afternoon tea.

High St. © 01424/772-727. Lunch £5–£7 ($10–$14). No credit cards. Mon–Sat 9:30am–4:30pm.

Gateway Restaurant TRADITIONAL BRITISH   The kitchen in this atmospheric place specializes in hearty and traditional home-cooked English food. Lunch specials usually include several old-fashioned pies: steak, ale, and mushroom; steak and kidney; and chicken, leek, and bacon. You can also get toasted sandwiches, an all-day brunch, or an afternoon cream tea.

78 High St. © 01424/772-056. Lunch £5–£8 ($10–$16); cream tea £4.95 ($10). No credit cards. Daily 9am–5:30pm.

Brighton

On the Sussex coast, a mere 50 miles (80km) south of London on the English Channel, Brighton is England's most famous and popular seaside town. Brighton was a small fishing village until the prince regent, a fun-loving dandy who reigned as George IV from 1820 to 1830, became enamored of the place and had the Royal Pavilion built. Where royalty moves, fashion follows, and Brighton eventually became one of Europe's most fashionable towns. The long terraces of Regency town houses you see everywhere in Brighton date from that period. Later in the 19th century, when doctors prescribed breathing sea air as a cure-all, the Victorians descended en masse, as did the world-weary simply looking for a little fun—and they still do. Today, Brighton is a popular place for conventions and weekend getaways. People come to hang out on the long stretch of beach, shop, stroll, and party the night away at clubs and discos.

However, Brighton is not everyone's cup of tea. Parts of the city are unkempt and unattractive, and one of the famous amusement piers is now a crumbling wreck and about to crash into the sea. Even so, medieval streets are lined with appealing shops, entire neighborhoods are being revitalized, and a sizeable gay and lesbian presence has re-energized the local scene, especially on weekends. Plus, Brighton is a "restaurant city," with lots of good places to dine. And it's so easy to reach from London that you might want to nip down just for an afternoon of a little sightseeing and a (bracing) dip in the sea.

If you want to spend more time in Brighton, we've recommended some hotels at the end of this chapter. If you do decide to linger awhile, consider combining this trip with a visit to nearby **Lewes and Monk's House** and **Charleston** (see trip 15). Or you can also combine a trip to Brighton with a visit to **Chichester** (see trip 6), just 30 miles (48km) west.

1 Essentials

VISITOR INFORMATION

Brighton's **Visitor Information Centre,** Royal Pavilion Shop, 4–5 Pavilion Buildings (© **0906/711-2255;** www.visitbrighton.com), in the Royal Pavilion, is about a 10-minute walk south from the train station. The center is open daily from 9:30am to 5pm.

Brighton Highlights

- Touring the extravagant Royal Pavilion.
- Promenading along the seafront.
- Visiting the Brighton Art Gallery's top-notch furniture collection.

SCHEDULING CONSIDERATIONS

You might want to time your visit to coincide with the **Brighton International Festival** (© 01273/292-950; www.brighton-festival.org.uk) in May. One of England's best-known arts festivals, it features a wide array of drama, literature, visual art, dance, and concert programs ranging from classical to hard rock. If you're into the nightlife scene of pubs, clubs, and discos, weekends in summer are definitely the best time to go—but also the busiest, so book ahead if you're staying overnight. If you're not into crowds (which can actually add to the fun of a trip to Brighton), visit on a weekday in spring or fall.

GETTING THERE

BY TRAIN

Over 40 direct trains a day depart from London's Victoria Station, with the first direct train departing at 4am (later on weekends), and the last direct train returning to London at 11:02pm. The trip takes about an hour; an off-peak (after 9:30am) return ticket costs about £18 ($36). For train schedules and more information, call **National Rail Enquiries** (© 08457/484950) or visit www.nationalrail.co.uk.

BY BUS

National Express (© 0990/808080; www.nationalexpress.com) runs hourly buses from London's Victoria Coach Station. A same-day return ticket for the 2-hour journey costs £10 ($20).

BY CAR

The M23 from central London leads to Brighton. The drive should take about 1 hour, but if roads are clogged, the trip may take twice as long.

GETTING AROUND

The center of Brighton is fairly compact, so the easiest way to get around is on foot; the walk from the train station to the Royal Pavilion takes about 10 minutes. **Brighton and Hove Bus Company** (© 01273/886-200) offers frequent service along the main streets; the local fare is £1.30 ($2.60). Taxis are usually available at the train station, or you can call **Streamline** (© 01273/747-474) to reserve one.

2 A Day in Brighton

Start your explorations at Brighton's one must-see attraction, the ❶ **Royal Pavilion** ✫✫✫ (© 01273/290-900; www.royalpavilion.org.uk). Set in a small landscaped park bounded by North Street, Church Street, Olde Steine, and New Road, the Royal Pavilion is one of the most extraordinary palaces in Europe. The prominent early-19th-century architect John Nash redesigned the original farmhouse and villa on

Brighton

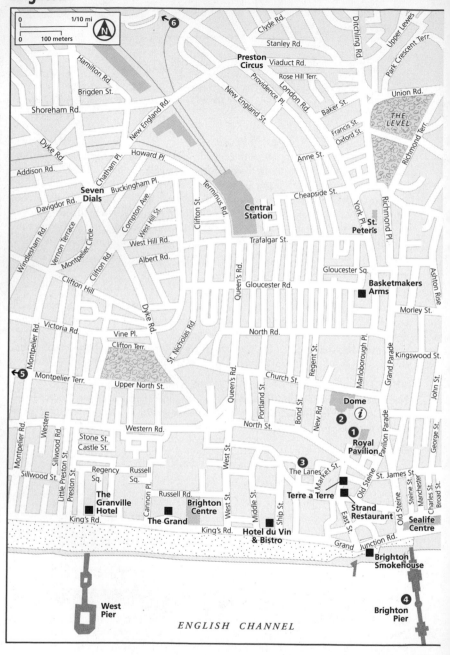

0 — 1/10 mi
0 — 100 meters

Clyde Rd.
Stanley Rd.
Preston Circus
Viaduct Rd.
Rose Hill Terr.
New England St.
Providence Pl.
London Rd.
Ditchling Rd.
Upper Lewes
Park Crescent Terr.
Hamilton Rd.
Brigden St.
Shoreham Rd.
New England Rd.
Baker St.
Union Rd.
Francis St.
Oxford St.
THE LEVEL
Richmond Terr.
Dyke Rd.
Addison Rd.
Chatham Pl.
Howard Pl.
Anne St.
Seven Dials
Buckingham Pl.
Davigdor Rd.
Compton Ave.
West Hill St.
Clifton St.
Terminus Rd.
Cheapside St.
Central Station
York Pl.
St. Peter's
Richmond Pl.
Windlesham Rd.
Vernon Terrace
Montpelier Circle
West Hill Rd.
Albert Rd.
Trafalgar St.
Gloucester Sq.
Ashton Rise
Clifton Hill
Clifton Rd.
Dyke Rd.
St. Nicholas Rd.
Queen's Rd.
Gloucester Rd.
Basketmakers Arms
Morley St.
Victoria Rd.
Vine Pl.
Clifton Terr.
North Rd.
Regent St.
Marlborough Pl.
Grand Parade
Kingswood St.
Montpelier Rd.
Montpelier Terr.
Upper North St.
Church St.
Portland St.
Bond St.
New Rd.
Dome
John St.
Western
Sillwood Rd.
Western Rd.
North St.
Dome
Royal Pavilion
Pavilion Parade
George St.
Stone St.
Castle St.
West St.
The Lanes
Market St.
St. James St.
Steine
Charles St.
Manchester
Broad St.
Little Preston St.
Preston St.
Regency Sq.
Russell Sq.
Cannon Pl.
Russell Rd.
Brighton Centre
Middle St.
Ship St.
Terre a Terre
Old Steine
East St.
Old Steine
Sealife Centre
Sillwood St.
The Granville Hotel
The Grand
King's Rd.
King's Rd.
Hotel du Vin & Bistro
Strand Restaurant
Grand Junction Rd.
Brighton Smokehouse
West Pier
ENGLISH CHANNEL
Brighton Pier

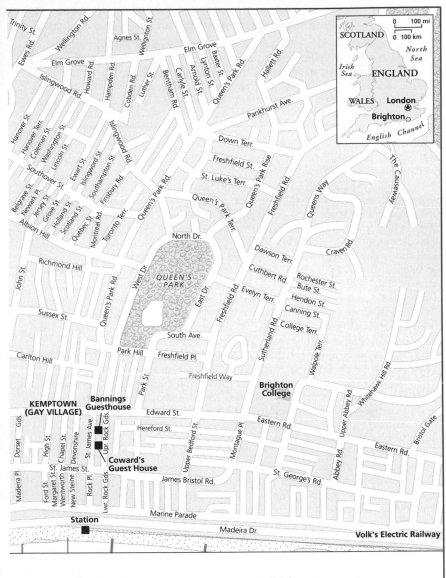

1 Royal Pavilion
2 Brighton Museum & Art Gallery
3 The Lanes

4 Brighton Pier
5 Hove Museum & Art Gallery
6 Preston Manor

Moments **Catcreep-ing through Brighton**

Exploring Brighton's catcreeps and twittens takes you into a secretive, hidden side of this otherwise flamboyant seaside town. Catcreeps are flights of steps connecting two roads at different levels on a hillside, and a twitten is a Sussex word used to describe a narrow path between two walls or hedges, or wall and hedge, usually leading from one street to another. You'll find catcreeps and twittens around The Lanes.

---

this site into an Indian fantasy of turrets and minarets for George IV (when the king was still prince regent). The fun- and food-loving George (from whom the Regency era got its name) lived here with his mistress, Lady Conyngham, until 1827, and filled the rooms, festooned with carvings of dragons and other whimsical creatures, with the elaborate furnishings and ornaments typical of the period. The Music Room is especially ornate, with a domed ceiling encrusted with seashells and red walls filled with Chinese scenes. The king's brother, William IV, and their niece, Queen Victoria, also used the pavilion, though Victoria found the place vulgar and later sold it to the city of Brighton for a song in 1850. Give yourself about an hour for a leisurely walk-through tour of the sumptuous and fantastically extravagant interior. The **Long Gallery** has a color scheme of bright blues and pinks; the **Music Room** has a domed ceiling of gilded, scallop-shaped shells; and the **king's private apartments** on the upper floors epitomize the Regency lifestyle of the rich and royal. **The Queen Adelaide Tea Room** is a nice spot for a light lunch or afternoon tea. The Royal Pavilion is open daily from 10am to 5pm (Apr–Sept 9:30am–5:30pm). Admission is £7.70 ($15) for adults, £5.90 ($12) for students and seniors, £5.10 ($10) for children under 16.

On the west side of the Royal Pavilion's gardens, on Church Street, you find the ❷ **Brighton Museum & Art Gallery** (✆ 01273/290-900). Admission is free to this small, attractive museum's interesting collections of Art Nouveau and Art Deco furniture, glass, and ceramics. There's also a fashion gallery. The museum is open Tuesday from 10am to 7pm, Wednesday through Saturday from 10am to 5pm, and Sunday from 2 to 5pm.

From the museum, head south on New Road, turning south on North Street, and south again on Market Street. This brings you to ❸ **The Lanes** *✿*, the warren of narrow streets that was Brighton's original fishing village. Today the area is filled with small shops. After you've browsed The Lanes, continue south on Market Street and then follow East Street down to the seafront. Brighton and neighboring Hove stretch along the English Channel, and the entire seafront is a pebbly public beach used for swimming and sunning. Stroll along the wide promenade and out to sea on the town's famous and tackily entertaining amusement area, ❹ **Brighton Pier** *✿*. The pier was built in the late 19th century when Brighton became a major holiday resort. At night, all lit up with twinkling lights, it's cheerily irresistible, even though you won't find much more than junk food and arcade games. Admission is free and it's open round-the-clock. Just below the pier you can board **Volk's Electric Railway** for a ride of about 1 mile (1.6km) along the beach in open-air cars; the railway has been hauling fun-lovers up and down the Brighton seafront since 1883 (it's England's oldest). Trains run from Easter to mid-September, daily 11am to 5pm (to 6pm Sat–Sun); the fare is £1.50 ($3) each way, £2.50 ($5) round-trip for adults; 70p ($1.40) each way, £1.20

($2.40) round-trip for children under 14.

ORGANIZED TOURS

At 8pm on the first Saturday of every month, a 90-minute **Ghost Walk** departs from Brighton Town Hall, The Lanes, visiting ancient graveyards and finishing at a haunted inn. For more information on this and other special guided walks, call ℭ **01273/888-596** or visit www.brightonwalks.com. You can buy your tickets (£6/$12) on the spot without advance reservations, but it's a good idea to call first to verify times.

MORE THINGS TO SEE & DO

❺ Hove Museum & Art Gallery   In the town that adjoins Brighton to the west, the Hove Museum is housed in an impressive Victorian villa and contains a good collection of 20th-century paintings and drawings, 18th-century furniture and decorative art, and the "Hove to Hollywood" film collection featuring footage of the town in 1900 shot by local moviemakers. (The British film industry started in Hove.) The museum is about a 15-minute walk from the Royal Pavilion.

19 New Church Rd. ℭ **01273/290-200.** Free admission. Tues–Fri 10am–5pm; Sat–Sun 10am–4:30pm.

❻ Preston Manor 𝒜   Though this handsome residence was built in 1738 on medieval foundations, what you see today is an early-20th-century refurbishment, a perfect example of the upper-class Edwardian lifestyle. Furniture, paintings, even table settings are in place, and you can explore the mansion from the basement kitchens to the attic nursery.

Preston Drove (2 miles/3km, north of city center off the London Rd.). ℭ **01273/292-770.** www.prestonmanor. virtualmuseum.info. £4.10 ($8.20) for adults, £2.40 ($4.80) for children under 16. Apr–Sept Tues–Sat 10am–5pm, Sun 2–5pm.

OUTDOOR ACTIVITIES

The entire seafront is an uninterrupted beach available for sunning and swimming, though the water in the English Channel is more than brisk and the pebbly shoreline not exactly conducive to lolling. If you're into sunbathing au naturel, you're in luck: Brighton has the only nude beach in England, about a mile (1.5km) west of Brighton Pier. You can walk there along the promenade above the beach or take Volk's Electric Railway (see "A Day in Brighton," above), along Madeira Drive to the marina.

3 Shopping

The Lanes, Brighton's original fishing village, is now a warren of narrow streets filled with small shops selling mostly tourist trinkets. North Laines has more interesting shops, including some trendy outfitters. Duke Street and Upper North Street are good for antiques. Shops in Brighton are generally open Monday through Saturday between 10am and 6pm, with a later closing on Thursday or Friday. During the summer tourist season, some shops are open on Sunday and closed on Monday.

4 Where to Dine

Basketmaker Arms PUB FARE   Some of Brighton's best pub grub—including delicious fish and chips on Fridays—is served in beamed rooms hung with old photos and at outside tables in good weather.

Cheltenham Place. ℭ **01273/689-006.** Main courses £4–£8 ($8–$16). MC, V. Mon–Fri noon–3pm and 5:30–8:30pm; Sat noon–10:30pm; Sun noon–10pm.

Brighton Smokehouse SEAFOOD   Many locals stop in at this little fish shop, located right on the beach, for a taste of inexpensive seafood. Crab sandwiches, chowders, and other tasty concoctions are served from a counter and eaten in the sea breeze at outdoor tables.

176 King's Arches. No phone. Sandwiches and soup from £4 ($8). No credit cards. Daily 10am–5pm.

Hotel du Vin Bistro ☞ MODERN FRENCH   The signature bistro of Brighton's most stylish new hotel (see "Extending Your Trip," below) is a sophisticated but comfortable spot with a menu that sticks to the basics. The two-course fixed-price menu is a good value and offers starters such as a salad of marinated goat's cheese and artichokes with pancetta, and main courses such as seared calves' liver or simple classics like coq au vin; a glass of wine is included.

In Hotel du Vin, Ship St. ☎ 01273/718-588. Reservations recommended. Main courses £15 ($30); fixed-price meal £15–£24 ($30–$48). AE, DC, MC, V. Daily noon–1:45pm and 7–10pm.

Strand Restaurant ☞ MODERN BRITISH/SEAFOOD   One of the hippest (and friendliest) places for dining is the bow-fronted Strand. The ever-changing menu is an extremely good value. Herby homemade vegetable soup, pâté, or mussels cooked with fresh cream, wine, and garlic may be followed by homemade fish cakes, or basil, leek and Parmesan risotto.

6 Little East St. ☎ 01273/747-096. Reservations recommended for dinner. Main courses £8–£10 ($16–$20). AE, DC, MC, V. Mon–Tues 6pm–midnight; Wed–Sat noon–midnight.

Terre à Terre ☞☞ VEGETARIAN   Considered the finest vegetarian restaurant in England, Terre à Terre elevates meatless cuisine into the art it should be but rarely is. The food is impeccably fresh and beautifully presented. You can eat your way through the menu with the Terre à Tapas, a superb selection of all their best dishes, big enough for two. On the menu, you'll find such imaginative dishes as heirloom tomato consommé, and wild garlic and goat's cheese risotto.

71 East St. ☎ 01273/729-051. Reservations essential on weekends. Main courses £12–£15 ($24–$30). DC, MC, V. Tues 6:30–10:30pm; Wed–Sun noon–10:30pm; Sun 10am–10pm.

5 Extending Your Trip

The Grand ☞☞☞   The grandest place to stay in Brighton is the Grand, a huge, dazzling-white resort hotel built on the seafront in 1864. The only five-star luxury hotel in Brighton, the Georgian-style property has 200 spacious and predictably gorgeous guest rooms with roomy tile bathrooms.

King's Rd., Brighton, E. Sussex BN1 2FW. ☎ 01273/224-300. Fax 01273/224-321. www.grandbrighton.co.uk. £120–£250 ($240–$500) double. Rates include English breakfast. AE, DC, MC, V.

The Granville Hotel ☞ 𝘒𝘪𝘥𝘴   Located opposite the West Pier, Granville's is a good choice if you're looking for a smaller, stylish, boutique hotel on the seafront. A former town house, this place has 25 individually designed rooms, all with private bathrooms and some with four-poster beds. The hotel is completely nonsmoking and welcomes families with children.

124 Kings Rd., Brighton, East Sussex BNT 2FA. ☎ 01273/326-302. Fax 01273/728-294. www.granvillehotel.co.uk. £85–£145 ($170–$290) double. Rates include breakfast. MC, V.

Hotel du Vin & Bistro ☞☞☞   A sophisticated new addition to Brighton's hotel scene, the ultra-stylish Hotel du Vin occupies a set of Mock Tudor and Gothic revival

Brighton's Gay & Lesbian Hotels & B&Bs

Several hotels and B&Bs in Brighton cater to gay and lesbian visitors. **Bannings** at Number 14, 14 Upper Rock Gardens, Brighton, Sussex BN2 1QE (© **01273/681-403**; www.bannings.co.uk), is a snug Georgian town house with six bedrooms, all with private bathrooms, that cost £70 to £90 ($140–$180) double, breakfast included. **Coward's Guest House,** 12 Upper Rock Gardens, Brighton, Sussex BN2 1QE (© **01273/692-677**; www.cowards brighton.co.uk), is a dapper, Regency-era town house that caters to men. It has six bedrooms with private bathrooms that rent for £70 to £90 ($140–$180) double, breakfast included.

buildings a stone's throw from the seafront. This is Brighton's most unique contemporary hotel, with an impressive three-story lobby, a signature French bistro (reviewed above), and 37 cool, uncluttered, and very comfortable bedrooms featuring marvelous beds with fine Egyptian linens, deep soaker tubs, and power showers.

Ship St., Brighton BN1 1AD. © **01273/718-588.** Fax 01273/718-599. www.hotelduvin.com. £145–£250 ($290–$500) double. Rates include breakfast. AE, DC, MC, V.

Cambridge

Cambridge, like Oxford, is forever linked with the venerable university that has flourished here on the banks of the River Cam for 7 centuries. Before the great university took root here, Cambridge was known to the Romans as a place to ford the Cam, and housed several monastic settlements in the Middle Ages. Obviously, the chance to step into a few of the 31 colleges and view their architectural wonders is what brings many visitors to Cambridge. But you're in for a pleasant surprise—this town that rises from marshy lands known as fens is itself a gem, an appealing blend of busy markets and shops, medieval architecture, and grassy riverside meadows and parklands. There's even a nice 21st-century buzz to the place, as dot.commers settle into what has become known as "Silicon Fen." You'll want to spend a whole day in Cambridge, so get an early start. To appreciate the city fully, plan on seeing the colleges as well as the town itself, with a walk through the market and along King's Parade and other cobbled streets, with a stop in a pub, and take time, too, to float down the Cam in a punt or to walk along the grassy riverside parklands known as the Backs. Before heading back to London, you might want to consider a trip out to the Imperial War Museum in Duxford. If you decide to extend your visit, see the last section in this chapter for nightlife and hotel recommendations.

1 Essentials

VISITOR INFORMATION

The **Tourist Information Centre,** The Old Library, Wheeler Street (© **01223/322-640;** www.visitcambridge.org/visitors), is behind the Guildhall and provides information on transportation and sightseeing, as well as useful maps. The office is open year-round, Monday to Friday 10am to 5:30pm, Saturday 10am to 5pm, and Sunday (Easter–Sept only) 11am to 4pm. To find out more about Cambridge University, including opening times for the colleges, it's best to surf the extensive website, www.cam.ac.uk, which has links to websites for each college; or call © **01223/337-733.**

SCHEDULING CONSIDERATIONS

What **colleges** you are able to see depends upon when you visit, as many close during exam periods (May–June) and are open for limited hours during terms, which in general run from mid-January to mid-March, mid-April to mid-June, and mid-October

Cambridge

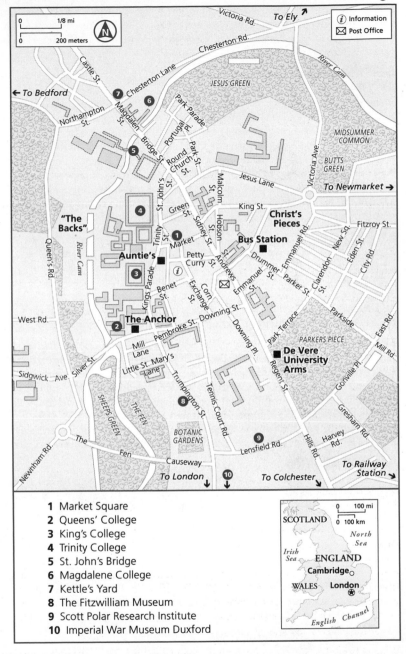

1 Market Square
2 Queens' College
3 King's College
4 Trinity College
5 St. John's Bridge
6 Magdalene College
7 Kettle's Yard
8 The Fitzwilliam Museum
9 Scott Polar Research Institute
10 Imperial War Museum Duxford

to mid-December. You'll only be able to hear the **King's College Choir** during terms and the first half of July. The colleges are most crowded with visitors during the summer holidays. Keep in mind that the **Fitzwilliam Museum** and **Kettle's Yard** are closed on Monday.

GETTING THERE
BY TRAIN

Trains depart from King's Cross Station as often as every 15 minutes throughout the day, but try to take a train at 15 minutes or 45 minutes past the hour—these are the fast trains and make the trip in just 45 minutes. (Other trains take a bit over an hour.) The first train from London departs at 5:45am and the last direct train returns to London at 11:19pm. The standard day return fare is £22 ($44). For more information, call **National Rail Enquiries** (✆ **08457/484950**) or go to www.nationalrail.co.uk. The Cambridge train station is located south of town on Station Road. You can walk or take a bus or taxi from the train station to Market Square and the center of town, about a mile (1.5km) away; buses run about every 15 minutes and the fare is 90p ($1.80).

BY BUS

Buses operated by **National Express** (✆ **08705/808-080;** www.nationalexpress.com) leave London's Victoria Coach Station for Cambridge every half-hour to hour throughout the day. Try to take a bus that makes the trip in less than 2 hours—some make more stops and take quite a bit longer. The day return fare is £10 ($20). An advantage to taking the bus rather than the train is the central location of the Cambridge bus station, on Drummer Street at the edge of the city-center pedestrian zone.

BY CAR

Cambridge is about 60 miles (97km) north of London on the M11. The trip usually takes a little over an hour. Parking in Cambridge is scarce and rather expensive. There are public lots scattered throughout the city center; these include Lion Yard Car Park, Grafton Centre Car Park, Park Street Car Park, and Queen Anne Terrace Car Park. You'll pay about £1.40 ($2.80) per hour for parking, and about £12 ($24) for 4 or 5 hours. The Park and Ride sites in outlying areas (well marked from entrances to the city) are less expensive, and regular bus service connects them with the city center.

GETTING AROUND

Cambridge (pop. 111,000) is an easily walkable city with two main streets. Trumpington Road—which becomes Trumpington Street, King's Parade, Trinity Street, and finally St. John's Street—runs parallel to the River Cam and provides easy access to

Cambridge Highlights

- Enjoying a concert by the internationally famous King's College Choir.
- Visiting the eclectic Fitzwilliam Museum, where you can see the first draft of Keats's "Ode to a Nightingale."
- Viewing the Tower at beautiful Queens' College, where the great scholar, Erasmus, lived from 1510 to 1514.
- Punting along the River Cam.

> **_Tips_ Cycling 101**
>
> The significant brainpower at Cambridge does not come into play when stu-
> dents mount bicycles, the town's most common form of transportation. Be on
> your guard when you step off curbs—always look both ways—and be on the
> lookout for cyclists roaring up behind you when you saunter down paths along
> the Backs and on such greenswards as Parker's Piece. Or follow the old adage,
> "If you can't beat them, join them," and rent a bicycle and pedal around town
> yourself. (See "Outdoor Activities," below.)

several of the colleges. Bridge Street, the city's main shopping zone, starts at Magda-
lene Bridge; it becomes Sidney Street, St. Andrew's Street, and finally Regent Street.
A Dayrider bus pass, good all day and available from any bus driver, costs £2.80
($5.60). Taxis are available at the train station; if you need one elsewhere in town, call
A1 Taxis (© **01223/525-555**) or **Cabco** (© **01223/312-444**).

2 A Day in Cambridge

You won't have time to see all the colleges, and some are not of great architectural
interest anyway. To see a nice swath of colleges from the outside and to get a sense of
the university's grandeur, take a stroll along the Backs—the meadows between the colleges and the River Cam.

Start at ❶ **Market Square** 𝄐. From there, follow King's Parade and take a right on
Silver Street to ❷ **Queens' College** 𝄐𝄐 (© **01223/335-511**), founded in 1448 and
named for Margaret of Anjou, the wife of Henry VI, and Elizabeth, wife of Edward
IV. The college straddles both banks of the River Cam, which you cross using the
famous wooden **Mathematical Bridge**—or infamous, as unfounded stories hold that
students have taken it apart and have been unable to reconstruct it. The bridge is one
of many architectural landmarks at Queens' College that include the handsome brick
16th-century **President's Lodge,** and **The Tower,** where the great scholar, Erasmus,
lived from 1510 to 1514. Hours vary seasonally, but the college is generally open to
the public from October to March, daily from 1:45 to 4:30pm; in July and August
daily from 10am to 4:30pm—check at the porter's lodge. The entrance fee is £1.50
($3). The college is closed from mid-May to mid-June.

Head back down King's Parade to ❸ **King's College** 𝄐𝄐𝄐 (© **01223/331-100**,
or 01223/331-155 for the chapel), founded by Henry VI in 1441 and justifiably
famous for its choir and the traditional Festival of Nine Lessons and Carols, which is
broadcast every Christmas Eve. Even without the presence of these heavenly voices,
the chapel is a fairly transcendental place, with its incredible fan vaulting, stained-glass
windows, and, behind the altar, Rubens's glorious _Adoration of the Magi,_ painted in
1634. Step into the small exhibition room to read about the chapel's history.

Try to attend a choral service for the full experience. You can normally hear Evensong Monday through Saturday at 5:30pm and Sunday at 10:30am and 3:30pm, but
only during university terms and during the first half of July; call to check. During
term, the college (including the chapel) is open Monday through Friday from 9:30am
to 3:30pm, Saturday from 9:30am to 3:15pm, and Sunday from 1:15 to 2:15pm. Out
of term, the college is open Monday through Saturday from 9:30am to 4:30pm, and

---

Fun Fact **Mad, Bad & Dangerous to Know**

According to legend, the poet Byron used to bathe naked with his pet bear in the large central fountain in Trinity College's Great Court. A bear? Well, Trinity did not allow students to keep dogs. The famous description of Byron as "mad, bad, and dangerous to know" was given to him later in life by Lady Caroline Lamb, one of Byron's many conquests.

Sunday from 10am to 5pm. The chapel is closed December 26 through January 1, and for recording sessions and rehearsals at other times (often without notice). Admission is £4.50 ($9) for adults, £3 ($6) for seniors, students, and children.

King's Parade turns into Trinity Street, which will lead you to ❹ **Trinity College** ✿✿✿ (✆ **01223/338-400**), the largest and wealthiest of Cambridge's colleges, founded by Henry VIII in 1546. (The king is irreverently commemorated in a statue on the Great Gate in which he clutches a chair leg instead of a sword—the alteration was a student prank.) Trinity has produced 31 Nobel Laureates, and famous alumni include former Indian prime minister Jawaharlal Nehru; the scientist Sir Isaac Newton; poets and writers Francis Bacon, Lord Tennyson, Lord Byron, Andrew Marvell, and John Dryden; and philosopher Bertrand Russell. The 2-acre (.8-hectare) Great Court—the largest enclosed courtyard in Europe—is the scene of the Great Court Run, the point of which is to run around the court in the time it takes the clock to strike noon, a scene you may remember from the movie *Chariots of Fire.* Pass through the hall at the west end of the court to Nevile's Cloister and the impressive **Wren Library,** designed by Sir Christopher Wren, the 17th-century architect of St. Paul's Cathedral in London. Wren also designed many of the furnishings in the library, and among busts of Sir Isaac Newton and other famous alumni you'll come upon a statue of Lord Byron, sculpted by Danish neoclassicist Bertel Thorvaldsen in the early 19th century and intended for Westminster Abbey. The college (not including the library) is open to the public daily from 10am to 5pm, but it closes during exams and at other periods, and certain parts may be closed the day you visit; ask at the porter's lodge before you pay admission, which is £2.20 ($4.40) for adults, £1.30 ($2.60) for seniors and students. The library is open free of charge to the public Monday to Friday from noon to 2pm and Saturday from 10:30am to 12:30pm. The college is closed for a week in June and all of September.

From the library, head toward the Backs and follow the Cam up to ❺ **St. John's Bridge** ✿, a replica of the Bridge of Sighs in Venice; the span joins the New Court of St. John's College, a 19th-century neo-Gothic fantasy of pinnacle and towers students call the "Wedding Cake," with the older, authentically Tudor section of the college, founded by Lady Margaret Beaufort, the mother of Henry VII, in 1511; the poet William Wordsworth was an alumnus of St. John's. Take St. John's Street to Magdalene (pronounced "maud-len") Street. It leads to ❻ **Magdalene College** ✿ (✆ **01223/ 332-100**), where the Pepys Library houses the diarist's collection of 3,000 volumes (open to the public 2 hr. a day; check with the porter); and **Jesus College** (✆ **01223/ 339-339**), founded in 1492 on the site of a nunnery. The chapel has been enlivened with stained-glass windows designed by Edward Burne-Jones and a ceiling by William Morris; both were leaders in the Arts and Crafts Movement of late-19th-century England. (You can admire the chapel during Evensong on Tues, Thurs, and Sat at 6:30pm.)

Continue up Magdalene until you reach the intersection of Castle and Northampton streets, where you'll find **❼ Kettle's Yard** 𝕽𝕽 (© 01223/352-124; www.kettles yard.co.uk), a very different kettle of fish. Jim Ede was the curator at the Tate during the 1920s and 1930s. He and his wife Helen acquired this collection of artworks, furniture, and decorative objects, which are displayed as he arranged them in his home. You'll find works by Ben Nicholson, Christopher Wood, and Alfred Wallis; and sculptures by Henry Moore, Henri Gaudier-Brzeska, Brancusi, and Barbara Hepworth. The gallery, meanwhile, hosts changing exhibitions of 20th-century art. Walking through the airy, light-filled rooms is a pleasure, and it's possible to sit and take in the surroundings, so try to visit early on a weekday when the house is least likely to be crowded. The house is open Tuesday to Sunday and Bank Holiday Mondays from 1:30 to 4:30pm (2–4pm in winter), and the gallery Tuesday to Sunday and Bank Holiday Mondays from 11:30am to 5pm. Admission is free.

ORGANIZED TOURS

The Tourist Information Centre (see "Visitor Information," earlier in this chapter) offers a **2-hour city walking tour** (£9/$18 per person) that includes colleges open to the public. The walks leave from the Tourist Information Centre at 1:30pm daily throughout the year; additional walks depart at 10:30am and 2:30pm Monday through Saturday from July through September, on Saturdays at 11:30am from October to March. For more information or to book a special guided tour, stop in this office or call **Blue Badge Guides** at © 01223/457-574.

City **Sightseeing** (© 01708/864340; www.citysightseeing.co.uk) offers an 80-minute open-top **bus tour** (£10/$20 per adult; £5/$10 per child 5–12). Buses depart daily from the train station starting at 9:45am and run every 15 to 20 minutes until 3 or 4pm, depending on the season.

MORE THINGS TO SEE & DO

❽ The Fitzwilliam Museum 𝕽𝕽   This eclectic treasure house shows off a horde of Egyptian and Greek antiquities, Chinese jades and bronzes, pages from Books of Hours, and the first draft of Keats's "Ode to a Nightingale," as well as china, glass,

---

Apostles of Knowledge

Of the many learned societies that have flourished at Cambridge over the centuries, few have become better known than **the Bloomsbury Group,** named for the district of London around the British Museum where this salon of writers, artists, and thinkers lived and often met. Most of the male members—E. M. Forster, Lytton Strachey, John Maynard Keynes, and Leonard Woolf among them—studied at Cambridge, and many belonged to the Apostles, a club founded at the university in the 1820s that met to discuss intellectual and philosophical issues. In London the group branched out to include women, most notably Vanessa Bell and Virginia Woolf (sisters of Thoby Stephens, a Cambridge Apostle). The group flourished into the 1930s. You will encounter the Bloomsbury Group in a rural setting if you visit Charleston and Monk's House, the homes of, respectively, Vanessa and Virginia, in Surrey, where the group often gathered (see trip 15).

majolica, silver, and clocks. Its treasure-trove of paintings ranges from medieval and Renaissance works to contemporary canvases and include Titian's *Tarquin and Lucretia,* Rubens's *The Death of Hippolytus,* brilliant etchings by van Dyck, rare Hogarths, and 25 Turners, as well as works by William Blake, the Impressionists, and the more recent artists Paul Nash and Sir Stanley Spencer.

Trumpington St. ℂ **01223/332-900.** www.fitzmuseum.cam.ac.uk. Free admission. Tues–Sat 10am–5pm; Sun 2:15–5pm.

❾ **Scott Polar Research Institute** 🐸   One of Cambridge's hidden gems of historical memorabilia commemorates Sir Robert Scott and his team, who died at the South Pole in 1912. Scott sailed from London in 1910 on the *Terra Nova* in an attempt to be the first explorer to set foot on the South Pole. He set the Union Jack on the pole in January 1912, but discovered that a Norwegian team had reached the goal just 1 month before. Scott and his expedition ran out of supplies and died as they made their way back across the ice shelf toward the *Terra Nova* but soon became heroes of arctic exploration. The gear, photos, and diaries of the doomed expedition are haunting and fascinating.

Lensfield Rd. ℂ **01223/336-540.** www.spri.cam.ac.uk. Free admission. Tues–Fri 11am–1pm and 2–4pm; Sat noon–4pm.

❿ **Imperial War Museum Duxford** 🐸🐸🐸   Duxford was a major air base during World War II and now houses the largest aviation museum in Europe, which is also one of Britain's most popular attractions. Vintage aircraft, tanks, a Concorde supersonic jet, and other equipment fill the grounds, and the American Air Museum, housed in a stunning new building, serves as a memorial to the 30,000 U.S. airmen who lost their lives flying on missions over Europe from British bases. All of the exhibits are well done, especially the Battle of Britain Exhibition and the Normandy Experience, which recounts the events of D-day. Duxford is of enormous interest to those who fought in World War II (and is especially popular with Americans who were based in England during the war), to aviation and military history buffs of all ages, and to anyone who wants to know more about the World War II experience in England. You can work a visit to Duxford into a 1-day trip to Cambridge fairly easily, using the convenient bus service from the city to the airfield (see below)—provided you give yourself a long day.

Duxford, outskirts of Cambridge at Junction 10 of M11 motorway. ℂ **01223/835-000.** www.iwm.org.uk. £14.95 ($30) adults, £11.50 ($23) seniors and students, free for children 15 and under. Mid-Mar to Oct daily 10am–6pm; Nov to mid-Mar daily 10am–4pm. Stagecoach bus C7 runs Mon–Sat every 30 min. 8:55am–4:35pm from the bus station on Emmanuel St. and the train station; for more information, call ℂ 0870/608-2608 or go to www.stagecoach bus.com. On Sun, take Myalls bus 132 from Cambridge bus station on Dummer St.

Moments **Picnic by the Cam**

If the weather's nice, go to Market Square for picnic provender (see "Shopping," below), and then head to the Backs for an idyllic stolen moment by the River Cam. Two of Cambridge's most famous landmarks—the Wren Library and King's Chapel—are especially impressive when viewed across the grassy expanse of the Backs.

OUTDOOR ACTIVITIES

"Punting," or pole-boating, is a Cambridge tradition. If you take to the River Cam early enough, you can enjoy a feeling of solitude as you witness the quiet colleges rise off the banks of the river. However, the carnival-like atmosphere that prevails on a warm day when students and visitors crowd the river is fun and an experience in itself. At the venerable Scudamore's **Punting Company** (© **01223/359-750;** www. scudamores.com), expect to pay £16 ($32) per hour on weekdays, £18 ($36) per hour on weekends, to hire a punt; you must leave a £60 ($120) refundable deposit. Scudamore's also organizes "chauffeured" punting tours of the college Backs and the riverside village of Granchester, with fees of about £12 to £15 ($24–$30) for adults, £10 ($20) for seniors and students, and £6 ($12) for children under 12. Punts are available at the **Mill Lane punting station,** next to Silver Street bridge (daily 10am–dusk Feb–Mar and Oct–Nov; daily 9am–dusk Apr–Sept; weekends only 10am–dusk Dec–Jan); **Jesus Green,** near the **Chesterton Foot Bridge** (weekends Apr–May and Sept–Oct 10am–dusk; daily June–Aug 10am–6pm); **Magdalene Bridge** (daily 10am–dusk Feb–Mar and Oct–Nov; daily 9am–dusk Apr–Sept; weekends only 10am–dusk Dec–Jan); and the **Main Boatyard,** Mill Lane (daily Apr–Sept 9am–dusk; weekends only Oct and Mar 10am–dusk).

You can join the rank and file of cycling students and rent a bike from **Geoff's Bike Hire** near the train station at 65 Devonshire Rd. (© **01223/365-629**). Rates are £7 ($14) for a day, £4 ($8) for half a day; the staff is really helpful and will provide a free leaflet on suggested cycling itineraries around town and through the nearby countryside.

3 Shopping

Every Saturday a crafts market takes over **All Saints Passage,** opposite Trinity Hall. On Sunday you'll find a farmers' market in **Market Square,** plus an art, crafts, and antiques market. A general market, selling everything from fish to fruit to fripperies, is open every day but Sunday in Market Square.

Stop at the **King's College Chapel Shop** (© **01223/331-228**) for souvenirs, books, postcards, and recordings of the King's College Choir. It's open Monday to Saturday from 9:30am to 3:45pm during university term, out of term Monday to Saturday from 9:30am to 4:50pm and Sunday from 10am to 4:15pm (winter) or 5:15pm (summer). The shop at the **Fitzwilliam Museum** (© **01223/470-474**) is also well worth a stop.

4 Where to Dine

The Anchor ☞ PUB   Looking out on a raft of punts and the willow-fringed river from a position opposite Queen's College, The Anchor is loaded with atmosphere— inside you'll find wooden beams, sloping ceilings, and odds and ends such as cider pots and prints. It serves such traditional homemade English pub grub as battered cod and plaice; lamb-and-vegetable or leek-and-potato pies; or sausage, eggs, and chips. Come here for real ale, as well as the usual selection of lagers and bitters.

Silver St. © 01223/353-554. £4–£8 ($8–$16). MC, V. Food served Mon–Thurs noon–7:45pm; Fri–Sat noon–3:45pm; Sun noon–2:30pm.

Auntie's ☞ TEAROOM   This tearoom is as much a tradition as the nearby market, and dispenses sandwiches, soups, and pastries to an interesting mix of town and gown.

1 St. Mary's Passage, off Market Sq. ⓒ 01223/315-641. Most items £3–£7 ($6–$14). MC, V. Mon–Fri 9:30am–5:30pm; Sat 9:30am–6:30pm; Sun 11am–5:30pm.

5 Extending Your Trip

You may want to extend your exploration of Cambridge into the evening hours, when the medieval streets can seem especially welcoming and you can find plenty of diversions in a pub or at one of many performances staged throughout the year. The main venue for music and theatre is **The Corn Exchange** on Wheeler Street (ⓒ **01223/ 357-851;** www.cornex.co.uk), which hosts visiting companies. The other place to see theatre is the **University Amateur Dramatics Club** on Park Street near Jesus Lane (ⓒ **01223/503-333**), where two student productions are performed nightly Tuesday through Saturday; it's closed in August and September. For music, check out the schedule of the **Trinity College Music Society** (ⓒ **01223/304-922;** www.tcms.org. uk), which presents 20 concerts each term, ranging from Renaissance to modern music, in the college chapel, Wren Library, and other interesting venues.

If you want to spend the evening nursing a pint or two in atmospheric surroundings, check out the 600-year-old **Pickerel Inn,** 30 Magdalene St. (ⓒ **01223/355-068**), the oldest pub in Cambridge; and **The Eagle,** on Benet Street (ⓒ **01223/505-020**), where airmen who drank here during World War II carved their names into the darkened ceiling of the back room—and often stop by to relive old times.

De Vere University Arms 😊😊😊   The best hotel in Cambridge lies behind an unappealing modern entrance on Regent Street. The original wing, though, is charmingly Victorian and faces Parker's Piece through large windows. The best guest rooms are the high-ceilinged ones in this wing, but all accommodations are gracious and traditionally furnished, and all have well-equipped modern bathrooms.

Regent St. ⓒ 01223/351-241. www.devereonline.co.uk. £85–£170 ($170–$340) double. Rates include English breakfast. AE, DC, MC, V.

Trip

5

Canterbury

*S*pinning the stories immortalized in *The Canterbury Tales,* Chaucer's pilgrims made their way to Canterbury to visit the shrine of Thomas Becket in Canterbury Cathedral. But Canterbury was a prominent place on the English map long before Chaucer wove his 13th-century tales. St. Augustine founded an abbey here in 597, after Ethelbert, King of Kent, granted him permission to preach Christianity. The evocative remains of St. Augustine's Abbey, one of Europe's great medieval centers of learning, are spread across a grassy field not far from the cathedral; both are now UNESCO World Heritage Sites. Pope Gregory I named Augustine the first archbishop of Canterbury, and the city has been the seat of the Anglican Church ever since.

The soaring cathedral that is the city's most famous feature began to rise in 1070, and it was there, in a corner of the northwest transept, that knights of Henry II murdered Thomas Becket, then archbishop of Canterbury, in 1170. Becket was canonized as a saint just 3 years later, at which point Canterbury became one of Europe's most popular pilgrimage centers. For nearly 400 years, until Henry VIII had the shrine destroyed in 1538, pilgrims from throughout England and Europe flocked to this medieval mecca in search of miracles and a bit of adventure. Bell Harry, the graceful cathedral bell tower that guided the pilgrims across the fields and orchards of the Kent countryside, will lead you to this appealing city, too. Canterbury Cathedral remains one of England's greatest and most venerable glories—its social and spiritual impact over the centuries has been profound.

Canterbury, on the River Stour in Kent, some 62 miles (99km) east of London, makes a perfect day trip. The cathedral is without a doubt the chief reason to visit, but there are also medieval buildings that will give you a glimpse into the pilgrim's world of 600 years ago, a host of small museums and attractions devoted to Canterbury's Roman and medieval past, and, of course, St. Augustine's Abbey, which even in ruin is one of the most venerable religious sites in England. No small part of the appeal of Canterbury is the absence of cars in most of the city center, making it easy to stroll around the city and slip into the past. You'll want to spend the better part of a day, coming down from London in the morning so you have plenty of time to enjoy the city. If you're a history buff or just enjoy the city's medieval ambience, you may want to spend more than a day here; if so, see the hotel recommendations at the end of this chapter.

Canterbury Highlights

• Exploring magnificent Canterbury Cathedral.
• Visiting the ancient grounds of St. Augustine's Abbey.
• Discovering the city's Roman past in the Roman Museum.

1 Essentials

VISITOR INFORMATION

The **Tourist Information Centre,** 12–13 Sun St. ((C) **01227/378-100;** www. canterbury.co.uk), is located opposite Christchurch Gate at the entrance to the cathedral precincts. Easter through October, the center is open Monday through Saturday from 9:30am to 5pm and Sunday from 10am to 4pm; November through Easter, it's open Monday through Saturday from 9:30am to 4pm.

SCHEDULING CONSIDERATIONS

You may want to time your visit so that you can take one of the informative **guided walks** offered daily at 2pm by the Tourist Information Centre (see "Organized Tours," below) or to hear **Evensong** sung in Canterbury Cathedral; it takes place at 5:30pm Monday through Friday, and at 3:15pm on Saturday. Canterbury is popular year-round with day-trippers and school groups from England and across the Channel. Crowds swell in summer and during school holidays (3 weeks at Christmas and at Easter, and a week in mid-Oct and mid-Feb). If you want to visit the **cathedral** in relative peace, arrive early and then return for Evensong, an atmospheric experience that even non-religious visitors will enjoy.

GETTING THERE
BY TRAIN

Canterbury has two train stations, both within easy walking distance of the city center. From London's Victoria Station, starting at 6:41am, direct trains run about every half-hour to Canterbury East; direct trains depart Canterbury for London until 9:40pm. Starting at 7am (later on weekends), direct trains from London's Charing Cross stop at Canterbury West, returning to London up until 9:13pm. The journey takes about 2 hours and costs about £22 ($44) for a day return. For train schedules and information, contact **National Rail Enquiries** ((C) **08457/484950**) or visit www. nationalrail.co.uk.

BY BUS

National Express ((C) **0990/808-080;** www.nationalexpress.com) offers frequent, direct bus service from London's Victoria Coach Station to Canterbury's bus station on St. George's Lane, a few minutes' walk from the cathedral. The trip takes 1 hour and 50 minutes; day return fare runs from £8 to £12 ($16–$24).

BY CAR

From London, take A2, then M2. The trip takes about 2 hours, but allot extra time if you're leaving London on a Friday night. Canterbury city center is closed to cars, but there are several parking areas close to the cathedral. The car parks in Sturry Road,

Canterbury

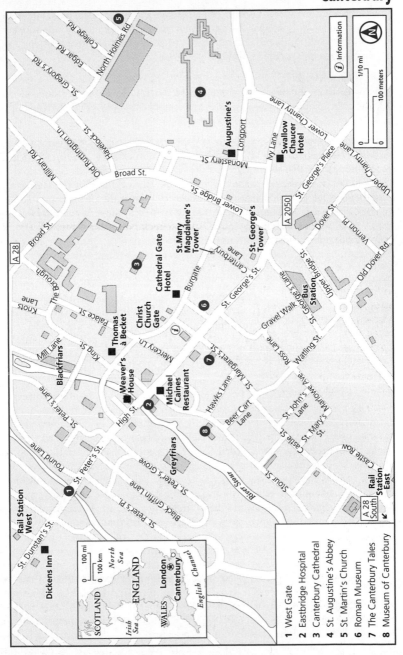

College Rd.
Edgar Rd.
St. Gregory's Rd.
North Holmes Rd.

⑤

Havelock St.
Old Ruttington Ln.
Military Rd.

Broad St.

Augustine's

④

Longport

Lower Chantry Lane

Ivy Lane

Swallow Chaucer Hotel

Monastery St.

St. George's Place

Upper Chantry Lane

Lower Bridge St.

A 2050

Broad St.

A 28

Knots Lane
The Borough

Palace St.
King St.

Christ Church Gate

Mill Lane

Blackfriars

St. Peter's Lane

Thomas à Becket

Cathedral Gate Hotel

③

Burgate

St.Mary Magdalene's Tower

Canterbury Lane

St. George's Tower

St. George's St.

Dover St.

Vernon Pl.

Old Dover Rd.

⑥

ⓘ

Mercery Ln.

Weaver's House

②

Michael Caines Restaurant

⑦

St. Margaret's St.

Hawks Lane

Gravel Walk

Ross Lane

Watling St.

Bus Station

Upper Bridge St.

George's Lane

High St.

⑧

Beer Cart Lane

Castle St.

St. John's Lane

St. Mary's St.

Marlowe Ave.

Rail Station West

St. Dunstan's St.

Dickens Inn

Pound Lane

①

St. Peter's Pl.

St. Peter's St.

Black Griffin Lane

St. Peter's Grove

Greyfriars

River Stour

Stour St.

Castle Row

A 28 South

Rail Station East

1 West Gate
2 Eastbridge Hospital
3 Canterbury Cathedral
4 St. Augustine's Abbey
5 St. Martin's Church
6 Roman Museum
7 The Canterbury Tales
8 Museum of Canterbury

Wincheap, and New Dover Road provide free Park and Ride service into Canterbury city center and back from 7am to 7pm Monday through Saturday. Parking vouchers, available from local shops and post offices, are needed for most on-street parking spots on the outskirts of Canterbury city center.

GETTING AROUND

Walking is the easiest way to get around Canterbury. Cabs are usually available outside the train stations, or you can order a taxi by calling **Lynx** (© **01227/464-232**) or **Cabwise** (© **01227/712-929**).

2 A Day in Canterbury

For a pilgrim's tour of Canterbury, enter the city through the ❶ **West Gate,** where St. Peter's Street crosses the River Stour. The gate has stood guard over the road to and from London for some 600 years, and hundreds of thousands of medieval pilgrims, on their way to visit St. Thomas Becket's shrine, passed through this gateway into the city. A spiral access stair leads up to the battlements for a panoramic view of the city and its cathedral. You might want to return here later in your tour to take a break in the beautiful gardens next to the gate, on the banks of the River Stour. The tower is open Monday through Saturday from 11am to 12:30pm and 1:30 to 3:30pm. Admission is £1.25 ($2.50).

Follow St. Peter's Street, which becomes High Street, and take a few minutes to visit ❷ **Eastbridge Hospital,** High Street (© **01227/471688**), founded in the 12th century to provide overnight lodging to pilgrims visiting the shrine of Thomas Becket. It has an undercroft, two chapels, and a refectory. The hospital is open Monday through Saturday from 10am to 4:45pm. Admission is £1 ($2) for adults, 50p ($1) for children.

Turn north on Mercery Lane and follow it to Christ Church Gate, where you enter the precincts of venerable ❸ **Canterbury Cathedral** ✸✸✸ (© **01227/762-862;** www.canterbury-cathedral.org). The origins of this massive and magnificent structure date back to A.D. 597, when St. Augustine arrived on a mission from Rome to bring Christianity to England. He founded a religious community in Canterbury at what has come to be known as St. Augustine's Abbey (see below), and established a church on the site of the present-day cathedral. The soaring edifice that rises on the site today, begun in 1070, is the first cathedral in England to be built in the Gothic style. The many additions made over the years include a central bell tower (nicknamed Bell Harry), where enormous bells have rung out the time since the 15th century. After overzealous knights of Henry II murdered Archbishop Thomas Becket in the cathedral in 1170 and he was canonized a few years later, pilgrims from all over Europe began to flock to his shrine; its location is marked in the Trinity Chapel near the high altar. The massive structure, built of soft gray stone from French quarries, is bathed in gentle light from the magnificent medieval stained-glass windows that depict the miracles of Christ. Henry II did his penance for Becket's murder (see "Thomas Becket vs. Henry II: A Medieval Power Struggle," below) in the crypt, beneath a magnificent bestiary carved into the capitals of the pillars—although he claimed never to have ordered the archbishop's execution. The cathedral houses the medieval royal tombs of Henry IV and Edward the Black Prince, but more stirring are the grooves that legions of pilgrims wore into the stone floor as they crawled past the shrine on their knees. Another Henry, the VIII, destroyed Becket's shrine and other parts of the cathedral after he was excommunicated and sought to destroy the power of the Church of

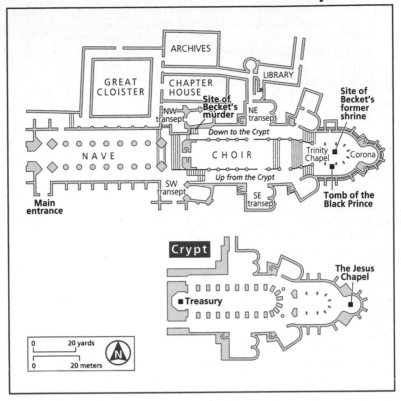

Rome, and Puritans ransacked the church during the English Civil War in the 1640s. These marauders spared much, however, except for the vibrant paintings that once covered the walls. You can see a fragment, depicting St. Paul and the viper, in the northeast corner. The cathedral is open daily 10am to 5pm (Nov–Feb until 4:30pm; July–Aug from 9:30am). Admission is £6.50 ($13) for adults; £5 ($10) for seniors, students, and children. King's School, the oldest public school in England, is housed in several fine medieval buildings (not open to the public) around the cathedral.

Follow Burgate east, crossing Lower Bridge Street and Monastery Street, to Longport, where you'll find the atmospheric ruins of ❹ **St. Augustine's Abbey** ✸✸ (✆ **01227/767-345**), one of the oldest Anglo-Saxon monastic sites in the country and, like the cathedral, a designated World Heritage Site. (It's about a 15-min. walk from the cathedral.) St. Augustine founded a monastic community here in A.D. 597, when he came to England to spread Christianity. The community flourished, and by 1500 the abbey was one of Europe's great centers of learning, with a 2,000-volume library. Henry VIII had the abbey, with its impressive Saxon and Norman churches and other buildings, destroyed when he broke with the Church in the mid–16th century, and commissioned a palace to be built on the grounds to house Anne of Cleves when she arrived from France to become his fourth wife. (The marriage was short-lived, and soon annulled; Anne was given Hever Castle as part of her settlement; see

Thomas Becket versus Henry II: A Medieval Power Struggle

Thomas Becket was born in Normandy in 1118, the son of a prosperous English merchant. He was sent to Paris for his education and from there to England, where he joined the household of Theobold, the archbishop of Canterbury. The archbishop, noting Becket's talents, sent him back to Paris to study law and upon his return made him archdeacon of Canterbury. In 1154, Theobold introduced Becket to the newly crowned king, Henry II. The two hit it off immediately, and Henry soon named Becket his chancellor. When Archbishop Theobold died in 1161, Henry saw the opportunity to increase his influence over the Church by naming his loyal advisor Becket to the highest ecclesiastical post in the land. Becket, who had never been ordained, was quickly invested as a priest, ordained a bishop, and made archbishop of Canterbury in 1162. But Becket and Henry clashed on the issue of the Church's right to try felonious clerics in their own religious courts of justice instead of those of the Crown, and eventually, in royal disfavor, Becket fled to France.

The two former friends met again in Normandy in 1170, and Becket was allowed to return to his post as archbishop. But another power struggle broke out when Becket refused to absolve two English bishops whom he had excommunicated for supporting the king. Henry, still in France, flew into a rage and purportedly shouted, "What sluggards, what cowards have I brought up in my court, who care nothing for their allegiance to their lord. Who will rid me of this meddlesome priest?" Henry later claimed it was an oath, not an order to kill, but his outrage inspired four knights to sail to England to rid the realm of its most annoying prelate. Arriving at Canterbury during the afternoon of December 29, the four immediately searched for the archbishop. Becket fled to the cathedral, where a service was in progress. The knights found him at the altar, drew their swords, and began hacking at their victim, finally splitting his skull.

The brutal act sent shock waves through medieval Europe and unnerved the king, who was blamed for inciting the murder. When miracles were reported at Becket's tomb, the former archbishop was canonized and hordes of pilgrims transformed Canterbury Cathedral into a shrine. Four years later, in an act of penance, the king donned sackcloth and walked barefoot through the streets of Canterbury while 80 monks flogged him with branches. Henry capped his atonement by spending the night in the martyr's crypt. St. Thomas remained a popular cult figure throughout the Middle Ages.

trip 11.) The extensive ruins of the abbey and the Tudor palace are set within a spacious park, and an intelligent audio tour offers insights into the extensive and complex history of the place. The site is open April through June Wednesday through Sunday 10am to 5pm; July and August daily 10am to 6pm; and September through March Sundays 11am to 5pm. Admission is £4 ($8) for adults, £3 ($6) for seniors and students.

Walk another 5 minutes east from St. Augustine's Abbey to North Holmes Road and you find the oldest parish church in England and another UNESCO World Heritage Site. No one knows for sure who founded **❺ St. Martin's Church** (✆ 01227/ 459-482), but it was already in existence when Augustine arrived from Rome to convert the Anglo-Saxon natives in A.D. 597 (and there's some archaeological evidence that the structure dates back to the time when Rome ruled England). The tiny church, named for the bishop of Tours, was given to Queen Bertha, the French (Christian) wife of (pagan) Saxon King Ethelbert of Kent, as part of her marriage contract. It's open daily from 9am to 5pm and admission is free.

Backtrack to Christchurch Gate on Burgate and follow Butchery Lane to the **❻ Roman Museum** ⚔ (✆ 01227/785-575). Two millennia ago, following their conquest of England, Romans were living in Canterbury, which they called *Durovernum Cantiacorum*. Their daily lives are chronicled through reconstructions, video presentations, and hands-on displays in this small but fascinating museum in the excavated Roman levels of the city between the cathedral and High Street. It's open Monday through Saturday from 10am to 5pm year-round, and on Sunday (June–Oct only) from 1:30 to 5pm. Admission is £3 ($6) for adults; £2 ($4) for seniors, students, and children.

Take St. George's Street north to St. Margaret's Street and turn left. **❼ The Canterbury Tales,** 23 St. Margaret's St., in St. Margaret's Church (✆ 01227/454-888; www.canterburytales.org.uk), re-creates scenes from *The Canterbury Tales,* Geoffrey Chaucer's spirited and sometimes bawdy stories about a group of medieval pilgrims on their way to visit Becket's shrine at Canterbury Cathedral. Animatronic figures bring the Wife of Bath, the knight, the miller, and several other pilgrims to life in a series of well-executed tableaux staged in the former church of St. Margaret, and an animated audio-tour retells the tales and presents the historical context of the pilgrimage to Canterbury. Informative and entertaining, yes, but it seems a bit odd to spend time and money on these theatrics when so much real history is in evidence just outside the door. The attraction is open daily from 10am to 5pm (Nov–Feb until 4:30pm). Admission is £7.50 ($15) for adults, £6.50 ($13) for seniors and students, and £5.50 ($11) for children.

Follow St. Margaret's Street to Hawks Lane and follow Hawks Lane to Stour Street. The **❽ Museum of Canterbury** (✆ 01227/452-747) is housed in the ancient Wool Priests' Hospital, and recently expanded into two adjacent buildings. The artifacts and interactive exhibits that shed light on Canterbury's long history and that are of most interest to the general visitor are in the old part of the museum; the new additions, such as the Rupert Bear Museum, are of interest only if you have children. The museum is open Monday through Saturday from 10:30am to 5pm, and 1:30 to 5pm on Sundays from July through September. Admission is £3.40 ($6.80) for adults; £2.25 ($4.50) for seniors, students, and children. Before you go, have a look at the collection of pilgrim badges from medieval souvenir shops—600 years ago, you might have bought one as a souvenir of your trip to Canterbury.

St. Thomas Becket's Shrine

Only one burning candle marks the spot where the shrine of St. Thomas Becket stood in Canterbury Cathedral. The most popular pilgrimage spot in England for nearly 400 years, it was destroyed by order of Henry VIII in 1538.

ORGANIZED TOURS

Guided walks of the city and cathedral leave from the Tourist Information Centre on Sun Street daily at 2pm. (Additional walks are held daily in July–Aug at 11:30am.) The cost is £4.50 ($9) for adults; £4 ($8) for seniors and students; £3 ($6) for children under 12; and £15 ($30) for families. The walks are a fun and informative way to learn more about Canterbury and its historic buildings.

Canterbury Historic River Tours, Weaver's House, 1 St. Peter's St. (© 07790/ 534-744; www.canterburyrivertours.co.uk), offers half-hour boat trips on the River Stour with commentary on the history of the buildings you pass. April through September, river conditions permitting, boats depart daily every 15 or 20 minutes from 10am to 5pm (from 11am on Sun). Tickets are £6 ($12) for adults, £5 ($10) for seniors and students, and £4 ($18) for children 5 to 15. Umbrellas are available in case of rain. The boats leave from behind the 15th-century Weaver's House (access via the Weaver's restaurant garden).

The **Canterbury River Navigation Company,** Westgate Gardens (© 01227/768-915), offers punt trips along the River Stour by experienced boatmen. A choice of scenic trips, including city trips, picnic trips, and wine-and-dine trips, are available seasonally. Boats leave from the slipway next to West Gate. The 1-hour City Trip costs £12 ($24) for adults, £4 ($8) for children.

OUTDOOR ACTIVITIES

The **Crab and Winkle Way** (www.crabandwinkle.org) is an attractive 7-mile (11km), one-way, nearly traffic-free walking and cycling route that follows part of the old Canterbury–Whitstable railway line. For a free detailed map covering the route and attractions along the way, ask for the Crab and Winkle Way brochure in the Canterbury Tourist Information Centre. **Downland Cycles** (© 01227/479-643), located in Canterbury West train station, rents bikes for £12 ($24) per day; you must reserve in advance.

3 Shopping

Canterbury Farmer's Market (Tues–Sat 8am–7pm, Sun 10am–4pm), located in the refurbished Victorian goods shed just outside Canterbury West train station, has stalls where local farmers sell produce and an enticing range of breads and cakes. Unique to Canterbury, the Farmer's Market also has a restaurant, **The Goods Shed** (© 01227/ 459-153), with a menu that changes twice daily to reflect the best seasonal produce available at the market. Food is prepared by top London chef Blaise Vasseur. Hours are the same as market hours.

A market with stalls selling more general goods, from clothes to gewgaws, is held on Wednesday and Friday from 8am to 4pm in Canterbury's city center.

4 Where to Dine

Augustine's ⚜ MODERN BRITISH   This fun, informal restaurant, set in a Georgian house on the way to St. Augustine's Abbey, is a neighborhood favorite and can be depended upon to serve up good cooking, including vegetarian dishes, using fresh, local ingredients.

1 and 2 Longport. © 01227/453-063. Main courses £12–£25 ($24–$50); fixed-price lunch £8.95 ($18). MC, V. Tues–Sat noon–1:30pm and 6:30–9pm; Sun noon–2pm. Closed Jan.

Michael Caines Restaurant ☆☆ TRADITIONAL/MODERN BRITISH   This elegant restaurant in the Abode Hotel is one of the best in Canterbury. Choose from a selection of traditional English dishes, try one of the more imaginatively conceived platters, or sample seasonal specialties such as grilled lemon sole or roasted breast of pheasant. Or dine on traditional pub fare in the Tavern.

Abode Hotel, High St. ✆ **01227/766-266.** Main courses restaurant £14–£20 ($28–$40); tavern £8–£15 ($16–$30). AE, DC, MC, V. Daily 7:30am–10pm.

Thomas à Becket PUB FARE   This cozy beamed room is a fine place to enjoy a pint and some excellent traditional English fare, such as bacon and liver casserole, or lamb and apple pie.

21 Best Lane. ✆ **01227/464-383.** Reservations recommended. £5–£9 ($10–$18). AE, DC, MC, V. Daily noon–11:30pm.

5 Extending Your Trip

Cathedral Gate Hotel ☆   If you want to stay near the cathedral, like the pilgrims of yore, you can't get any closer than this 27-room hotel adjoining Christchurch Gate (one of the gates into the cathedral precincts). Dating from 1438, the hotel has comfortable and modestly furnished rooms and an overall ambience of sloping floors, massive oak beams, and winding corridors. With the cheapest rooms, you'll be sharing a bathroom.

36 Burgate, Canterbury, Kent CT1 2HA. ✆ **01227/464-381.** Fax 01227/462-800. www.cathgate.co.uk. £40–£98 ($80–$196) double. Rates include continental breakfast. AE, DC, MC, V.

The Swallow Chaucer Hotel   Originally a Georgian residence, the Chaucer stands opposite Canterbury's ancient city walls, about a 10-minute walk from the city center. This is a small, pleasant, recently refurbished hotel with 42 comfortable rooms, all of them different in size and layout (and all named for characters in Chaucer's novels), some with views over the city's rooftops to the cathedral.

63 Ivy Lane (off Lower Bridge St.), Canterbury, Kent CT1 1TU. ✆ **01227/464427.** Fax 01227/450397. www.swallowhotels.com. £75–£110 ($150–$220) double. AE, DC, MC, V.

Chichester

Chichester, about 70 miles (113km) south of London near the Sussex coast, is a handsome town of medieval and 18th-century houses on beautiful lanes and streets. And despite the quiet, country air that prevails in Chichester, the town also boasts four attractions, any one of which would draw visitors: a beautiful Norman cathedral, with a graceful steeple that can be seen from far out at sea; Pallant House, one of Britain's finest galleries of modern art; the Chichester Festival Theatre, one of the country's most acclaimed stages, regularly hosting England's leading actors; and Fishbourne Roman Palace, a massive, 2000-year-old domestic complex, graced with exquisite mosaics.

You can visit these sights while soaking in the pleasant atmosphere of Chichester, enjoying its lively streets and lanes that are still largely surrounded by Roman and medieval walls. Many of these byways, including the town's four major thoroughfares, follow the grid the Romans laid out for their city of Noviomagus Reginorum, which later became the major city of the Kingdom of Sussex. You can spend a pleasant full day in Chichester, but you may want to linger long enough to enjoy Evensong in the cathedral or even a performance at the Festival Theatre before returning to London. You could also combine a trip to Chichester with a visit to **Brighton** (see trip 3), just 30 miles (48km) east along A27 and easily reached by trains along the coast, which run about every half-hour.

Chichester Highlights

- Walking along streets laid out by the Romans and lined with medieval to 18th-century houses.
- Exploring Chichester Cathedral, one of England's most remarkable Norman edifices.
- Seeing the magnificent mosaics at Fishbourne Roman Palace.
- Enjoying 20th-century British art at the Pallant House Gallery.
- Attending a performance at the Festival Theatre.

Chichester

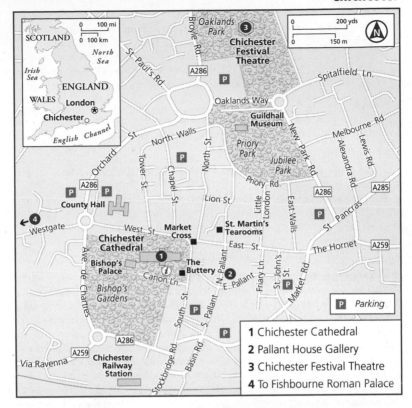

Parking

1 Chichester Cathedral
2 Pallant House Gallery
3 Chichester Festival Theatre
4 To Fishbourne Roman Palace

1 Essentials

VISITOR INFORMATION

Chichester is about 70 miles (113km) southwest of London and 30 miles (48km) west of Brighton along the Sussex coast. The **Tourist Information Centre,** 29a South St. (*© 01243/775-888;* www.chichesterweb.co.uk), is open April to September, Monday 10:15am to 5:15pm, Tuesday to Saturday 9:15am to 5:15pm, and Sunday 11am to 3:30pm; October to March it's open Monday 10:15am to 5:15pm and Tuesday to Saturday 9:15am to 5:15pm.

SCHEDULING CONSIDERATIONS

A visit to Chichester from April through September can include a performance at the city's acclaimed **Festival Theatre,** and in July of every third year the city hosts the **Southern Cathedrals Festival,** with performances by the choirs of Chichester, Winchester, and Salisbury cathedrals. Any time you visit, try to be in town long enough to enjoy **Evensong** in the cathedral (5:30pm Mon–Sat and 3:30pm Sun). The cathedral also hosts free lunchtime concerts on Tuesdays at 1:10pm November through February. Chichester is especially pleasant on a day of good weather, since a visit can include walks out to **Fishbourne Roman Palace** and along **the Salterns Way** (see below).

BY TRAIN

From London's Victoria and Waterloo Stations, trains depart about every half-hour throughout the day for Chichester. The trip takes 1½ hours and the fare is £18.50 ($37). The first train leaves London as early as 4am and the last train returns from Chichester to London at 11:15pm. For train information, call **National Rail Enquiries** at ℂ **08457/484950** or go to www.nationalrail.co.uk.

BY CAR

The trip from London takes about 1¾ hours, depending on traffic. Follow A3 south to Hindhead, and from there a well-marked route on A287 and A286 into Chichester.

GETTING AROUND

Chichester train station is on the edge of the town center, a short walk from the cathedral and most other sights.

Fishbourne Roman Palace is about 1½ miles (2.4km) west of Chichester. A pleasant walk follows the town streets onto the Lavant to Bosham cycle way, which leads through fields and passes through the site. You can also take a bus (no. 11, 56, or 700) from the front of the cathedral and get off at Salthill Road, which leads through a suburban neighborhood to the site. Fare is about £1.60 ($3.20).

2 A Day in Chichester

Most of the center of Chichester is closed to traffic, making it a pleasure to stroll and admire the city's delightful old streets. The urban grid still follows the plan the Romans laid out, and four main streets (appropriately named South, North, East, and West) bisect the town at right angles to one another and meet at the medieval Market Cross. From here, it's just a short walk down West Street to ❶ **Chichester Cathedral** 𝆑𝆑𝆑 (ℂ **01243/812-482;** www.chichestercathedral.co.uk), begun in 1076 on the site of a Roman shrine and completed just 32 years later, creating a unified assemblage of Norman grandeur, topped by a graceful spire, that has remained remarkably untouched over the years. Two recent additions include a stained-glass window by 20th-century painter Marc Chagall, depicting Psalm 150, "O praise God in his holiness . . . let everything that hath breath praise the Lord," and a painting by another 20th-century artist, Graham Sutherland (whose work you will also see at the Pallant House Gallery), in the Chapel of St. Mary Magdalene. These works are surrounded by many fine Romanesque sculptures, including a 12th-century relief of the rising of Lazarus, and exquisite stained glass, some of it from the 14th century. The cathedral is open from 7:15am to 6pm in winter (until 7pm in summer). Guided tours are conducted Monday through Saturday at 11:15am and 2:30pm and last 45 minutes.

From the Market Cross, it's a short walk east of East Street to North Pallant Street and ❷ **Pallant House Gallery** 𝆑𝆑𝆑, 9 North Pallant (ℂ **01243/774-557;** www.pallant.org.uk), one of Britain's greatest showplaces of modern art. Works by Barbara Hepworth, Graham Sutherland, Duncan Grant, and other leading British artists of the 20th century hang in stunningly designed galleries, which also display an extensive collection of 18th-century porcelain from London's acclaimed Bow Factory. The gallery is open Tuesday through Saturday 10am to 5pm (until 8pm on Thurs), and Sunday 12:30 to 5pm. Admission is £6.50 ($13) for adults, £3.50 ($7) for students, and £2 ($4) for children 6 to 15; admission is half price on Tuesdays and on Thursday evenings.

Chichester's other great cultural institution, the ❸ **Chichester Festival Theatre** (② **01243/784-437**; www.cft.org.uk), is at the end of North Street. Founded in 1962 under the stewardship of Sir Laurence Olivier, who served as the first artistic director, the theatre has seen performances by almost every major British actor, including Alan Bates, Julie Christie, Alec Guinness, John Gielgud, Anthony Hopkins, Derek Jacobi, Joan Plowright, Diana Rigg—to name just a few. You can see Britain's leading actors of today in award-winning productions during the Festival season from April through September, and the theatre hosts visiting troupes and performances the rest of the year.

In the little village of Fishbourne, now a suburban neighborhood about a mile (1.6km) west of the city center, you'll find some of the remains the Romans left behind: ❹ **Fishbourne Roman Palace** 𝕲𝕲𝕲, Salthill Road (② **01243/785-859**; www.sussexpast.co.uk/fishbourne), a remarkable palace that's as grand as those of Imperial Rome. Built around A.D. 50, it's the largest domestic building to be uncovered in Britain, and contains 20 remarkably well-preserved mosaic floors; in the most exuberant, a cupid rides on the back of a dolphin. Excavations have also uncovered an underground heating system and an elaborate bath, and the garden has been planted as it would have been in Roman times. The palace is open daily late January to mid-December from 10am to 4pm (or later, in the spring/summer; call ahead or check the website), and 10am to 4pm Saturdays and Sundays only from mid-December to late January. Admission is £6.80 ($14) for adults, £5.80 ($12) for seniors and students, £3.60 ($7) for children, and £17.40 ($35) for families of two adults and two children. To reach the palace on foot, follow West Street to the edge of the city center, and from there the well-marked Lavant to Bosham cycle way leads about a mile (1.6km) west to the site; you can also take a bus (no. 11, 56, or 700) from the front of the cathedral and get off at Salthill Road, then walk about ¼ mile (.4km) to the palace.

ORGANIZED TOURS

Excellent **guided walking tours** introduce you to the streets and sights of Chichester. They cost £3.50 ($7) and leave from the **Tourist Information Centre,** 29a South St. (② **01243/775-888**), May through September Tuesdays at 11am and Saturdays at 2:30pm, and October to April Saturdays at 2:30pm.

OUTDOOR ACTIVITIES

Salterns Way is a cycle and walking route that leads from the center of Chichester to Chichester Harbor, a distance of about 11 miles (17km). Along the way, the route passes through fields, woods, and marshlands, before coming to the harbor on the Sussex Coast. On summer weekends, you might find kiosks renting bicycles in the train station parking lot, or ask about bike rentals at the tourist office.

3 Shopping

The Cloisters Shop, in the cathedral's handsome and newly restored cloisters (② **01243/812-482**), offers a fairly predictable selection of notecards and souvenirs, but a standout is the excellent selection of CDs of the cathedral's acclaimed choir.

4 Where to Dine

The Buttery at the Crypt ✿ TRADITIONAL   A vaulted room is the atmospheric setting for an excellent range of sandwiches and desserts.

12a South St. ✆ **01243/537-033**. www.thebuttery.org. Sandwiches £2.20–£3.20 ($4.40–$6.40). MC, V. Mon–Sat 8:30am–5pm; Sun 10am–4pm.

St. Martin's Tearooms ✿✿✿ TRADITIONAL   It's almost worth the trip to Chichester just to enjoy a light lunch of salmon sandwiches, salads, or tea in these atmospheric beamed rooms, warmed by wood fires and overlooking a lovely garden.

3 St. Martin's St. ✆ **01243/786715**. www.organictearooms.co.uk. Sandwiches from £3 ($6); main courses £4–£6 ($8–$12). MC, V. Mon–Fri 10am–6pm; Sat 9am–6pm.

Trip

7

Dover Castle

*T*he strategic importance of this spot atop the White Cliffs, facing the Continent from high above the English Channel, has been appreciated for more than 2,000 years. Within a mighty ring of walls, the oldest and most important fortification in England houses a Roman pharos (lighthouse), a magnificent keep built by Henry II, and secret tunnels burrowed into the chalky cliffs during World War II. An exploration of the compound provides a short course on British history—along with breathtaking views over the White Cliffs, the busy docks below (England's main port for shipping to and from the Continent), and, on a clear day, across the English Channel all the way to France.

The castle began as an Anglo-Saxon fortress and took on much of its present appearance in the 12th century, when Henry II strengthened the massive fortifications and built the Keep, the largest in Britain. Dover Castle soon came to be known as the "key of England," because any enemy who took it would have easy access to the rest of the island. An ongoing threat came from French forces just across the Channel, against whom Henry III and the monarchs who followed him built more walls and towers. The Napoleonic Wars spurred the extension of a labyrinth of defensive tunnels that housed thousands of soldiers to fend off an invasion, and the underground complex was expanded to serve as a shelter and the headquarters of military operations during World War II.

Given the extensive and remarkably well-preserved fortifications, a visit to the castle will be especially fascinating for anyone interested in military history. All visitors, though, will be swept away by the sheer scope of British history in evidence here, from the Roman pharos, said to be the oldest structure in Britain, to the tunnels used as bunkers in World War II, where a tour is now accompanied by explosions, the droning of airplanes, and air raid sirens. Plan on devoting a full day to this trip, giving yourself time to tour the castle at leisure (3–4 hr.) and for a walk atop the White Cliffs.

1 Essentials

VISITOR INFORMATION

Dover is 78 miles (126km) southeast of London. **Dover Castle** (© **01304/201-628;** www.english-heritage.org.uk), at the eastern edge of the city atop the famous White Cliffs, is open daily April through September from 10am to 6pm; October from 10am

Dover Castle

1 Pharos
2 Saxon church
3 The Keep
4 Medieval tunnels
5 Wall walk
6 Admiralty Look-Out
7 Secret Wartime Tunnels

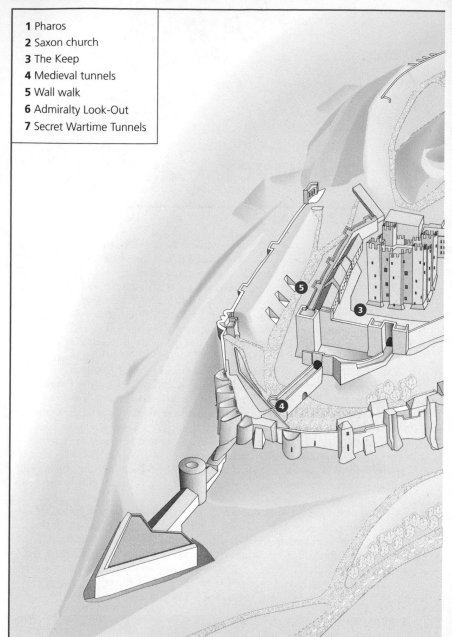

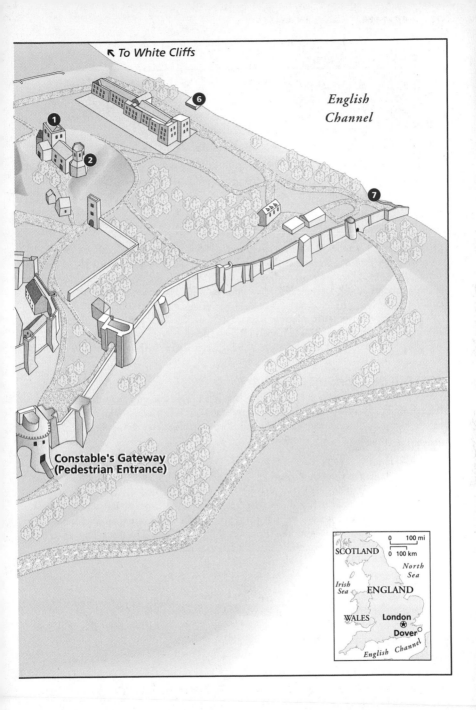

↖ To White Cliffs

English Channel

**Constable's Gateway
(Pedestrian Entrance)**

SCOTLAND

*North
Sea*

*Irish
Sea*

ENGLAND

WALES

London

Dover

English Channel

0   100 mi
0   100 km

Dover Castle Highlights

- Visiting the ancient Roman pharos (lighthouse) and stepping inside the 1,000-year-old Saxon church.
- Exploring the Keep of King Henry II, where you'll see the remains of the Great Hall and a chapel dedicated to Thomas Becket.
- Walking along the walls that circle the castle.
- Enjoying the view from Admiralty Look-Out.
- Taking a tour of the Secret Wartime Tunnels, which were constructed during World War II.

to 5pm; and November through March from 10am to 4pm. The castle is closed December 24 through December 26 and January 1. Admission is £9.70 ($20) for adults, £7.40 ($15) for students and seniors, £4.70 ($9.50) for children ages 5 to 15, free for children under 5, and £24.50 ($49) for families of up to two adults and three children.

The **Dover Visitor Information Centre** (© **01304/205-108;** www.whitecliffs country.org.uk), in the Old Town Gaol on Biggin Street, is open Monday through Friday from 9am to 5:30pm, Saturday and Sunday from 10am to 4pm (Oct–Mar closed Sun).

SCHEDULING CONSIDERATIONS

Dover is not a place to save for a rainy day. You'll get soaked as you cross the vast castle compound, and the White Cliffs not only lose their luster in the rain, but exploring them can be uncomfortable and, due to slippery paths, even dangerous.

GETTING THERE
BY TRAIN

Trains run about every half-hour throughout the day from both Victoria and Charing Cross stations in London to Dover Priory Station, with the first direct train leaving Victoria at 7:05am and the first direct train leaving Charing Cross at 5:30am; the last direct train for Victoria leaves Dover at 10:52pm and the last direct train for Charing Cross leaves Dover at 10:03pm. The trip takes about 1¾ hours. The cheap day return fare is about £25 ($50). For more information, contact **National Rail Enquiries** (© **08457/484950**) or visit www.nationalrail.co.uk.

BY BUS

Coaches operated by **National Express** (© **08705/808080;** www.nationalexpress. com) run hourly or half-hourly from London's Victoria Coach Station to Dover town center starting at 7am; the last bus leaves Dover at 11:30pm. The trip takes about 2½ hours and the day return fare is £12 ($24).

BY CAR

The trip from London takes about an hour and a half, depending on traffic. Take the M25 to the M20 for the speedy drive down to Folkstone, then the A20 to Dover. As you approach Dover on the A20, there is a well-marked exit to the castle, where you'll find several free car parks.

GETTING AROUND

It's easy to reach the castle from the train station on foot; the route is well marked and takes about 15 minutes. Stagecoach buses nos. 90, 91, and 111 make the trip from the bus station in the town center to the entrance of the castle; a **Dayrider ticket,** good all day, costs £2.80 ($5.60). The taxi fare is between £5 and £6 ($10–$12). There's a taxi stand outside the station, but to ensure that a car will be available when you arrive, arrange a pickup in advance by calling **Heritage Taxis** at Ⓒ **01304/225-522.**

2 A Day at Dover Castle

Dover Castle can easily overwhelm you: A lot of history has happened within these massive walls, and the complex is vast (70 acres/28 hectares) and crowded with sites. The most satisfying way to see the castle is to let history be your guide and to tour the compound in chronological order. Begin at the highest point in the castle, a rise crowned with the rather humble-looking ❶ **pharos (lighthouse)** 𝕶𝕶 the Romans constructed to guide their ships across the Channel. It's said to be the oldest structure in Britain. Next to it stands a ❷ **small stone church (St. Mary-in-Castro)** 𝕶 that, despite some clumsy restoration, is solidly Saxon (note the characteristic thick walls and few windows), built a thousand years ago.

Between 1160 and 1180, Henry II transformed Dover into one of the mightiest fortifications in Europe. At the heart of Henry's medieval defenses is the ❸ **Keep** 𝕶𝕶𝕶, where you can step into the hulking remains of the Great Hall and two graceful stone chapels, one dedicated to Thomas Becket, murdered in Canterbury Cathedral by Henry's knights in 1170 (see trip 5). The Keep is still the social center of the castle, and houses a restaurant, a shop, and a theatre that stages "The 1216 Siege Experience," a sound-and-light show (included in the admission fee) that dramatizes the French attempt to seize the castle. By 1216, the French had, in fact, invaded southeast England, and Louis, the French Dauphin, controlled London and the Tower. Dover,

Fun Fact The Cinque Ports

Beginning in the 11th century, the port towns of Dover, Hastings, Hythe, Romney, and Sandwich formed the Confederation of Cinque Ports to defend themselves against invasion from the Continent and to protect their lucrative trading routes on the Channel. Dover became the headquarters of the confederation in the 13th century, by which time the Cinque Ports was a formidable organization that enjoyed considerable privileges, including exemption from taxation. As the towns grew increasingly rich and powerful, the monarchy decided it was wise to keep a hand in the control of the Cinque Ports by appointing a warden to oversee them. Notable figures who have held this title include the duke of Wellington, Sir Winston Churchill, and H. M. Queen Elizabeth, the late queen mother. The post comes with a castle, Walmer, 7 miles (10km) north of Dover.

under the command of Hubert de Burgh, held out for several months, long enough for English troops to rally and, in August 1217, defeat the French and regain London and the rest of the southeast. Also in the Keep are rooms filled with furniture, documents, and other effects of Henry VIII, who came to Dover in 1539, when he had just been excommunicated because of his divorce from Catherine of Aragon (a divorce she neither wanted nor accepted) and European sentiment had turned against him. The king was seeking assurance that the castle could withstand an invasion that then seemed inevitable.

Just south of the Keep is an ingenious series of ❹ **medieval underground tunnels** 𝒦 that allowed soldiers to get from one part of the castle to another during a siege. The castle's greatest strength, though, is the ❺ **series of walls** 𝒦𝒦𝒦 that completely encircle the compound. You can make a complete circuit of the castle on them, stopping to enjoy the view of the port and the Channel from ❻ **Admiralty Look-Out** 𝒦 (you'll get a definite sense of the castle's strategic importance from this vantage). Next, tour the ❼ **Secret Wartime Tunnels** 𝒦𝒦𝒦. This 18th-century tunnel system, first used by British soldiers housed here to ward off a French invasion during the late-18th-century Napoleonic Wars, was pressed into use in 1940, when it became the command center for Operation Dynamo, which evacuated 340,000 British troops from Dunkirk, across the Channel in France, when it became clear they could not fend off the German army. The complex proved to be virtually bombproof, and in 1942 the British War Cabinet began to expand the tunnels—by war's end the tunnels comprised an underground city and housed barracks, military headquarters, a communications center, and a hospital. At one point, during the Cold War, there were plans to use the tunnel system as a nuclear shelter, but those were abandoned when the government figured out the chalk cliffs offered little protection from radiation. You can view the complex only on hour-long guided tours accompanied by dramatic sound-and-light effects; the last tour departs an hour before the castle closes.

ORGANIZED TOURS

A **City Sightseeing** (𝒞 **01708/866000**; www.citysightseeing.co.uk) double-decker sightseeing bus operates in Dover from mid-May to mid-September. With hop-on/hop-off service, it travels from Dover Priory train station to the castle entrance, with additional stops that include Market Square and the White Cliffs. The tour also provides a look at Dover's extensive docks. Buses operate daily from 10am to 4pm, and the fares are £6.50 ($13) for adults, £5.50 ($11) for seniors and students, and £3 ($6) for children 5 to 15.

MORE THINGS TO SEE & DO

There's not much to capture your interest in Dover, as the old town was leveled by World War II bombers and assaulted again by ugly postwar rebuilding. But before you board the train for the trip back to London, you might want to take a short walk around the small town center. The **Maison Dieu** (in the town hall on Biggin St.;

Tips **A Perch with a View**

Climb up to Admiralty Look-Out and enjoy the view. The vista of the White Cliffs, often shrouded in a light mist, rising above the choppy seas of the Channel, is exhilarating.

Start Walking!

If you want some bracing exercise in the sea air, approach your day in Dover as a good hike: Climb the mile or so from the station to the castle, cover the 70-acre (28-hectare) castle compound on foot, walk the half-mile or so to the White Cliffs, and follow the trails across the top for several miles. Wear good walking shoes, carry water, and dress appropriately for the season—that means layered clothing for warmth for much of the year, rain gear just about any time, and light clothing and sunscreen for rare but memorable warm summer days.

Tues–Sat 10am–4:30pm and Sun 2–4:30pm) dates to 1221 and was built as a hostel for pilgrims traveling from the Continent to Canterbury. Admission is free. In the 1,800-year-old **Roman Painted House,** New Street (✆ **01304/203-279;** Apr–Sept Tues–Sat 10am–5pm, Sun 2–5pm), frescoes and a heating system beneath the floor are remarkably well-preserved. Admission is £2 ($4) adults, 80p ($1.60) seniors and children.

OUTDOOR ACTIVITIES

One of the most exhilarating and enjoyable walks in England is atop the famous **White Cliffs of Dover** (✆ **01304/202-756;** www.nationaltrust.org.uk). From a parking area about a quarter of a mile (.5km) beyond the castle (follow the signs from the castle entrance), a 2.5-mile (4km) path follows the top of the chalk cliffs, rendered white by fossilized marine life that millennia ago floated in a tropical sea, to South Foreland Lighthouse. In 1898, Guglielmo Marconi made the first shore-to-ship radio transmissions from the top of the lighthouse, which is open daily in July and August, and Thursday through Monday from March 1 to June 30, from 11am to 5:30pm. Admission is £2 ($4) for adults, £1 ($2) for children under 16, and £5 ($10) for families of up to two adults and three children. The bracing sea air, the looming presence of the mighty castle, the busy traffic in the shipping lanes far below, and the views 17 miles (27km) across the English Channel to France make this a walk you will long remember.

3 Where to Dine

White Cliffs Teashop ✿ CAFETERIA/LIGHT FARE   This simple cafeteria in a handsome glass pavilion at the entrance to the National Trust's White Cliffs walk is a delightful place for a snack or light meal. Sandwiches, a few hot dishes, desserts, and beverages can be enjoyed in the airy dining room or on the terrace.

White Cliff Visitors Centre. ✆ **01304/202-754.** Most items £3–£7 ($6–$14). DC, MC, V. Mar–Oct daily 10am–5pm; Nov–Feb daily 11am–4pm.

Trip 8

Greenwich

*T*ime is of the essence in Greenwich, a town and borough of Greater London, about 4 miles (6.5km) east of the city center. The world's clocks are set according to Greenwich Mean Time, and visitors from around the globe flock here to stand on the Prime Meridian, the line from which the world's longitude is measured. The main attractions in Greenwich, parts of which have been designated a World Heritage Site by UNESCO, are the Old Royal Observatory, the Queen's House, and the National Maritime Museum, all located in Greenwich Park, and the Royal Naval College, a grouping of historic buildings on the River Thames. The *Cutty Sark,* a 19th-century clipper ship, is another popular attraction but is closed for renovation until late 2008.

Greenwich offers enough to keep you fully occupied for a day and, with its attractions, acres of parkland, and riverside setting, is a great outing for kids. Though Greenwich is a suburb of London and easy to reach—if pressed for time, you can get to Greenwich quickly by underground or light rail—a village-like atmosphere prevails. You might want to consider traveling to or from Greenwich by boat to get a look at London from the waters of the Thames.

1 Essentials

VISITOR INFORMATION
The **Greenwich Tourist Information Centre,** Pepys House, Cutty Sark Gardens (© **0870/608-2000**), is open daily from 10am to 5pm.

SCHEDULING CONSIDERATIONS
All the main sights in Greenwich are open daily from 10am to 5pm. There is always a crowd at the **Prime Meridian**—that's part of the fun—but if you want to straddle the two halves of the earth without company, make your way to the **Old Royal Observatory** as early in the morning as possible. If you want to visit the **outdoor markets,** Saturday is the best day because you can hit all three (antiques, food, and crafts).

GETTING THERE
BY LIGHT RAIL
The most interesting route to Greenwich is by **Docklands Light Rail** from Tower Hill Gateway (the Docklands Station near the Tower of London), which takes you

Greenwich

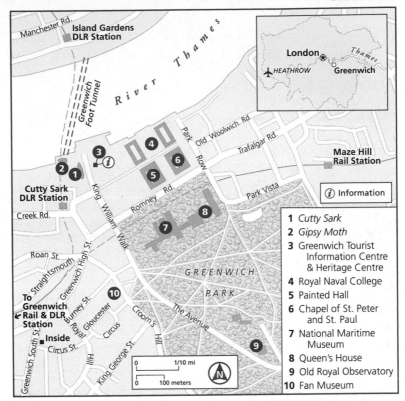

Legend:

1 *Cutty Sark*
2 *Gipsy Moth*
3 Greenwich Tourist Information Centre & Heritage Centre
4 Royal Naval College
5 Painted Hall
6 Chapel of St. Peter and St. Paul
7 National Maritime Museum
8 Queen's House
9 Old Royal Observatory
10 Fan Museum

ⓘ Information

past Canary Wharf and all the new Docklands development. Take the light rail to Island Gardens, the last stop, and then walk through the Victorian foot tunnel beneath the River Thames to Greenwich. You emerge next to the *Cutty Sark*. The fare is £4 ($8) adults.

BY UNDERGROUND

North Greenwich is a stop on the **Jubilee Underground line,** but it's too far to walk into town from the Tube station. Bus no. 188, which stops right outside the Tube station, will take you into Greenwich for £2 ($4); ask the driver to let you off near the *Cutty Sark*.

BY FERRY

Thames River Services (*ⓒ* **020/7930-1616;** www.westminsterpier.co.uk) runs a year-round fleet of boats from Westminster Pier to Greenwich Pier; the journey takes about 1 hour. If you want to enjoy views of London from the water, this is a fun and easy way to do so. A return ticket is £9.40 ($19) adults, £4.70 ($9) children, and £26 ($52) families (two adults/two children). The boat landing is next to the *Cutty Sark*.

GETTING AROUND

All the attractions in Greenwich are signposted, and you can easily reach them on foot. The Old Royal Observatory, Royal Maritime Museum, and Queen's House are

Greenwich Highlights

- Climbing aboard the clipper ship *Cutty Sark.*
- Visiting the Old Royal Observatory.
- Exploring Greenwich Park, home of the National Maritime Museum and Queen's House.
- Enjoying the heroic architecture of the Royal Naval College.

located in Greenwich Park. If you're dealing with young kids or have mobility impairments, be aware that the Old Royal Observatory sits atop a hill and the pathway up to it is a bit of a climb.

2 A Day in Greenwich

Start your day in Greenwich at the ❶ *Cutty Sark* ✦ (② 020/8858-3445), berthed on King William Walk next to the River Thames. Last of the tea-clipper sailing ships, the *Cutty Sark* was launched in 1869 and used for the lucrative tea trade in the China Sea. Designed for speed, the vessel could cover almost 400 sea miles a day. Later, it carried wool from Australia. It was restored in 1922 and was used as a training ship until the end of World War II. The ship contains historic maritime memorabilia; the Long John Silver Collection of merchant ship figureheads is the largest in the country. *Note:* The ship had been closed for restoration since a fire struck on May 21, 2007, causing major damage. It is scheduled to reopen in late 2008. Until that time, you can visit an adjacent exhibition. Admission to the Visitor Centre exhibition is £2 ($4) per person. Berthed a few yards away is the ❷ *Gipsy Moth,* built in 1966 for Sir Francis Chichester, who sailed the craft single-handedly around the world; the boat is not open to the public.

From the *Cutty Sark,* make your way to the adjacent ❸ **Greenwich Tourist Information Centre,** Pepys House, Cutty Sark Gardens (② 0870/608-2000), and spend a few minutes in the **Heritage Centre,** where you can learn more about Greenwich's royal and maritime past. From the Heritage Centre it's a short walk to the ❹ **Royal Naval College** ✦ (② 0800/389-3341), a majestic grouping of buildings that occupies the site of Greenwich Palace, which stood here from 1422 to 1620 and was the birthplace of Henry VIII, Mary I, and Elizabeth I. Badly damaged by Oliver Cromwell's troops during the Civil War in the 17th century, the palace was torn down and replaced in 1696 with a naval hospital designed by Sir Christopher Wren. Its 4 blocks, named after King Charles II, Queen Anne, King William III, and Queen Mary II, are split into two sections so as not to block the view of the river from Queen's House in Greenwich Park (see below). UNESCO recognized the architectural and historical importance of the college in 1997 by naming it a World Heritage Site. The Navy moved out of the college in 1998, and the various buildings are now home to the University of Greenwich and other public organizations. Stop in to see the magnificent ❺ **Painted Hall** ✦, designed by Wren and completed in 1704 (the incredible painted ceilings, however, were executed by Sir James Thornhill from 1707–26), and the neoclassical ❻ **Chapel of St. Peter and St. Paul** ✦, with an immense altarpiece, *The Preservation of St Paul after Shipwreck at Malta*, painted by the American-born artist Benjamin West. The rooms are open daily from 10am to 5pm and admission is free.

From the Royal Naval College, cross Romney Road and take the path to the ❼ **National Maritime Museum** *✿* (✆ **020/8312-6608;** www.nmm.ac.uk), where Britain's seafaring past is charted in recently revamped galleries. Highlights include Prince Frederick's amazing gilded barge, built in 1732 for the eldest son of George II; Queen Mary's royal barge from 1689; and a collection of intricate ship models. An enormous collection of Lord Nelson memorabilia is also on display, including the bullet-pierced coat he was wearing when he was killed by a sniper's bullet at the Battle of Trafalgar on October 21, 1805. The museum is open daily from 10am to 5pm and admission is free.

Adjacent to the National Maritime Museum is the splendidly restored ❽ **Queen's House** *✿* (✆ **020/8858-4422**), designed in 1616 by the innovative Inigo Jones, considered to be the founder of English classical architecture, and later used as a model for the American White House. The first classical building in England (mostly Palladian in style, with lots of columns and marble), Queen's House was commissioned by Anne of Denmark, the wife of James I, and completed in 1635 (with later modifications). You can visit the royal apartments on a self-guided tour; the house has become a kind of art gallery with a number of fine paintings (many featuring marine and naval themes). Queen's House is open daily from 10am to 5pm and admission is free.

The vast expanse of Greenwich Great Park, the first Royal Park to be enclosed (1433), begins directly behind the Maritime Museum and Queen's House. There have been deer in the park since the 15th century. After leaving Queen's House, make your way up the park's hill to explore the ❾ **Old Royal Observatory** *✿✿* (✆ **020/8312-6608**), founded in 1675 by Charles II as part of his quest to determine longitude at sea by time instead of by the stars (the first structure in Britain built purely for scientific research). Clockmaker John Harrison eventually solved the problem in 1763, and received £20,000 ($40,000) for his pains. Of particular interest inside the observatory is the collection of Harrison's original 18th-century chronometers (marked H1, H2, H3, and H4). All time is measured from the **Prime Meridian Line** *✿✿* (longitude 0°), marked by a brass strip outside the observatory. You can stand astride the meridian (with a foot in each hemisphere) and set your watch precisely by the falling time-ball (every day at precisely 1pm), which is how shipmasters have set their chronometers since 1833. The observatory is open daily from 10am to 5pm; admission is free.

ORGANIZED TOURS

The Tourist Information Centre in Greenwich (see "Visitor Information," above) offers daily 1½-hour **walking tours** of the town's principal sights at 12:15pm and

---

Tips The Four Corners of the World

In the Painted Hall of the Royal Naval College, have a look at the paintings beyond the arch in the upper hall. They are meant to reflect Britain's triumph as a maritime power, with figures representing Europe, Africa, Asia, and America (the four corners of the world) acclaiming Queen Anne and her husband Prince George of Denmark. America is dressed in the regalia of an Indian chief, while Asia has a camel, Africa a lion, and Europe a white horse.

2:15pm. Walks leave from the information center and cost £4 ($8). Reservations aren't necessary, but it's a good idea to call first to verify the schedule. These walks are a good way to learn more about Greenwich and its importance in English history.

MORE THINGS TO SEE & DO

❿ Fan Museum   The Fan Museum is the only museum in the world devoted entirely to every aspect of fans and fan making, and it's primarily of interest to those with an interest in social history or decorative design. Home to more than 3,500 predominantly antique fans from around the world dating from the 11th century to the present day, its collections are displayed in changing exhibitions that present fans in their historical, sociological, and economic contexts. Afternoon tea is served on Tuesday and Sunday from 3 to 4:30pm for £3.50 to £4.50 ($7–$9).

12 Crooms Hill. ℂ **020/8305-1441.** www.fan-museum.org. Admission £3.50 ($7). Tues–Sat 11am–5pm; Sun noon–5pm.

3 Shopping

Greenwich Market is an essential part of a weekend visit to this historic maritime borough. Greenwich's upscale character is reflected in the quality of goods for sale: from fine antiques to collectors' oddities, old and new. The **Central Market,** which is a treasure-trove of antiques, vintage clothing, and music stalls (Sat–Sun 9am–5pm), and the **Food Market** (Sat 10am–4pm) are on Stockwell Street, just off Greenwich High Road, opposite St. Alfege's Church. The **Craft Market** (Thurs 7:30am–5pm and Fri–Sun 9:30am–5:30pm) is in College Approach.

4 Where to Dine

Inside Ⓖ MODERN BRITISH   The menu changes weekly at this neighborhood restaurant with a quiet, low-key ambience that's just a cut below posh. For starters you might try the lamb kabob or scallops on risotto. Main courses generally include dishes such as roast chicken or lamb, fresh fish, and vegetarian options such as truffle button-mushroom risotto. The prices are somewhat high but so is the quality of the cooking.

19 Greenwich South St., SE 10. ℂ **020/8265-5060.** Main courses £11–£17 ($22–$34); set-price meals £12–£20 ($24–$40). MC, V. Wed–Fri noon–2:30pm; Tues–Sat 6:30–11pm; Sat–Sun brunch 11am–1pm.

Pavilion Tea House Ⓖ ⒦ⁱᵈˢ LIGHT MEALS/SNACKS   This light-filled aerie, perched on top of the hill beside the Old Royal Observatory, is a great spot for a casual lunch, a simple snack, or afternoon tea. Service is fast and friendly, and the quality of the food is high. Lunch on homemade soups with crusty bread, a warm onion tart, or a tuna niçoise salad; snack on cupcakes or cherry trifle. Kids are welcome and there are outdoor tables in summer.

Greenwich Park, Blackhearth Gate, SE 10. ℂ **020/8858-9695.** Main courses £3–£8 ($6–$16). MC, V. Mon–Fri 9am–6pm; Sat–Sun 9am–7pm.

Hampstead

*H*ampstead is an attractive village, now swallowed up in the giant London metropolis, that has attracted many writers, artists, architects, musicians, and scientists over the years. John Keats, Robert Louis Stevenson, the painter John Constable, D. H. Lawrence, Karl Marx, Sigmund Freud, and John Le Carré have all called Hampstead home. The Oscar-winning actress Glenda Jackson *(Women in Love)* is currently Hampstead's Member of Parliament.

The original village, just 20 minutes by Tube from central London, is a picturesque place to explore, loaded with charming Regency and Georgian houses, old roads, alleys, steps, and courts. Many Londoners come for weekend jaunts on Hampstead Heath, an 800-acre (320-hectare) expanse of high heathland that serves as one of London's most popular and picturesque parks. You should join them: A walk on the Heath will make you feel like you've spent time in the English countryside. Be sure, though, to also visit Hampstead's historic houses and museums—they provide insights into residents from Keats to Freud and are quite extraordinary. You could easily spend a day in Hampstead, but it's close enough to central London that you can easily pop in for a couple of hours.

1 Essentials

VISITOR INFORMATION

Hampstead is part of Greater London and does not have its own tourist information center. The **Britain and London Visitor Centre,** 1 Regent St. SW1 (www.visitbritain. com or www.visitlondon.com) is open Monday to Friday from 9:30am to 6:30pm, Saturday and Sunday 10am to 4pm.

SCHEDULING CONSIDERATIONS

Fenton House is closed between November and March. The **old western cemetery** at Highgate is open only to guided tours. (See tour times below.) The best time to tour **the Heath** is in spring and summer, or in winter, after a snowfall; in fall, like in other London-area parks, you'll find the area soggy and brown rather than bright with flaming colors.

Hampstead Highlights

- Visiting Fenton House, with its air of 18th-century gentility, and 2 Willow Rd., the architect Erno Goldfinger's 1939 International Style house.
- Rambling through Hampstead Heath.
- Viewing the Regency-era library and the Rembrandt and Vermeer paintings in Kenwood House.

GETTING THERE
BY UNDERGROUND
The fastest and easiest way to get to Hampstead is by Underground. Ride the Northern Line to Hampstead Station; the trip takes about 20 minutes from central London.

GETTING AROUND
The pleasures of Hampstead village and the Heath can only be appreciated on foot. To reach Kenwood House and Highgate Cemetery, both described below, you can take bus no. 210, which runs from the Archway, Golders Green, Hampstead, and Highgate Underground stations. By bus it takes approximately 10 minutes to reach Kenwood House, about 20 minutes to reach Highgate Cemetery; you can reach Kenwood House on foot in about 30 minutes once you're in Hampstead Heath, but the trek to Highgate is much longer.

2 A Day in Hampstead

From the Hampstead Underground station, walk north on Holly Hill to Hampstead Grove. ❶ **Fenton House** ᚱ (© **020/7435-3471;** www.nationaltrust.org.uk), set in a walled garden on the west side of Hampstead Grove, was built in 1693 and is one of the earliest, largest, and finest houses in Hampstead. Displayed within are fine collections of Asian and European porcelain, needlework, and furniture, and an important collection of early keyboard instruments, including a 1612 harpsichord that Handel probably played. Fenton House is open March, Saturday and Sunday from 2 to 5pm, and April through October, Wednesday to Friday from 2 to 5pm and Saturday and Sunday from 11am to 5pm. Admission is £5.20 ($10) for adults, £2.60 ($5) for children 16 and under; a joint ticket for admission to Fenton House and 2 Willow Rd. is £7 ($14).

Backtrack to the Underground station and take Flask Walk north to New End Square. Here you'll find ❷ **Burgh House** (© **020/7431-0144;** www.burghhouse. uk), a handsome Queen Anne house that serves as Hampstead's center for meetings, concerts, and art exhibitions. It's also home to the local history museum, with a permanent display about the great landscape artist John Constable, who lived and worked in Hampstead. Burgh House is open Wednesday to Sunday from noon to 5pm. (It's closed 2 weeks at Christmas.) Admission is free.

From Burgh House, walk north on Well Walk and enter ❸ **Hampstead Heath** ᚱᚱ, 800 acres (320 hectares) of high heath, park, wood, and grassland that separate the

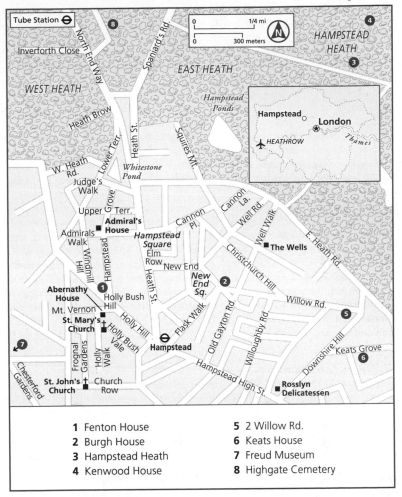

Hampstead

Tube Station ⊖

0 ─── 1/4 mi
0 ─── 300 meters

HAMPSTEAD HEATH

North End Way
Inverforth Close
Spaniard's Rd.
EAST HEATH
WEST HEATH
Heath Brow
Hampstead Ponds

Heath St.
Lower Terr.
Squires Mt.
W. Heath Rd.
Whitestone Pond
Judge's Walk
Grove
Upper Terr.
Admiral's House
Cannon Pl.
Cannon La.
Well Rd.
Well Walk
Admirals Walk
Hampstead Square
Elm Row
New End
The Wells
Windmill Hill
Christchurch Hill
E. Heath Rd.
Abernathy House
Holly Bush Hill
Heath St.
New End Sq.
Willow Rd.
Mt. Vernon
Holly Hill
Flask Walk
Old Gayton Rd.
St. Mary's Church
Holly Bush Vale
Holly Walk
⊖ **Hampstead**
Willoughby Rd.
Downshire Hill
Keats Grove
Chesterford Gardens
Frognal Gardens
Hampstead High St.
Rosslyn Delicatessen
St. John's Church
Church Row

Hampstead
London
HEATHROW
Thames

1 Fenton House	**5** 2 Willow Rd.
2 Burgh House	**6** Keats House
3 Hampstead Heath	**7** Freud Museum
4 Kenwood House	**8** Highgate Cemetery

villages of Hampstead and Highgate. If you ascend Parliament Hill, the highest point on Hampstead Heath, on a clear day, you can see St. Paul's and even the hills of Kent south of the Thames. People come to walk, fly kites, sunbathe, swim, picnic, and jog.

Follow the footpaths through the Heath to reach palatial ❹ **Kenwood House** 🐾🐾 (🕾 **020/8348-1286**) in the northwestern section of the Heath. Built as a gentleman's country home, Kenwood was enlarged and decorated in neoclassical style by Robert Adam, starting in 1764. The impressive art collection includes a Rembrandt self-portrait and Vermeer's *The Guitar Player*. During the summer, open-air concerts are given beside the lake. The house is open daily from 11am to 5pm (Nov–Mar until 4pm). Admission is free.

Backtrack through the Heath and follow Heath Road southeast, exiting near the eastern end of Willow Road. ➎ **2 Willow Rd.** ⨳ (✆ **0207/435-6166;** www.national trust.org.uk), the home of Hungarian architect Erno Goldfinger and his wife, the artist Ursula Blackwell, is now a National Trust property and can be visited. Built by Goldfinger in 1939 and still filled with his furniture, books, and modern art collection, the house is a fascinating example of the sleekly functional Modern Movement architecture (note the large windows characteristic of the style). The house is open early March through late March on Saturday only noon to 5pm; late March through mid-June Thursday through Saturday noon to 5pm; mid-June through late October Thursday through Friday noon to 5pm (with additional Sat hours mid-June to late Nov noon–5pm). Admission is £4.90 ($10) for adults, £2.50 ($5) for children 16 and under, and a joint ticket with Fenton house is £7 ($14). It was from Goldfinger, by the way, that Ian Fleming got the name for one of his most famous James Bond novels.

From Willow Road, head south on Downshire Hill and east on Keats Grove to reach ➏ **Keats House,** Wentworth Place (✆ **020/7435-2062;** www.cityoflondon. gov.uk/keats). The Romantic poet John Keats lived in this charming Regency cottage for only 2 years (1818–20) of his short life, but it was here that he wrote one of his most celebrated poems, "Ode to a Nightingale," and fell in love with Fanny Brawne, his neighbor's daughter (they were engaged, but he died of tuberculosis before they could marry). On display are manuscripts, including his last sonnet ("Bright star, would I were steadfast as thou art"), first editions, diaries, letters, and memorabilia. The house is closed for refurbishment until October 2008, but is generally open Tuesday through Sunday from noon to 5pm (Nov–Mar until 4pm). Admission is £3 ($6) for adults, £1.50 ($3) for seniors and students.

ORGANIZED TOURS

The **Heath & Hampstead Society** (www.heathandhampsteadsociety.org.uk) organizes a 2-hour walk on the first Sunday afternoon of every month except January. The walks start from Burgh House, New End Square, and are open to the public; there is a suggested donation of £2 ($4). Times are either 10:30am or 2:30pm. For further information, e-mail info@heathandhampsteadsociety.org.uk.

MORE THINGS TO SEE & DO

➐ **Freud Museum** ⨳   After he and his family left Nazi-occupied Vienna as refugees in 1938, Sigmund Freud (1856–1939) lived, worked, and died in this spacious three-story redbrick house. Rooms on view contain original furniture, letters, photographs, paintings, and personal effects of Freud and his daughter, Anna (who lived here for 44 years). In the study and library, you can see the famous couch (remarkably Middle Eastern in style) and his large collection of Egyptian, Roman, and Asian antiquities. From the Hampstead Underground station, walk south along Fitzjohn's Avenue, turning west on Nutley Terrace and south on Maresfield Gardens; the walk takes about 15 minutes.

20 Maresfield Gardens, NW3. ✆ 020/7435-2002. www.freud.org.uk. Admission £5 ($10) adults, £3 ($6) seniors and students. Wed–Sun noon–5pm.

➑ **Highgate Cemetery** ⨳   Serpentine pathways wind through this beautiful cemetery, which opened in 1829 and quickly became the fashionable place for Londoners

An Inspiring Stroll

A snowy walk on Hampstead Heath inspired C. S. Lewis to write *The Lion, the Witch and the Wardrobe*. These 800 acres (320 hectares) of half-wild, half-manicured green in northwest London do feel like a parallel universe. Sundays are like a fiesta: Lie back and listen to the bandstand concerts on Parliament Hill, with its unparalleled view across the capital. People fly kites or wield a mean Frisbee. Others fish, swim, or race model boats in the ponds.

to be buried. You have to take a tour to visit the old western part of the cemetery; the eastern section was added 3 decades later. Victorian funerary rituals were extraordinarily elaborate—witness the tomb-lined Egyptian Avenue, which leads up to the catacombs in the Circle of Lebanon. Scientist Michael Faraday, poet Christina Rossetti, and many other famous figures are buried here in an atmosphere that is part fright-night movie, part woodsy wildlife sanctuary. The grave of Karl Marx, marked by a gargantuan bust, lies in the eastern cemetery, as does that of novelist George Eliot, whose real name was Mary Anne Evans. The cemetery is still very much in use. *Note:* No children under 8 can enter the western side, and video cameras or tripods are not allowed in either the eastern or western sides.

Swain's Lane, N6. ℂ 020/8340-1834. www.highgate-cemetery.org. East Cemetery £3 ($6); Western Cemetery £5 ($10), £1 (50¢) for children 8–16. East Cemetery Apr–Oct Mon–Fri 10am–5pm, Sat–Sun 11am–5pm, last admission a half-hour before close; Nov–Mar Mon–Fri 10am–4pm, Sat–Sun 11am–4pm, last admission a half-hour before close. West Cemetery tours Mar–Nov Mon–Fri 2pm, Sat–Sun 11am, noon, 1, 2, and 3pm; bookings accepted for weekday tours only. Tube: Archway.

OUTDOOR ACTIVITIES

Hampstead Heath is full of specialized recreational opportunities, but if you're visiting for the day, chances are you'll just be walking. The **Highgate Men's Pond** in Hampstead Heath is the closest thing London has to a beach; it has an enclosed sun deck for sunbathing, and swimmers share the water with lots of quacking ducks and algae. The nearby **Kenwood Ladies' Pond** is for women only. These outdoor ponds are open year-round from dawn to dusk. Admission is £2 ($4). For further information on sports facilities and outdoor recreation in Hampstead Heath, visit the City of London website at **www.cityoflondon.gov.uk.**

3 Where to Dine

Giraffe *Kids* INTERNATIONAL   Check out the Hampstead branch of this appealing chain if you want delicious, reasonably priced food and a casual, friendly, and completely nonsmoking atmosphere. The menu wanders the globe, from English herby sausages to Moroccan-spiced meat dishes to French dishes laden with garlic. There's a kids' menu and lots of daily specials.

46 Rosslyn Hill. ℂ 020/7435-0343. Reservations recommended; not accepted for weekend lunch. Main courses £5–£10 ($10–$20). AE, MC, V. Mon–Fri 8am–11pm; Sat 9am–11pm; Sun 9am–10:30pm.

Rosslyn Delicatessen *GG* MODERN BRITISH/FRENCH   One of London's best delis is conveniently close to Hampstead Heath and provides all the fixings for a picnic. The gourmand owners offer a tempting array of cheeses, prepared dishes, wines, and desserts.

56 Rosslyn Hill. ℂ 020/7794-9210. Sandwiches and prepared dishes £4–£8 ($8–$16). AE, MC, V. Daily 10am–8pm.

The Wells ⭐ MODERN BRITISH/FRENCH/MEDITERRANEAN   A stylish gastropub restaurant in an old house between High Street and the Heath, The Wells is Hampstead at its gentrified best. The menu changes often, but you'll find main courses such as roast lamb, pan-fried salmon with tomato and paprika couscous, fresh crab and black olive risotto, and deep-fried fishcakes.

30 Well Walk. ℂ 020/7794-3785. Main courses £9–£15 ($18–$30); fixed-price lunch £15–£25 ($30–$50). MC, V. Daily noon–3pm and 7–9:30pm.

Trip 10

Hampton Court

Cardinal Thomas Wolsey, Henry VIII's lord chancellor, began building Hampton Court in 1514. But the cardinal got on Henry's bad side when he opposed the king's request for a divorce from Catherine of Aragon, and the incident provided a convenient excuse for the greedy Tudor monarch to nab Hampton Court for himself and make the property a royal residence, a status it held from 1525 until 1760. Henry's fifth wife, Catherine Howard, supposedly haunts the place to this day. The palace appealed even to the anti-royalist Oliver Cromwell, Lord Protector of the Commonwealth during the Civil War. He sold Hampton Court in 1645, but arranged to buy the palace back and spent many weekends here. George III, who came to the throne in 1760, more or less abandoned Hampton Court, preferring Windsor Castle (see trip 24). Queen Victoria opened the palace to the public in 1838, and extensive renovations over the years have returned Hampton Court to its Tudor grandeur. One of the greatest tragedies to befall the palace was a massive 1986 fire in the King's Apartments, but even that section of the palace is now completely restored.

Located in East Moseley, Surrey, 13 miles (21km) west of London on the north side of the River Thames, Hampton Court is one of the easiest and most rewarding day trips from London. You can visit Hampton Court as a half-day trip if traveling by train or car, or make a visit a full day's outing if you choose to reach the palace by boat (just like Henry VIII and Elizabeth I would have done).

1 Essentials

VISITOR INFORMATION
The **Information Centre** (© **0870/752-7777;** www.hrp.org.uk) in the Clock Court is open the same hours as the palace: April through October daily 10am to 6pm, November through March 25 daily 10am to 4:30pm. It's closed December 24 to 26 and January 1. Admission to the palace is £13 ($26) for adults, £10.50 ($21) for seniors and students, and £6.50 ($13) for children 5 to15.

SCHEDULING CONSIDERATIONS
The last admission to the **palace** is at 5pm in summer, 3:30pm in winter. On Sunday, visitors are welcome to attend **choir services** in The Chapel Royal at 11am and 3:30pm. If you want to take one of the **free tours** given throughout the day by costumed guides,

Hampton Court Highlights

- Wandering through the enormous palace.
- Exploring the riverside gardens and Maze.

it's essential to sign up as early as possible (see "Organized Tours," below). You will probably be surprised by all there to see at Hampton Court, so allow plenty of time for your visit—4 hours for even a quick tour of the palace and gardens, longer if you want to linger in the galleries, in the maze, and on the garden paths.

GETTING THERE
BY TRAIN
The fastest, easiest, and most direct route to Hampton Court is by train from London Waterloo to Hampton Court. Trains depart Waterloo at 12 and 42 minutes past each hour (some trains require an easy change at Surbiton) and return to London from Hampton Court throughout the day and into the evening at 24 and 54 minutes past the hour. The journey takes 30 minutes, and the standard day return fare is £9.20 ($18). For more information, call **National Rail Enquiries** (⟨ **08457/484950**) or visit www.nationalrail.co.uk. The palace entrance is a 5-minute walk from the station.

BY BOAT
If you have plenty of time, you can ride in the wake of many a British monarch and take a boat to Hampton Court; the journey (boats leave from Westminster Pier) takes almost 4 hours. From April to October, boats usually depart at 11am and noon; contact **Westminster Passenger Service** (⟨ **020/7930-2062;** www.wpsa.co.uk) for more information. One-way fares (you can return to London by train) are £13.50 ($27) for adults, £9 ($18) for seniors, £6.75 ($14) for children 5 to 15, and £33.75 ($68) for families (two adults, two children).

BY CAR
The palace is located on the A308 and is well signposted; follow the brown tourist attraction road signs. From the M25, take either exit 10 onto the A307, or exit 12 onto the A308. The palace is also accessible via the A3 and then the A309. The trip from central London only takes 30 to 60 minutes, depending on traffic. Parking is available on-site for £3.50 ($7). Alternative parking is available nearby at Hampton Court Green, Bushy Park, and Hampton Court Station.

GETTING AROUND
Hampton Court is a 5-minute walk from the train station (follow the signs).

2 A Day in Hampton Court
From the time the palace was first built until the 1660s, **Hampton Court** ✸✸✸, like most of the great houses near London, was approached by water. ❶ **The West Front** of the palace, where visitors enter today, was begun by Cardinal Wolsey (ca.1475–1530) and completed for Henry VIII (though when the king showed up at Hampton Court, he entered through the gardens). The wings to the left and right of

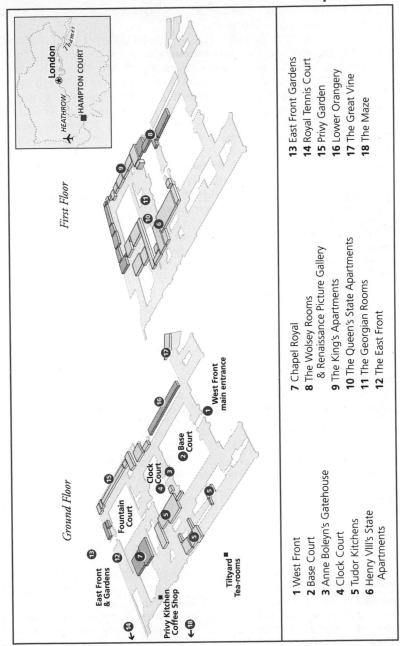

First Floor

Ground Floor

West Front
main entrance

Base
Court

Clock
Court

Fountain
Court

East Front
& Gardens

Privy Kitchen
Coffee Shop

Tiltyard
Tea-rooms

1 West Front
2 Base Court
3 Anne Boleyn's Gatehouse
4 Clock Court
5 Tudor Kitchens
6 Henry VIII's State
 Apartments

7 Chapel Royal
8 The Wolsey Rooms
 & Renaissance Picture Gallery
9 The King's Apartments
10 The Queen's State Apartments
11 The Georgian Rooms
12 The East Front

13 East Front Gardens
14 Royal Tennis Court
15 Privy Garden
16 Lower Orangery
17 The Great Vine
18 The Maze

London
Thames
HEATHROW
HAMPTON COURT

the gatehouse were added by Henry VIII and once contained the Great House of Ease-ment (communal lavatories) and the kitchens.

The ❷ **Base Court,** the first courtyard, contained lodgings for Cardinal Wolsey's guests and large household. Note the turrets surrounding the courtyard, which sport the insignia of Henry VIII and Elizabeth I. Pass through ❸ **Anne Boleyn's Gatehouse** (built in the 19th c., long after the beheaded queen's death), on the far side of Base Court, and you enter ❹ **Clock Court,** the principal Tudor courtyard and the heart of both Wolsey's and Henry VIII's palaces. Over the gateway you can see Wolsey's coat of arms and the famous Astronomical Clock made for Henry VIII in 1540 (note the sun revolving around the earth—the clock was built before Galileo and Copernicus debunked that myth).

Start your tour in ❺ **The Tudor Kitchens** ✷✷, a complex of some 50 rooms on the north side of Clock Court set up as if in the process of preparing food for a great feast in 1542. Cardinal Wolsey had 600 people in his household, and Henry VIII had twice that. The kitchens continued to serve the royal court until 1660, when servants lost their right to be fed at the king's table and were put on wages instead.

From the Clock Court, make your way to ❻ **Henry VIII's State Apartments** ✷✷. **The Horn Room,** originally a waiting place for servants bringing food to The Great Hall next door, is decorated with elk horns, including the large fossilized antlers of a prehistoric great elk found in Ireland and presented to Charles II (reigned 1660–85). In **The Great Watching Chamber,** the Yeomen of the Guard were stationed to con-trol access to the king. The room's decorated ceiling incorporates the arms and badges of Henry VIII and his third and favorite wife, Jane Seymour. Probably the most famous room in Hampton Court is **The Haunted Gallery,** which tradition holds is haunted by the ghost of Catherine Howard, Henry VIII's fifth wife. Only 15 months after her marriage in 1540, the young queen was charged with adultery and arrested. According to legend, she managed to escape from her rooms and run along the gallery toward the chapel, where the king was at Mass. Guards seized her and dragged her screaming back to her rooms; she was later executed at the Tower of London.

❼ **The Chapel Royal** ✷✷✷, built by Wolsey and in use for over 450 years, still has the Royal Pew where the monarch and his companions would sit, and a magnificent vaulted ceiling, installed in 1536. Henry VIII married his final wife, Catherine Parr, here in 1543. The vast oak screen was carved by Grinling Gibbons and installed by Sir Christopher Wren in the 18th century when the chapel was refitted for Queen Anne (1702–14).

❽ **The Wolsey Rooms** ✷✷, on the south side of the palace, were part of Cardinal Wolsey's private lodgings in the 1520s. The two small rooms in this suite are lined with 16th-century linenfold paneling, so-called because it was intended to reproduce the effect of draped fabric on the walls. The plain Tudor-style fireplaces also date from Cardinal Wolsey's time. These rooms, and the adjacent **Renaissance Picture Gallery** ✷✷✷, are now used to display 16th- and early-17th-century paintings from the Royal Collection, including works by Lucas Cranach, Pieter Bruegel, Correggio, Agnolo Bronzino, Lorenzo Lotto, Parmigianino, and Titian.

Though Henry VIII (1491–1547) is the dominant personality associated with Hampton Court, much of his palace was lost at the end of the 17th century when William III (reigned 1689–1702) and Mary II (reigned 1689–94) commissioned Sir Christopher Wren to rebuild Hampton Court. From The Wolsey Rooms, follow signs to ❾ **The King's Apartments** ✷✷, which Wren built for William III at the end of the 17th century. **The King's Staircase,** the most spectacular in the palace, was decorated in about 1700 by the Italian painter, Antonio Verrio. The former **Guard Chamber** is decorated with a display of more than 3,000 arms, mostly muskets, pistols, bayonets, and swords. Even when the king was not present, courtiers would show their respect by bowing to the empty throne beneath its canopy in **The King's Presence Chamber.** The principal ceremonial room in the palace was **The King's Privy Chamber,** where ambassadors were received and court functions held. The magnificence of William's apartments is most apparent in **The Great Bedchamber,** with its gilded furniture, mirrors, painted ceiling, and carvings. **The King's Backstairs** lead down to a series of smaller, more intimate rooms that formed **The King's Private Apartments.**

From The King's Apartments, make your way to ❿ **The Queen's State Apartments** ✸✸✸. These rooms were begun by Sir Christopher Wren at the end of the 17th century for William III's wife, Mary II (reigned 1688–94), but were completed in succeeding reigns. The apartments you see today were used by Queen Caroline between 1716 and 1737 for entertaining important visitors, receiving petitions, and holding court entertainments. **The Queen's State Bedchamber** is still furnished with its original state bed (complete with 18th-c. mattresses). The magnificent **Queen's Gallery** was built as Queen Mary's private gallery and later adopted by King William as his private gallery.

⓫ **The Georgian Rooms** ✸✸ were used by Caroline, wife of George II (reigned 1727–60), and are displayed as they were during the last visit of the full court to the palace in 1737. The **Communication Gallery** linking the King's and Queen's apartments is hung with portraits known as The Windsor Beauties, painted by Sir Peter Lely between 1662 and 1665 and representing the most beautiful women at the court of Charles II (reigned 1660–85). The **Cartoon Gallery** ✸✸✸, one of the first picture galleries in Britain, was built for William III by Sir Christopher Wren to display Raphael's large drawings of the Acts of the Apostles. The original cartoons were lent by Queen Victoria to the Victoria and Albert Museum in 1865; today you see a set of copies painted in 1697.

As you leave the palace to enter the gardens behind, have a look at the palace's magnificent ⓬ **East Front.** The exterior of Sir Christopher Wren's building at Hampton Court is probably the best and most famous expression of the baroque style in England, and was intended to rival Louis XIV's palace of Versailles.

The Hampton Court **gardens** ✸✸✸ are a delightful mix of 500 years of royal gardening history. In Henry VIII's time, ⓭ **The East Front Gardens** area was parkland but was gradually enclosed and laid out as a great semicircular parterre (ornamental garden) with 12 marble fountains. Queen Anne (reigned 1702–14) added the surrounding semicircular canals in 1710. At the north end of the Broad Walk is ⓮ **The Royal Tennis Court** ✸, built in the 1620s and still in use today. ⓯ **The Privy Garden,** the king's private garden on the south side of the palace facing the river, has been

---

⌒*Moments* Real Tennis

Make sure your visit to the gardens includes a look at **The Royal Tennis Court** built for James I in 1626. It's still in use, and if you're lucky you'll see players engrossed in a match of Real Tennis, a complex game that's quite different from modern lawn tennis and makes use of the court's side walls and roof.

restored to the way it appeared when it was completed for William III in 1702 (note the elaborate ironwork screen). ⑯ **The Lower Orangery** 𝕱𝕱𝕱, originally built to house Mary II's collection of botanical specimens, was later converted into a gallery to display Andrea Mantegna's *Triumphs of Caesar,* a sequence of nine paintings that depict the triumphs of the Roman emperor Julius Caesar (104–44 B.C.). Painted at the Italian court of the Gonzagas in Mantua between 1484 and 1505, the paintings were acquired by Charles I in 1629 and probably arrived at Hampton Court in 1630, where they have been ever since. ⑰ **The Great Vine** 𝕱, planted in 1768 by landscape designer Lancelot "Capability" Brown, is the oldest known vine in the world and still produces 500 to 700 pounds (230–320 kilograms) of grapes each year. The grapes are harvested at the end of August and sold in the palace shops. ⑱ **The Maze** 𝕱𝕱𝕱, made up of a thousand yews planted in 1702 on the north side of the palace, covers a third of an acre (the paths wind for nearly half a mile/.8km) and is one of the most popular attractions at Hampton Court. You can climb the tower in the center of the maze for a view of the grounds.

ORGANIZED TOURS

Costumed guides give excellent free tours of the State Apartments, usually beginning at 11am and running hourly until 3:30 or 4pm. These 30-minute tours must be booked in advance at the Information Centre in the Clock Court. If you want to take one, sign up as soon as you arrive or you may be disappointed. An **audio guide,** available free from the Information Centre, provides a wealth of information and anecdotes about the history and contents of the building and the monarchs who lived there.

OUTDOOR ACTIVITIES

Daily (except Christmas) from the first Saturday in December to mid-January, you can rent ice skates and cut figure eights on the **Hampton Court Palace Outdoor Ice Rink** set up near the West Front of the palace. Tickets for timed-entry 1-hour sessions, including skate rental, cost £10 ($20) for adults, £7.50 ($15) for children under 16, and can be reserved in person at the Hampton Court box office or in advance by contacting Ticketmaster (© **0870/0601778;** www.ticketmaster.co.uk).

3 Shopping

The **Barrack Block Shop,** located in the former palace barracks, sells an extensive range of gifts from china to children's stationery as well as guidebooks and postcards. **The Garden Shop,** overlooking the gardens on the East Front of the palace, has a selection of garden-themed merchandise including books and garden accessories. The **Tudor Kitchens Shop,** next to The Tudor Wine Cellar, offers specialty food products and traditional kitchen equipment.

4 Where to Dine

Pop into the Tudor-themed (think wooden tables, and 16th-c.-style chandeliers) **Privy Kitchen Coffee Shop** near The Tudor Kitchens for tea, coffee, pastries, or a light lunch. The coffee shop is open from 10am to 5pm (Nov–Mar until 4pm). The **Tilt-yard Café** (© **020/8943 3666**), in the palace gardens, is a buffet cafe-restaurant with a slightly upscale atmosphere that serves hot and cold drinks, sandwiches, salad lunches, and hot meals; there's also a coffee bar. It's open 10am to 5:30pm (Nov–Mar until 4:30pm).

Hever Castle

With its time-mellowed stone, towers, moat, and drawbridge, Hever looks exactly what it is—a medieval castle that's played a colorful part in British history for more than 800 years. Hever dates to 1270, when William de Hever built the stone gatehouse and the bailey encircled by a moat. Sir Geoffrey Bullen bought and enlarged the castle in 1462, and Hever was the childhood home of his granddaughter Anne Boleyn, the second wife of Henry VIII. Hever passed on to Anne (who eventually lost her head) and to Henry, who gave the house to his fourth wife, Anne of Cleves, as part of the couple's divorce settlement.

By the early-20th-century Hever had fallen into near ruin, and was ripe for the picking by an American with visions of living like British royalty. William Waldorf Astor (1848–1919), heir to an American fur-trading fortune, bought Hever in 1903, restored it, filled the castle with acres of luxurious paneling, and created the property's stunning classical and natural gardens. Hever is a pleasure to visit: Warm, welcoming, and with a painting, piece of statuary, or captivating vista waiting to be enjoyed around every corner and along every garden path. Plus, you can combine a visit here with a walk in the country or a visit to another fascinating noble dwelling nearby, Penshurst Place. If you're traveling by car and have the stamina to tour another house, you can combine a visit to Hever and Penshurst with a stop at **Knole** (see trip 13), the enormous ancestral home of the Sackville clan. Knole is in Sevenoaks, about 15 miles (24km) north of Hever Castle via winding country lanes.

1 Essentials

VISITOR INFORMATION

Hever Castle (© **01732/865-224**) is 30 miles (48km) southeast of London, in the Kent countryside between the towns of East Grinstead and Sevenoaks. The castle is off B2026, a small country lane, about 3 miles (5km) southeast of the village of Edenbridge. It is open April through October daily from noon to 6pm (grounds open at 11am and last admission is at 5pm); and March, November, and December Wednesday to Sunday from 11am to 3pm (grounds open at 11am and last admission is at 2pm). Admission to the castle and gardens is £10.50 ($21) for adults, £8.80 ($18) for seniors, £5.70 ($12) for children 5 to 14, and £26.70 ($54) for families of up to two adults and two children.

Hever Castle Highlights

- Touring the library and other comfortable rooms created for Viscount Astor.
- Seeing what Anne Boleyn wrote in her Book of Hours.
- Strolling through the Italian Gardens, which took 1,800 workers 4 years to create.
- Taking in the breathtaking view of the castle, along with its moat and towers, as you approach the castle from the main gates.

SCHEDULING CONSIDERATIONS

Especially nice times to visit Hever are **Spring Garden Week** in mid-March, **Rose Week** in late June, and **Autumn Color Week** in mid-October. During these weeks the castle gardeners are on hand to point out seasonal highlights on the grounds, where gardens bloom in full color. If you're planning a visit to **Penshurst Place** as well, keep in mind that it's closed in winter. (See below for more information.)

GETTING THERE
BY TRAIN

From London's Victoria Station, trains depart hourly throughout the day for Hever Station. The trip takes 50 minutes and requires a change at East Croydon, East Grimstead, or Hurst Green. (Be sure to ask where to transfer before you board the train at Victoria, since there may not be a conductor or ticket taker on board the train.) The first train leaves London at 6:47am and the last train returns from Hever to London at 10:05pm, and trains leave about once an hour; the fare is about £15.50 ($31) standard day return. An alternative to Hever Station is Edenbridge Town Station, located 3 miles (5km) from the castle; a taxi is available from this station. On Sundays things can get a bit confusing: The train may not stop at Edenbridge Town Station but at Edenbridge Station (ask before you board), in which case you can also call for a taxi. For train information, call **National Rail Enquiries** at ✆ **08457/484950** or go to www.nationalrail.co.uk.

BY CAR

The trip from London takes under an hour, depending on traffic. From the M25, take Junction 5 and follow A22 about 5 miles (8km) south to Bindley Heath; from there you will follow small country lanes (B2029, B2028, and B2026) east for about 8 miles (13km) to Hever Castle. (The route from A22 is well marked with signs.)

GETTING AROUND

Hever train station is in the countryside, about a mile from the castle. You can walk along country lanes to the castle, but in good weather it's far more pleasant to follow the well-marked footpath through fields and woods. There is no taxi service from Hever Station, but you can take a taxi from Edenbridge Station or Edenbridge Town Station. Make your taxi arrangements in advance from London because there is no taxi stand at the station, and cabs are often busy; call **Edenbridge Cars** (✆ **01732/864-009**) or **Rely On Cars** (✆ **01732/863-800**).

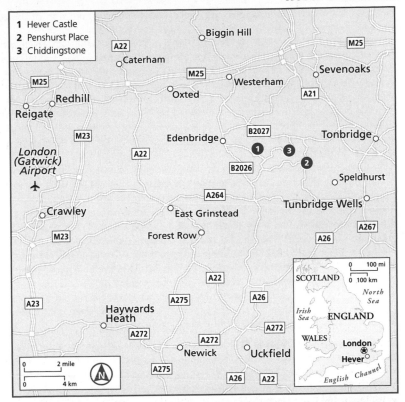

1 Hever Castle
2 Penshurst Place
3 Chiddingstone

Biggin Hill

A22
Caterham

M25

M25
Redhill
Reigate

M25
Westerham
Sevenoaks

Oxted

A21

M23
Edenbridge
B2027
Tonbridge

A22
❶ ❸
❷

B2026
Speldhurst

London
(Gatwick)
Airport
✈

A264
Tunbridge Wells

Crawley
East Grinstead

M23
Forest Row
A26
A267

A22
SCOTLAND

0   100 mi
0   100 km

A23
A275
A26
North
Sea

Haywards
Heath
Irish
Sea
ENGLAND

A272
A272
WALES

0   2 mile
0   4 km
N
A272
Newick
A275
Uckfield
A26
A22
London
✹
Hever

English Channel

2 A Day at Hever Castle

You must follow a set route through ❶ **Hever Castle** ⚜⚜, but you can do so at your own pace. Guides are posted in every room—take advantage of their knowledge; they are a gold mine of information, which they are pleased to share with inquisitive visitors.

The ground floor, where William Astor fashioned his living quarters, is lavishly furnished in exquisite early-20th-century taste—you will wish you could cross the velvet ropes and settle into one of the deep armchairs in the drawing room, morning room, or library. Hever, in fact, remained a private home until 1983. The castle was for many years the home of William Astor's son, John Jacob Astor (1886–1971), who served in the British Parliament, owned the London *Times* newspaper, and was named the 1st Baron Astor of Hever in 1956; he and his wife, Violet Astor, are buried on the grounds.

The next floor is less appealing, but as you make your way through a maze of rooms filled with historic bric-a-brac, you'll come upon some treasures. In a small exhibition room at the top of the stairs is a **Book of Hours** signed by Anne Boleyn, in which the young and ill-fated queen prophetically wrote, *"Le temps viendra"* ("The time will come"). When Anne, the mother of Queen Elizabeth I, failed to produce a male heir, Henry trumped up charges of an incestuous affair with her brother and had the siblings beheaded. Henry's bedroom is richly paneled and furnished as it was during his rare visits to the castle. In it hangs a much-reproduced portrait of the king attributed to Hans Holbein.

You can trace the history of Henry's marriages in the **Long Gallery,** peopled with mannequins of the monarch's six wives, beginning with his first queen, Catherine of Aragon. When the pope refused Henry's request to divorce Catherine and marry Anne Boleyn, Henry broke with the Catholic Church and formed the Church of England, with himself as head. Anne of Cleves, Henry's fourth wife, lived at Hever after the king divorced her and married Catherine Howard. The 13th-century **Gatehouse,** the last stop on the tour, is filled with a grisly collection of torture devices and explicit diagrams showing how defenders once poured boiling oil onto invaders through "murder holes" in the floor.

William Astor employed as many as 1,800 workers, who toiled for more than 4 years creating the castle's gardens, among the finest in England, on what was once marshland. (Clearly, the fantastically wealthy heir, who became a viscount, was not without feudal ideas—he housed his staff in a mock Tudor village that you can't visit but you can see across the lawns to the rear of the castle.) It's hard not to feel rather grandiose as you stroll through the **Italian Gardens,** which surround a 35-acre (14-hectare) lake that a crew of 800 laborers dug out over a 2-year period; the gardens are appointed with a stunning collection of classical sculpture and portions of the triumphal arch that the Roman emperor Claudius erected on the nearby coast in A.D. 52. If you have children in tow and want to enjoy these formal but welcoming gardens in peace, send them off to amuse themselves in the **Yew Maze** and the **Water Maze,** in which a misstep will get them doused in a spray of water.

MORE THINGS TO SEE & DO

❷ Penshurst Place ⨂⨂   This remarkably intact medieval manor house dates from the 13th century, and has at its heart the Baron's Hall. Stone-floored, with a chestnut-paneled ceiling and built around a massive octagonal hearth, the hall is considered one of the finest interiors remaining from the Middle Ages. Many of the grander staterooms and the Long Gallery upstairs date from the 16th century, when King Edward VI presented the house to the Sidney family. The most famous member of this clan is Sir Philip Sidney, soldier, courtier, poet, and personification of an Elizabethan gentleman, and his descendants live here still. The walled and terraced gardens are perfect places in which to spend part of a warm afternoon.

A Show for All Seasons

Except for the darkest days of winter, the gardens at Hever always put on a show of color. Crocuses and snowdrops come up in March, and daffodils and tulips in April, when the camellias also start to flower. Wisteria, rhododendrons, and azaleas bloom in May and June, and in July the 3,000 bushes in the walled Rose Garden reach full flower, and, along with many of the other flowering shrubs, thrive throughout August. Japanese maples, beeches, and other trees begin to turn in September, and the spectacle of fall foliage, accented with the dahlia borders, doesn't wind down until late October.

The Six Wives of Henry VIII

Among the lures of Hever Castle is its connection to King Henry VIII and his many marriages. Wax figures of Henry's queens are lined up in the Long Gallery, and they provide an illuminating lesson in a juicy episode in English history. **Catherine of Aragon** (1485–1536), the daughter of King Ferdinand and Queen Isabella of Spain, had been married to Henry's brother Arthur, and upon his death a year after the marriage, Catherine became betrothed to Henry, who was then too young to marry. After 20 years of marriage, Catherine failed to produce a male heir (she had one daughter, who would later reign as Mary I, or "Bloody Mary"), and Henry sought to annul the union. The pope refused, so Henry installed a new archbishop of Canterbury, Thomas Cranmer, to carry out his wishes, thereby creating the Church of England. Catherine never accepted the divorce and until her dying day always thought of herself as Henry's wife.

Henry next married **Anne Boleyn** (1500–36), whose family lived at Hever. The young queen produced a daughter (who would become Elizabeth I) but no male heir, and Henry became convinced the union was doomed. He had Anne executed on (trumped-up) grounds of adultery and 11 days later married **Jane Seymour** (1509–37), who within the year finally gave Henry a son (the future Edward VI) but died in childbirth. Henry next married **Anne of Cleves** (1515–57) to further his alliances with Germany, but was dissatisfied with this queen (whom he thought was horse-faced) and soon arranged for a divorce (amicable enough that Anne frequently socialized with Henry's later wives); Hever was part of Anne's settlement.

Sixteen days after freeing himself of Anne, Henry married **Catherine Howard** (1521–42), more than 30 years his junior. The king had his young queen, who was a first cousin of Anne Boleyn, executed when he discovered she was taking lovers. In 1543, Henry married **Catherine Parr** (1512–48), who outlived the king by only a year—but long enough to marry Thomas Seymour, brother of Henry's third queen.

You won't be able to get from Hever to Penshurst easily via public transportation. If you are not driving, you can arrange for a taxi or you can walk, following public footpaths; see "Outdoor Activities," below. From Penshurst, you can return to London's Victoria Station by train (changing at Redhill). The trip takes about 70 minutes. There is a train every half-hour, and the last departure is at 11:22pm. The cheap day single ticket (one-way from Penshurst to London) is about £10 ($20).

In the village of Penshurst, 5 miles (8km) southeast of Hever, on B2176. ✆ 01892/870-307. House and grounds: £7.50 ($15) adults, £7 ($14) seniors and students, £5 ($10) children, £21 ($42) families.

OUTDOOR ACTIVITIES

Well-maintained public footpaths crisscross the countryside all around Hever. One of the most pleasant walks takes you through woods and fields from the church near the castle gate for about 1.5 miles (2.5km) to ❸ **Chiddingstone** ✿, a charming village of half-timbered houses that looks so perfectly English you expect to see Miss Marple or another character from British fiction step out of a doorway. There's a castle, complete with banner flying from a turret, but it's ersatz 19th century (open to the public some days during the summer). If you're feeling energetic, you can continue to Penshurst (see above), but stop at the post office or a shop on the main street and ask for detailed directions; it can be really hard to find your way on the intersecting footpaths.

3 Where to Dine

King Henry VIII ✿ PUB   Named for the monarch who's rather infamously linked with Hever Castle just up the road, this handsome, paneled pub serves sandwiches and meat pies, along with curries and other daily specials. The satisfying Sunday-roast lunch, when you can enjoy lamb, beef, or other substantial fare in front of a fire, adds a very nice touch to a day's outing from London.

Hever Rd., near castle entrance. ⓒ **01732/862-457.** Main courses £4–£9 ($8–$18). DC, MC, V. Food served Mon–Sat noon–2:30pm and 6:30–9:30pm; Sun noon–3pm and 6–9pm.

Kew Gardens

Located 9 miles (14km) southwest of central London, the Royal Botanic Gardens, Kew—more familiarly known as Kew Gardens—are a feast for the eyes (and noses) of garden lovers. Kew's connections with royalty began with Frederick, Prince of Wales, who leased Richmond Lodge and its adjoining property in 1730 and had a hand in laying out the grounds. But it was Frederick's widow, Caroline; his son, George III; and daughter-in-law, Augusta, who really developed Kew. They set about creating a vast pleasure garden and their work was aided by botanists who began to bring exotic plants to Kew from all over the world. The architect William Chambers decorated the royal estate with pavilions, temples, and even a pagoda. In the 1760s, renowned landscape artist Capability Brown (who also designed the gardens at Hampton Court; see trip 10) redesigned the gardens, which were becoming an important center of research as well as a royal estate, and in 1840 the Royal Botanic Gardens were taken over by the nation. Recognizing the historical importance of the gardens, UNESCO designated Kew Gardens a World Heritage Site in 2003. Kew is today not only one of the world's most beautiful gardens, but also a renowned center of research in plant diversity, habitat restoration, and rainforest survival. Displays throughout the gardens highlight Kew's colorful history as well as the vital work that continues here. Since Kew is just a half-hour ride from the center of London, you can visit the gardens on a half-day trip, but you may well want to spend more time here and take a walk along the River Thames to Ham House.

1 Essentials

VISITOR INFORMATION
The **Victoria Gate Visitor Centre** (www.rbgkew.org.uk) on Kew Road provides information and remains open the same hours as the Royal Botanic Gardens, daily 9:30am to 5:30pm (6:30pm in summer, 4:15pm in winter).

SCHEDULING CONSIDERATIONS
The gardens are open daily from 9:30am to dusk, but the glass conservatories close an hour before the gardens themselves. The gardens are interesting year-round, but for overall peak blooming, visit between April and July. Kew Palace is open April through

Kew Gardens Highlights

• Exploring the world-famous plant collections in the Royal Botanic Gardens.

• Visiting the glasshouse conservatories, some new, some dating back to the Victorian era.

September daily from 9:30am to 4:15pm. The gardens are closed December 25 and January 1.

GETTING THERE
BY UNDERGROUND
By far the easiest way to get to Kew is to take the District Line Underground to Kew Gardens. The trip from central London takes about half an hour. (Take a train marked Richmond, not one marked Ealing, Broadway, or Wimbledon.) From the Kew station it's a 5-minute walk west on Lichfield Street to the garden entrance on Kew Road. For **Transport for London** information, call ℂ **020/7222-1234** or visit www.tfl.gov.uk.

BY BOAT
Traveling by boat is a scenic and leisurely way to reach Kew Gardens from London. From April to late September, boats operated by the **Westminster Passenger Service Association** (ℂ **020/7930-2062;** www.wpsa.co.uk) leave from London's Westminster Pier daily at 10:30 and 11am, noon, and 2pm. Return fares for the 90-minute journey are £16.50 ($33) for adults, £11 ($22) for seniors, £8.25 ($17) for children 5 to 15, and £41.25 ($83) for families (two adults, two children). The last boat from Kew back to London usually departs around 5:30pm (depending on the tide).

BY CAR
Kew Gardens is well signposted from all the major local roads. The drive from London can take about half an hour, but you may find yourself stuck in traffic for much longer—it's faster and easier to come by Underground. The South Circular (A205) passes the northeast corner of Kew Gardens; and Kew Road (A307) forms the eastern border. There is a car park near the Brentford Gate, reached via Ferry Lane off Kew Green near the Main Gate; parking costs £3.50 ($7) for a full day. Free parking is available on Kew Road (A307) after 10am every morning; this provides easy access to the garden's principal entrance at Victoria Gate.

GETTING AROUND
Exploring the nooks and crannies of the Royal Botanic Gardens is best done on foot, but the grounds are extensive and to see everything on foot requires at least 3 hours. You can get a 40-minute overview of the 300-acre (120-hectare) gardens by taking the **Kew Explorer** (ℂ **020/8332-5615**), a hop-on/hop-off people-mover that makes eight stops within the gardens. Tickets are £3.50 ($7) for adults, £1 ($2) for children under 17. You can purchase a ticket at any of the garden's ticket gates or from the driver of the vehicle. The main boarding point is close to the Victoria Gate Visitor Centre and the Palm House.

Kew Gardens

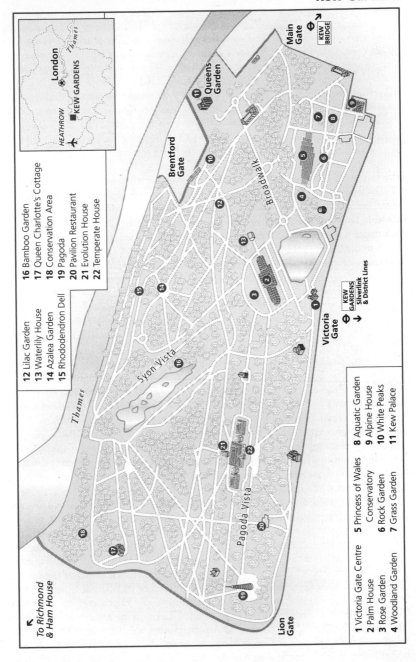

To Richmond
& Ham House

Thames

Syon Vista

Pagoda Vista

Lion
Gate

Brentford
Gate

Broadwalk

Victoria
Gate

KEW
GARDENS
Silverlink
& District Lines

Queens
Garden

Main Gate

KEW
BRIDGE

London
KEW GARDENS
HEATHROW
Thames

12 Lilac Garden
13 Waterlily House
14 Azalea Garden
15 Rhododendron Dell

16 Bamboo Garden
17 Queen Charlotte's Cottage
18 Conservation Area
19 Pagoda
20 Pavilion Restaurant
21 Evolution House
22 Temperate House

1 Victoria Gate Centre
2 Palm House
3 Rose Garden
4 Woodland Garden

5 Princess of Wales
    Conservatory
6 Rock Garden
7 Grass Garden

8 Aquatic Garden
9 Alpine House
10 White Peaks
11 Kew Palace

2 A Day in Kew

There are four entrances to the **Royal Botanic Gardens, Kew** 𝕣𝕣𝕣 (© 020/8332-5622; www.rbgkew.org.uk). **Victoria Gate** on Kew Road is the largest entrance and nearest to the Kew Gardens Underground station. The **Main Gate** on Kew Green is the nearest entrance to the Kew Bridge train station and Kew Pier riverboat stop. The **Brentford Gate** is adjacent to the car park and a 10-minute walk along the riverbank from Kew Pier. **Lion Gate,** the southernmost gate on Kew Road, is nearest to the Pagoda and the Pavilion Restaurant. Admission to the gardens is £12.25 ($25) for adults, £10.25 ($21) for seniors and students, and free for children 5 to 16. The gardens are open daily from 9:30am to dusk (6:30pm in summer, 4:15pm in winter, 5:30pm fall and spring).

For a good and fairly complete walk encompassing the main garden areas and glasshouse conservatories, you'll need 3 to 4 hours. Start at the ❶ **Victoria Gate Visitor Centre,** where you can pick up detailed maps and information. Then head west to the famous ❷ **Palm House** 𝕣𝕣𝕣, which acts as a centerpiece to the gardens. Dramatic and elegant, this glass and iron curvilinear structure is one of the world's premiere examples of Victorian design. Built between 1844 and 1848, it was constructed to house tropical trees, shrubs, and palms. Beneath the Palm House is the Marine Display, with tanks containing fish, coral, and algae: the beginnings of plant life on earth. To one side of the Palm House is the ❸ **Rose Garden** 𝕣, created in 1923 and a major focal point for visitors, especially June through September, the peak flowering months. The garden houses 54 rose beds, each containing a different variety of rose.

From the Rose Garden, make your way north to the ❹ **Woodland Garden.** This area illustrates the change in vegetation between forest and alpine zones. A deciduous tree canopy of oaks and birches supports climbing plants and provides shade for deciduous shrubs such as rhododendrons, which in turn protect ground-cover plants, including hellebores, primulas, Himalayan blue poppies, and North American trilliums. A short walk to the northwest brings you to the ❺ **Princess of Wales Conservatory** 𝕣, named in honor of the garden's founder, Augusta, the princess of Wales, and Diana, Princess of Wales, who opened the Conservatory in July 1987. This contemporary glasshouse has 10 climatic zones, ranging from arid to moist tropical. The hot and humid area contains swamp and riverine habitats and displays giant Amazonian waterlilies. In contrast, the arid zone houses plants tolerant of desert conditions, particularly cacti and other succulents.

Just east of the conservatory is the ❻ **Rock Garden,** originally built in 1882 and designed to resemble a mountain valley in the Pyrenees. The site was recently redesigned to include moist gullies, water features, and other special environments that allow for the cultivation of a variety of alpine, Mediterranean, and woodland plants. Adjacent, to the north, is the ❼ **Grass Garden,** designed in 1982 and displaying some 550 species of grasses. Continue toward the northeast corner of the gardens and you'll reach the ❽ **Aquatic Garden,** which opened in 1909 (its design was reportedly inspired by the sunken gardens at Hampton Court Palace; see trip 10) and is famous for its 40 different varieties of waterlily. Nearby, in the northeastern corner of the gardens, is the strikingly modern ❾ **Alpine House** 𝕣𝕣, opened in 2005 and displaying Kew's significant collection of alpine plants. From late winter to May, corresponding with the flowering season of the plants being displayed, you'll see collections of crocus, fritillaria, narcissus, primula, and saxifrage.

Heading west across the park toward the River Thames, you come to ❿ **White Peaks,** a restaurant and gift shop (see "Where to Dine," below). Immediately to the west is ⓫ **Kew Palace,** George III's family home and used by the royal family between 1729 and 1818. The small redbrick palace is the last survivor of several important royal residences at Kew; closed for several years for restoration, the palace reopened in 2006 and can now be visited from April through September (for more information on the palace, check out the Historical Royal Palaces' website at www.hrp.org.uk). The **Queen's Garden,** behind Kew Palace, is a 17th-century-style garden with parterres of low boxwood hedges enclosing plantings of lavender, sage, and rosemary. Next to the parterres is a sunken nosegay garden planted with the fragrant flowers used to make posies or nosegays in the 17th century.

From the palace, backtrack to White Peaks and continue southeast to the ⓬ **Lilac Garden** ✿, at its fragrant best in May. Completely renovated in 1993, the new garden has 105 specimens of hardy lilacs ranging from the oldest species to modern cultivars and hybrids. Just east of the Lilac Garden you'll find the ⓭ **Waterlily House** ✿, the hottest and most humid glasshouse at Kew (and also notable for its striking ironwork). In summer it houses tropical ornamental aquatic plants and giant waterlilies; it's closed in winter.

South of the Waterlily House is the ⓮ **Azalea Garden,** with its profusion of hardy azaleas that provide a blaze of springtime color. Zigzagging back toward the Thames, you reach the famous ⓯ **Rhododendron Dell** ✿✿, planted with over 700 specimens of hardy, spring-flowering, shade-loving rhododendrons, some of them unique hybrids found only at Kew. The Rhododendron Dell was carved out of a riverside flood plain by the great landscaper Capability Brown in 1773. It became the Rhododendron Dell when Sir Joseph Hooker (arguably Britain's most important botanist and a former director of Kew Gardens) began bringing back rhododendrons from his Himalayan expeditions in the 1850s. The best time to visit is during late May, when most of the rhododendrons are in flower.

In the neighboring ⓰ **Bamboo Garden,** over 120 individual specimens of hardy bamboo have been brought together from regions all over the world. From here, continue south past Kew's artificial lake to ⓱ **Queen Charlotte's Cottage.** This cottage began as a small, single-story building within the grounds of Richmond Lodge, which Queen Charlotte received as a wedding gift when she married George III in 1761. It was used as a summer house. Queen Charlotte's Cottage is not open to the public except once a year on the May Day Bank Holiday. The nearby ⓲ **Conservation Area** contains one of the finest spring-flowering bluebell woods in the London area. The woods are managed as a nature reserve.

Walk east from Queen Charlotte's Cottage and you'll reach the ⓳ **Pagoda** ✿✿, completed in 1762 and a charming reminder of the passion for Chinoiserie in English garden design in the mid–18th century. Close by is the ⓴ **Pavilion Restaurant.**

The Chinese Pagoda

The Chinese Pagoda in Kew Gardens is a strange but oddly endearing sight. In 1761, when it was built, the Pagoda was the most accurate reconstruction of a Chinese building in Europe. It is 163 feet (49m) high and contains nothing but a staircase. Unfortunately, it's closed to the public.

A Walk to Richmond & Ham House

If you'd like an add-on to your trip to Kew, from the gardens, a path follows the Thames for about 2 miles (3km) to the appealing town of **Richmond-upon-Thames** ⚑, where handsome brick Regency houses line the streets and cafes overlook the river. If you admire the new riverfront development here, you're in good company—Prince Charles, a critic of much modern British architecture, has applauded the neoclassical assemblage of new buildings on the river. The town is surrounded by the oaks and pastures of Richmond Park, a vast hunting ground that Charles I set aside in 1637. Deer still roam the 2,500 acres (1,000 hectares), and a former royal residence, White Lodge, built by George II in 1729, houses the Royal Ballet School.

Another mile or so upriver is **Ham House** ⚑⚑ (© **0208/940-1950**), a 17th-century Stuart palace with elaborate gardens and sumptuous Restoration period interiors; even the dairy is elaborate, and iron cows' legs support the marble counters. The house is notable as a center of political intrigue during the Civil War: William Murray, who lived in the house when King Charles I was exiled in 1642, was a staunch royalist, and his daughter Elizabeth became a leading member of the Sealed Knot, a secret society dedicated to restoring the monarchy. Perhaps a result of the scheming that once went on in its grand salons, Ham is said to be the most haunted house in England and special ghost tours are sometimes offered. Ham House is open April through October, Saturday to Wednesday from 1 to 5pm; gardens are open year-round, Saturday to Wednesday 11am to 6pm. Admission to the house and gardens costs £9 ($18) for adults, £5 ($10) for children.

(See "Where to Dine," below.) North and slightly west of the restaurant, you come to ㉑ **Evolution House,** a walk-through exhibition of plant evolution over 3,500 million years. ㉒ **Temperate House,** just east of Evolution House, is the world's largest ornamental glasshouse, and holds a collection of subtropical plants. The main center block and the octagons at each end were built between 1860 and 1862; the end blocks were added between 1860 and 1899. The world's largest indoor plant, the Chilean winepalm, is displayed within.

From Temperate House you can walk back to Victoria Gate in about 5 minutes.

ORGANIZED TOURS

Free, hour-long **guided walking tours** of Kew Gardens leave year-round (except Christmas and New Year's Day) at 11am and 2pm from the Guides' desk, just inside the Victoria Gate Visitor Centre. Tour groups are limited to 20 people on a first-come, first-served basis; register with the guide 15 minutes before the tour. These walks provide an excellent introduction to the gardens.

3 Shopping

The shops at **Victoria Gate** and **White Peaks** (© **020/8332-5653** for both) sell many exclusive products, including kitchenware and stationery lines designed for the Royal

Botanic Gardens using illustrations from the Kew archives. There is also a comprehensive selection of horticultural books. The **Garden Shop** (© **01444/894-073**), at the entrance to the garden, is open from March to October and sells a wide range of interesting and unusual plants and garden items. (*Note:* Live plants cannot be brought into the U.S.)

4 Where to Dine

The **Orangery Restaurant** (© **020/8332-5186**), located close to the Main Gate in a historic building with pretty views of the gardens, offers morning coffees, lunches (including cooked-to-order stir-fries and pasta), and afternoon teas. It's open daily from 10am to 1 hour before closing; prices for main courses range from £6 to £12 ($12–$24). The same prices and hours apply at **White Peaks,** Kew's newest venue, which offers chargrilled steak sandwiches and sausages, plus baked potatoes with various toppings and fresh baked pastries. The **Victoria Gate Coffee Shop,** in the Victoria Gate Visitor Centre, serves cappuccino and espresso, handmade pastries and cakes, ice cream, handmade sandwiches, and warm panini in a casual, coffee-shop setting. It opens at 9:30am and closes 30 minutes before the garden; a sandwich costs from £3.50 to £6 ($7–$12).

The **Pavilion Restaurant** (© **020/8332-5186**), located near the Pagoda, is the garden's largest restaurant and provides alfresco dining in warm weather; in it you'll find a self-service cafeteria offering hot meals, a fresh salad bar, desserts, and hot and cold drinks. It opens at 10am and closes an hour before the gardens; it's also closed during the winter months. Main courses at lunch range in price from £4 to £8 ($8–$16).

Knole

*O*ne of Britain's largest and grandest houses covers 4½ acres (1.8 hectares) and has 365 rooms, as well as a courtyard for every day of the week and a staircase for every week of the year. Large, yes, but Knole is certainly not homey—indeed, the house has always been meant to impress rather than charm, and its labyrinthine rooms and galleries are a treasure-trove of Stuart furniture, textiles, and portraits by such masters as Anthony van Dyck, Thomas Gainsborough, and Sir Joshua Reynolds.

Thomas Bouchier, archbishop of Canterbury, commissioned the construction of Knole on the site of a medieval farm in 1456. The palace was home to four of Bouchier's successors, until the early 16th century, when Henry VIII took a liking to the house and seized it from Archbishop Thomas Cranmer. Henry's daughter, Elizabeth I, gave Knole to her cousin, Thomas Sackville, the 1st Earl of Dorset, and the Sackvilles have lived here ever since.

The enormous house is both somber and, seen with the sun warming its stone and marble, beautiful. Vita Sackville-West, the 20th-century novelist and poet, described Knole as a "very old woman who has always been beautiful, who has had many lovers and seen many generations come and go." You will share this sense of history as you tour the rooms and admire the furnishings that generations of Sackvilles have acquired over the centuries. As you walk through the 1,000-acre (400-hectare) deer park and see the sprawling house across the lawns you will also come to appreciate Vita's comment that Knole "is above all an English home. It has the tone of England; it melts into the green of the garden turf, into the tawnier green of the park beyond, into the blue of the pale English sky."

Because you can board a train in London and find yourself standing in the Great Hall at Knole in less than an hour, you can easily do this day trip in half a day—unless, that is, you want to explore more of British history on a visit to Ightham Mote or Chartwell, two other nearby historic houses.

1 Essentials

VISITOR INFORMATION

Knole is in the town of Sevenoaks, about 30 miles (48km) southeast of London. The **house** (© 01732/462-100; www.nationaltrust.org.uk), in a large deer park at the south end of town, is open mid-March to late October, Wednesday to Sunday from

Knole

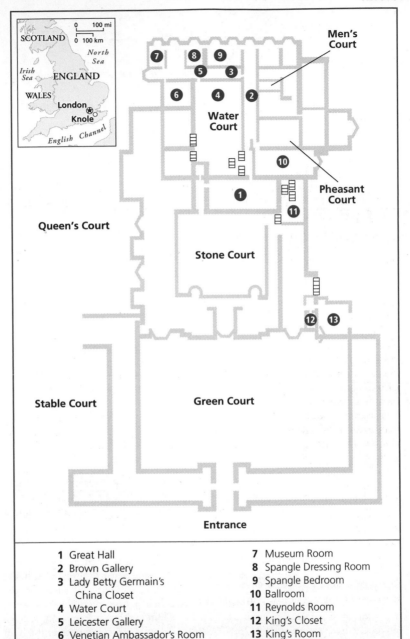

Men's Court

Water Court

Queen's Court

Pheasant Court

Stone Court

Stable Court

Green Court

Entrance

1 Great Hall
2 Brown Gallery
3 Lady Betty Germain's
China Closet
4 Water Court
5 Leicester Gallery
6 Venetian Ambassador's Room

7 Museum Room
8 Spangle Dressing Room
9 Spangle Bedroom
10 Ballroom
11 Reynolds Room
12 King's Closet
13 King's Room

Knole Highlights

• Walking through the Deer Park.

• Touring the Great Hall, with its embellished staircase and minstrels' gallery.

• Viewing the Count Ugolino painting and other works by Reynolds in the Reynolds Room.

• Seeing the rare silver furniture in the King's Room.

noon to 4pm; the last entry is at 3:30pm. The Deer Park is open year-round. Admission is £8.50 ($17) for adults, £4.25 ($8.50) for children, and £21.30 ($43) for families of up to two adults and three children.

SCHEDULING CONSIDERATIONS

On the first Wednesday of the month from May to September, the **private gardens of the Sackville family** are open to the public from 11am to 4pm. Behind the mile (1.6km) of ragstone walls surrounding the garden are an Orangery, formal borders, lawns, pools, a knot garden, and the so-called "Wilderness," in which mossy paths wind beneath beech trees. Admission to the garden costs £2 ($4) for adults, £1 ($2) for children.

GETTING THERE
BY TRAIN

Trains run about every 15 minutes to half-hour throughout the day from London's Charing Cross Station to Sevenoaks, with the first train leaving London at 5:30am on weekdays (6am on weekends) and the last train returning from Sevenoaks at 11:22pm. The trip takes about 35 minutes. The saver day return fare is about £8 ($16). For more information, call **National Rail Enquiries** at ℂ **08457/484950** or go to www. nationalrail.co.uk.

BY CAR

Sevenoaks is about 3 miles (4.8km) off M25, the London ring road, and the trip from the center of the city takes about 45 minutes, a little less if traffic is light. Leave the M25 at Junction 5 and follow the signs into Sevenoaks. The entrance to Knole is at the south end of the town center off A225 Tonbridge Road.

GETTING AROUND

Knole is about a mile from the train station, and can be reached by an easy walk through the center of Sevenoaks. An especially picturesque way to approach the house is to follow Webb's Alley off High Street, which leads to a footpath that crosses the Knole Deer Park to the house. **Bus no. 402** runs hourly from the train station past the entrance to Knole; the fare is £1 ($2). For additional bus information, call the **Sevenoaks bus station** at ℂ **01732/743-040.** There's a taxi stand outside the train station, but to ensure that a car will be available when you arrive, arrange a pickup in advance by calling **Beeline Radio Taxis** at ℂ **01732/456-214.**

2 A Day at Knole

The self-guided tour of the immense house includes only 13 rooms, but even so, you'll feel as though you're covering acres. After approaching the house through the enormous Deer Park, you'll pass into the ❶ **Great Hall** 𝖦𝖦𝖦 through two courtyards. (Part of this entrance wing was added by Henry VIII, who acquired Knole in 1538.) Thomas Bouchier, archbishop of Canterbury, who built the house between 1456 and 1480, used to dine on the dais at the far end of the cavernous hall. When Thomas Sackville took possession of Knole in 1603, he enhanced the dining experience by adding a gallery where his private orchestra would play throughout the meal. He also embellished the Great Staircase with carvings and murals to impress his guests as they climbed to the first-floor staterooms.

One of Thomas Sackville's most accomplished descendants was Vita Sackville-West, the 20th-century poet and novelist. She grew up at Knole and loved the house, but as a woman could not inherit it. Instead she bought nearby Sissinghurst and created one of England's most famous gardens (see trip 21). Vita's friend and fellow novelist Virginia Woolf set her novel *Orlando* at Knole, and you'll find the novel especially evocative after visiting the house; you can read a page or two in the facsimile edition on view in the Great Hall.

The staterooms at Knole are laid out as apartments comprising long galleries, bedchambers, and dressing rooms. As you pass through the first of these arrangements, the ❷ **Brown Gallery** 𝖦 and the adjoining ❸ **Lady Betty Germain's China Closet** 𝖦𝖦 (which houses a notable collection of Delft), look out the window into the ❹ **Water Court** 𝖦𝖦—this half-timbered courtyard surrounded by bow windows is one of the few charming nooks and crannies at Knole.

In the nearby ❺ **Leicester Gallery** 𝖦 (named for the Earl of Leicester, a 16th-c. owner of Knole who was a favorite of Elizabeth I), pay close attention to the full-length portrait of James I; the king is sitting on an X-framed chair exactly like the one beneath the painting. Another piece of notable furniture is in the ❻ **Venetian Ambassador's Room** 𝖦—the bed is said to be the one in which King James II awoke at Whitehall on December 18, 1688, the day William of Orange took the crown and forced James into exile. A less imposing but nonetheless notable piece of furniture is the Knole settee in the adjoining ❼ **Museum Room** 𝖦. This high-armed, high-backed couch may look

From *Orlando*

Virginia Woolf based the title character of her novel *Orlando* on her friend Vita Sackville-West, and she modeled Orlando's home in Kent on Knole, Vita's beloved childhood home. In Woolf's words, "It looked a town rather than a house, but a town built, not hither and thither, as this man wished or that, but circumspectly, by a single architect with one idea in his head. Courts and buildings, grey, red, plum colour, lay orderly and symmetrical; the courts were some of them oblong and some square; in this was a fountain; in that a statue; the buildings were some of them low, some pointed; here was a chapel, there a belfry . . . while smoke from innumerable chimneys curled perpetually into the air."

> ⎛ *Tips* **A Bird's-Eye View**
>
> Ramble through Knole's Deer Park over hills and through woods. Find a high spot and look over the sea of roofs and courtyards—you'll agree with novelist Virginia Woolf that Knole is "a town rather than a house."

familiar; the design is still popular and often reproduced. The harpsichord in the ❽ **Spangle Dressing Room** ✿ is one of the oldest in England, but your attention will probably be drawn to the 17th-century bed in the adjoining ❾ **Spangle Bedroom** ✿✿, covered with thousands of silver panels intended to sparkle in the sunlight.

In the next rooms hang Knole's famous paintings. A van Dyck portrait of a teenaged Frances Cranfield, who married a 17th-century owner of Knole, is in the ❿ **Ballroom** ✿, and a collection of paintings by Sir Joshua Reynolds hangs in the appropriately named ⓫ **Reynolds Room** ✿✿✿. If you know your Dante, you might recognize the horrible scene of a starving Count Ugolino contemplating eating his dead children. One of the more curious portraits is of Wang-y-Tong, page to the third duke of Dorset, who owned Knole for the last half of the 18th century and was Reynolds's patron.

The last two rooms commemorate royalty—the ⓬ **King's Closet** ✿ does so humbly, with what is euphemistically called a "seat of easement" used by Charles II or James II; and the ⓭ **King's Room** ✿✿ shows off a grandiose bed made for Charles, as well as a set of rare silver furniture. Though the remarkable ensemble is lit dimly (to preserve the gilt), the set is one of Knole's great treasures and, like the house itself, in a somewhat musty manner suggests the grandeur of bygone times.

The **Deer Park** ✿✿✿ that surrounds Knole is a relic of the Middle Ages, built as a private hunting ground and one of the few such parks to survive—many others around England were transformed into the picturesque landscapes that came into vogue in the 18th century. In fact, the only changes to the rolling parklands around Knole were wrought by nature. In 1987 a fierce windstorm roared through Kent, toppling more than 70% of the trees, many of them ancient oaks. An ambitious replanting program has restored the park, maintaining its timeless appearance.

MORE THINGS TO SEE & DO

From Knole you can visit nearby Ightham Mote and Chartwell. Chartwell is accessible by bus no. 401, which runs from Sevenoaks train station only on Sunday, every 2 hours between 9:53am and 5:53pm; the fare is £2 ($4). To reach Chartwell at other times, and to reach Ightham Mote, it's necessary to take a taxi; the fare to each is about £6 ($12) one-way. To reserve a taxi, call **Beeline Radio Taxis** at ☎ **01732/456-214.**

Ightham Mote ✿✿✿   One of the oldest residences in England and one of the best-preserved medieval dwellings in the world dates to 1330. Unlike the cold staterooms at Knole, the Great Hall and other rooms of this moated manor exude warmth and familiarity and are filled with textiles, paneling, and furnishings accumulated over the centuries. The gardens are beautiful, and the extensive grounds are laced with footpaths.

Ivy Hatch, 6 miles (9.5km) east of Sevenoaks. ☎ **01732/810-378.** www.nationaltrust.org.uk/places/ighthammote. £8.60 ($17) adults, £4.30 ($8.60) children, £21.50 ($43) families. Early Mar to late Oct Sun–Mon and Wed–Fri 10am–5:30pm.

Chartwell ★★★   For more than 40 years, Sir Winston and Lady Churchill made this handsome brick house their home, entertaining world leaders and engaging in their private pursuits. Here England's wartime prime minister wrote his history of the English-speaking peoples and other books, and painted his accomplished watercolors. Together the couple transformed the 80-acre (32-hectare) grounds, and their gardens continue to flourish. Anyone who admires the larger-than-life Churchill will enjoy seeing the house where he relaxed and pursued his many interests, and a visit also provides a look at how the wealthy upper classes once lived—and, in the case of a privileged few, still do.

2 miles (3.2km) south of Westerham (fork left off B2026 after 1½ miles/2.5km), about 7 miles (11km) southwest of Sevenoaks. © **01732/868-381**. www.nationaltrust.org.uk/places/chartwell. £9.80 ($20) adults, £4.90 ($10) children, £24.50 ($49) families. Mid-Mar to late Oct Wed–Sun 11am–5pm (also Tues July–Aug).

3 Where to Dine

Greggs ★ LIGHT FARE/TRADITIONAL BRITISH   You can eat simply or rather lavishly in this attractive room in the center of Sevenoaks. Soups, pastas, and salads are served on a good-value fixed-price "Market Garden" lunch menu, but calves' liver, steaks, and other hearty British fare are also available. Sunday lunch is very popular with locals.

28–30 High St. © **01732/456-373**. Most items £16–£17 ($32–$34); fixed-price lunch menu £12–£15 ($24–$30). DC, MC, V. Tues–Sat 12:30–2:30pm and 6:30–9:30pm; Sun noon–2:45pm.

Leeds Castle

"*T*he loveliest castle in the world," as Leeds bills itself, is lovely indeed, a vision of turrets, towers, and light gray stone that seems to float in the middle of a swan-filled lake. On the extensive and manicured grounds, streams bubble through copses, exotic flowers bloom in well-tended gardens, and a maze hides a secret grotto. Leeds has a long history, too: It traces its roots to the 9th century, when Leed, a minister of the king of Kent, built a wooden fortress here on two islands in the River Len, and it was transformed into a royal palace for Edward I in 1278; the castle's vineyard, still producing grapes, is listed in the 11th-century *Domesday Book*. King Henry V imprisoned his stepmother, Queen Joan, at Leeds on charges of witchcraft, then turned the castle over to his wife, Catherine de Valois. Henry VIII made substantial improvements to Leeds for his first queen, Catherine of Aragon. The castle was later the country seat of Lord Culpeper, colonial governor of Virginia. A wealthy Anglo-American heiress, Olive, Lady Baillie, purchased the castle in 1926, restoring some of Leeds to its medieval splendor and creating in other parts of the castle one of the most sophisticated and tasteful homes of 20th-century Britain. So, a visit to Leeds provides a dose of English history with a glimpse into the lives of a privileged few.

While Leeds is beautiful and the setting for a great many moments in Britain's past, it is also a heck of a lot of fun. Mazes enliven the gardens, balloons take off from the grounds, fireworks frequently burst overhead, strains of orchestras float through the woods during summer concerts. All in all, Leeds is probably the showiest castle in the land. To take advantage of the place in all its glory, try to arrange a visit on a day when the weather will permit you to enjoy the grounds as well as the castle.

1 Essentials

VISITOR INFORMATION

Leeds is located 7 miles (11km) east of the town of Maidstone and about 40 miles (64km) southeast of London. Unlike many historic homes in Britain, the **castle** is open year-round: April to October from 11am to 7pm (last admission at 5:30pm); and November to March from 10:15am to 5pm (last admission at 3:30pm). Entrance to the castle and grounds costs £14 ($28) for adults, £11 ($22) for seniors and

Leeds Castle

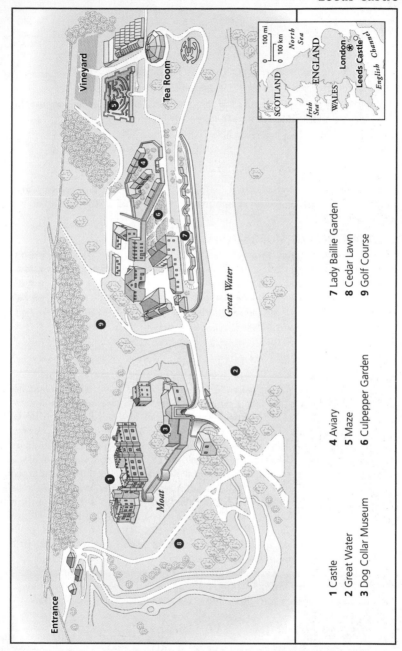

Entrance

Vineyard

Tea Room

Moat

Great Water

1 Castle
2 Great Water
3 Dog Collar Museum

4 Aviary
5 Maze
6 Culpepper Garden

7 Lady Baillie Garden
8 Cedar Lawn
9 Golf Course

SCOTLAND

ENGLAND

WALES

London

Leeds Castle

North Sea

Irish Sea

English Channel

0   100 mi
0   100 km

Leeds Castle Highlights

- Touring the sumptuous 20th-century living quarters of the castle.
- Exploring the medieval chapel with its paintings and carvings.
- Discovering the weird grotto, hidden in the maze.
- Strolling through Culpeper Garden, a colorful and delightfully informal bower, and the Mediterranean-style Lady Baillie Garden.
- Visiting charming Bearsted village.

students, £8.50 ($17) for children 4 to 15, and £39 ($78) for families of up to two adults and three children. For more information, call © **01622/765-400** or visit www. leeds-castle.com.

SCHEDULING CONSIDERATIONS

You may or may not want to arrange your visit to Leeds Castle to coincide with one of the many events the castle hosts. These include a **Flower Festival** in early April, a **food and wine festival** in May, **open-air concerts** on summer evenings, a **hot-air balloon and antique car exhibition** in September, and an extravagant **Guy Fawkes fireworks display** on or around November 5. Try to avoid **weekends,** especially in summer when crowds can be legion.

GETTING THERE
BY TRAIN
The closest train station to Leeds Castle is the one in the village of Bearsted, about 7 miles (10km) away. The trip from London's Victoria Station takes just over an hour, and the standard day return fare is about £14 ($28). You'll save money and hassle by purchasing an "all in one" ticket from Southeastern rail; it's available at any ticket window at Victoria Station. The ticket, which includes train travel to Bearsted, bus transport between the station and the castle, and admission to the castle and grounds, costs £26 ($52) for adults, £14 ($28) for children 4 to 15. There are some 20 trains a day from London; the first train to Bearsted is at 6:10am and the last train returns to London at 10:32pm; trains run every half-hour during rush hour and every hour throughout the rest of the day and evening. A bus meets trains throughout the day for the trip from the train station to the castle; if you don't have an all-in-one ticket, you'll pay a round-trip (return) bus fare of £4 ($8). The first bus leaves the train station at 10:30am after meeting the 9:18am train from London. From March to October, the last bus returns to the train station from the castle at 6pm (reaching the station in time for the 6:24pm train to London). From November to February, the last bus returns to the train station at 4pm (in time for the 4:24pm train to London). For more information, call **National Rail Enquiries** at © **08457/484950** or go to www.nationalrail.co.uk.

BY BUS
Another way to visit Leeds Castle is on a special **National Express** coach that departs from London's Victoria Coach Station at 9am each day the castle is open. It arrives at the castle at 10:25am, and departs the castle at 3:05pm to arrive back at London's

Victoria Coach Station at 4:50pm. The fare, including transportation and admission to the castle and grounds, is £21 ($42) for adults and £14 ($28) for children 4 to 15. For more information, call © **08705/808080** or visit www.nationalexpress.com.

BY CAR

The trip from London takes just under an hour, depending on traffic. Take the M25 to the M20, then take exit 8 and follow the signs to the castle entrance. Parking is free.

GETTING AROUND

A free, open-air bus travels from the main entrance to the castle (a distance of about a quarter mile) and other attractions on the grounds. It is, however, much more enjoyable to walk along the paved paths that curve around ponds and cross lawns and woods.

2 A Day at Leeds Castle

To get a good overview of the extent and grandeur of Leeds, and to enjoy views of its moat, turrets, and towers, walk around the grounds before entering the ❶ **castle** ✿✿. The prescribed castle tour begins in the dank and dull Norman cellars, then continues into medieval rooms that include the 15th-century bathroom of Catherine of Valois, the young wife of Henry V; Catherine was French, and clearly was pampered—the room is surprisingly well equipped and luxurious, and invites an interesting comparison with the sumptuous Russian onyx bathroom in another wing that Lady Baillie had installed in the 1920s.

Interiors at Leeds are intimate and appealing—**Henry VIII's Banqueting Room** ✿✿, one of many additions the king made to the castle, is handsome, not overwhelming, and overlooks the grounds through a large bay window. One of the pleasures of exploring the castle is coming upon treasure after treasure: In the Banqueting Room, the prize is a spring scene by Pieter Bruegel the Younger; in the **Chapel** ✿✿ are exquisite limewood carved panels and four paintings by the late-14th-century Florentine Niccolò di Pietro Gerini that depict the Passion of Christ—they are some of the earliest known works on canvas. Probably the most charming of the castle's many works of art is Giambattista Tiepolo's *The Punchinello's Kitchen,* which hangs above the mantle in the Yellow Drawing Room and provides an 18th-century view of the Venice Carnival.

In addition to its medieval splendor, Leeds gives visitors a look at a privileged mid-20th-century lifestyle that has all but disappeared. The rooms that Lady Baillie renovated are comfortably luxurious, proving that you don't have to be a king or queen to

---

⟮*Tips*⟯ Up, Up & Away

You can elevate your experience of Leeds Castle (www.leeds-castle.com) by climbing aboard the basket of a hot-air balloon and ascending to float over the Kent countryside. Trips are operated April 1 through November 1 and cost £120 ($240) for weekday morning flights, £135 ($270) for weekday afternoon flights, and £150 ($300) for weekend flights; the prices include entrance to the castle and gardens, as well they should.

live like one, though it helps to have a king's ransom at your disposal. Lady Baillie, an heiress to the Whitney millions, paid £472,973 for the castle in 1926. She outbid another interested buyer, William Randolph Hearst, the American newspaper czar.

After the castle tour, return to the grounds and take some time to relax in a nice spot—the benches overlooking the lake known as the ❷ **Great Water** 𝖆 are a good choice. As you tour the grounds, at each turn you seem to come upon another attraction. These can be somewhat surprising, such as the ❸ **Dog Collar Museum** 𝖆, where canine accessories going back more than 400 years are on display; and the ❹ **aviary** 𝖆𝖆, whose state-of-the-art pavilions house more than 100 parakeets, macaws, and other feathered species. Lady Baillie was a collector of birds, and the black swans she introduced to England in the 1930s still swim in the castle moat. This aviary, built in her memory, is one of the world's leading avian breeding labs and has successfully bred many rare species.

The most popular attraction at Leeds is the ❺ **maze** 𝖆𝖆𝖆, planted with 2,400 yew trees and leading to a fantastically macabre Grotto filled with mythical beasts crafted from shells and minerals. Two of the most pleasant spots on the grounds are the ❻ **Culpeper Garden** 𝖆𝖆, a colorful and delightfully informal bower; and the ❼ **Lady Baillie Garden** 𝖆𝖆, where Mediterranean plantings cascade down lakeside terraces.

Fun Fact   **Royals & Americans**
_____

Leeds Castle traces its origins to the days of William the Conqueror and became a royal home when Edward I, the founder of the British Parliament, acquired the estate around 1290. The castle remained in the hands of the monarchy for the next 3 centuries. Among the royal tenants who left their mark on Leeds is Catherine of Valois, who received the castle upon the death of her husband, Henry V, in 1422; her bedroom and bathroom are on view in the old Keep, known as the Gloriette. (Catherine, then only 21, fell in love with Owen Tudor, clerk of her wardrobe, and they secretly married— their son Edmund was the father of King Henry VII, founder of the Tudor dynasty.) Catherine of Aragon, first wife of Henry VIII, also lived at Leeds, and the fireplace in the Queens Gallery is emblazoned with part of her symbol, the pomegranates of Aragon. A portrait of Edward VI, Henry VIII's only male heir (whom he had with his third queen, Jane Seymour), hangs above the fireplace; notice his misshapen ear.

Leeds's connection with America began in 1663, when Thomas, the second Lord Culpeper, purchased the castle; Lord Culpeper's father had been granted more than 5 million acres (2 million hectares) in Virginia, and Culpeper later became governor of the colony. His daughter, Catherine, married into the Fairfax family, who eventually inherited the Culpeper lands in Virginia and the castle, which they held until the end of the 18th century. One reminder of the castle's American connections is on the grounds—a sundial that's designed to show the time in Virginia.

Moments **Lazing on the Lawn**

You won't tire of the vista of Leeds rising from the moat that surrounds it. An especially nice outlook is the one from the ❽ **Cedar Lawn,** just off the main drive. Stretch out and enjoy the view.

MORE THINGS TO SEE & DO

Before boarding the train back to London, take an hour or so to wander around **Bearsted** *☆☆*. (The train station is at the edge of the village, only a 5-min. walk from the center.) The village surrounds a large, beautifully maintained green, and on the east side you'll see a distinctive Kentish scene: the steep, conical roofs of oast houses, used for drying hops. (The ones here have been converted to residences.)

OUTDOOR ACTIVITIES

On the grounds is a ❾ **9-hole golf course** built for Lady Baillie in the 1920s. The course is open daily. Weekday fees are £19.50 ($39) for adults, £16.50 ($33) for seniors. On weekends, the fee for all players is £13 ($26). Clubs are available for rent. For more information, call the pro shop at ✆ **01622/767-828.**

3 Where to Dine

The White Horse *☆* PUB   At this historic village pub, far more appealing than the dining options on the castle grounds, you can find a cozy nook in front of the fire or at a window overlooking the lovely green. Both pub fare and substantial meals are served.

Bearsted Green. ✆ **01622/738-365.** Most items £4–£10 ($8–$20). DC, MC, V. Food served Mon–Sat noon–2:30pm and 6:30–9:30pm; Sun noon–3pm and 6:30–9pm.

Monk's House & Charleston

*T*hese two evocative houses are known as "Bloomsbury in Sussex": During the early years of the 20th century they were the country retreats of the artistic, intellectual, and literary set known as the "Bloomsbury Group" for the London neighborhood where many of them lived. The designer/painter Vanessa Bell (1871–1969), her husband the art critic Clive Bell (1881–1964), and her friend and sometime lover Duncan Grant (1885–1978), who would become one of Britain's most renowned 20th-century painters, moved to Charleston, a rambling and derelict old farmhouse, in 1916. Vanessa and Duncan painted many of the furnishings and surfaces in fanciful patterns and hung works by Picasso and Renoir, creating an artistic setting in which they lived until their deaths many years later.

Vanessa's sister, the novelist Virginia Woolf (1882–1941), and her publisher husband Leonard (1880–1969) bought modest and "unpretending" Monk's House in the nearby village of Rodmell in 1919. The couple spent summers at Monk's House and

Monk's House & Charleston Highlights

- Touring the village of Rodmell, where Monk's House is located.
- Exploring the Sitting Room at Monk's House, where you will have to resist the urge to plop down and read a book.
- Strolling through the garden and orchard at Monk's House (especially in the autumn, when you may be able to pick fruit in the orchard).
- Seeing Vanessa Bell's bedroom at Charleston, the most comfortable room in the house.
- Viewing the Dining Room at Charleston, which the residents outdid themselves designing.

Monk's House & Charleston Area

SCOTLAND

North Sea

Irish Sea ENGLAND

WALES

London ⊛

Lewes ○

English Channel

0   100 mi
0   100 km

A272

Uckfield ○

Newick ○

Chailey Green ○

Little Horstead ○

South Chailey ○

Plumpton Green ○

A275

Barcombe Cross ○

Ouse

A26

Cooksbridge ○

Plumpton ○   B2116

Offham ○

Ringmer ○

B2192

A27   Stanmer ○

3
5 **4** ○ Lewes

A27

Glynde ○

Falmer ○   Kingston ○

A27

A270

2
South Charleston ○

Woodingdean ○   Rodmell ○   **1**
■ MONK'S HOUSE

Brighton

Rottingdean ○

Telscombe ○

A26

Saltdean ○

Newhaven ○

Peacehaven ○

ENGLISH   CHANNEL

0   1 mile
0   2 km

Ⓝ

1 Monk's House
2 Charleston
3 Lewes
4 Lewes Castle
5 Anne of Cleves House

moved here year-round in 1940, when their London home was destroyed in the Blitz. Virginia wrote several of her novels here. In 1941 she drowned herself (she is generally thought to have suffered from bipolar disorder) in the nearby River Ouse.

A visit to one or preferably to both of these beautifully maintained houses is a delightful and enlightening experience. The houses are more than literary and artistic shrines—they evoke a lifestyle, an intellectual climate, and a heady period in English history. The members of the Bloomsbury Group who inhabited the rooms of both houses epitomized the early-20th-century avant-garde and had a profound influence on painting, design, fiction, economics, politics, and feminism.

The base for visiting both houses is Lewes, founded by the Normans above the banks of the River Ouse soon after 1066 and now an appealing medieval and Georgian town where narrow lanes called "twittens" surround the ruins of a Norman castle. Allow a full day if you plan on visiting both houses, and get an early start. In addition to travel time and time for leisurely tours of Monk's House and Charleston, you'll want to allow an hour or two to walk around Lewes, and maybe pay a visit to the castle and to the house where Anne of Cleves, fourth wife of Henry VIII, lived after her divorce from the king. Fans of poet Percy Bysshe Shelley may want to make this an overnight trip for a chance to stay in the Shelley family home. (See the last section of this chapter.) If you plan to spend more than a day in **Brighton** (see trip 3), which is just 8 miles (13km) southwest of Lewes, you might want to consider visiting the houses as part of that trip.

1 Essentials
VISITOR INFORMATION
Monk's House and Charleston are on the Sussex Downs, near the town of Lewes, which is about 50 miles (80km) south of London and 8 miles (13km) northeast of Brighton. **Monk's House** (✆ **01372/453-401;** www.nationaltrust.org.uk), in the village of Rodmell, 4 miles (6.5km) southwest of Lewes, is open from early April to the end of October, Wednesday and Saturday from 2 to 5:30pm. Admission is £3.30 ($6.60) for adults, £1.65 ($3.30) for children under 16, and £8.25 ($17) for families of up to two adults and two children. **Charleston** (✆ **01323/811-265;** www. charleston.org.uk), in open country 7 miles (11km) east of Lewes off A27, is open late March through June and September through October, Wednesday and Saturday from 11:30am to 5pm and Thursday, Friday, and Sunday from 2 to 5pm; July through August, Wednesday through Saturday from 11:30am to 5pm and Sunday from 2 to 5pm. During these times the house is also open on Bank Holiday Mondays from 2 to 6pm. The last admission is 1 hour before closing. Admission costs £6.50 ($13) for adults, £4.50 ($9) for seniors and students; "Sisters" theme tours that include a look at the kitchens and Vanessa Bell's studio (Fri only) are £7.50 ($15).

SCHEDULING CONSIDERATIONS
You'll have to plan your trip carefully because Wednesday and Saturday afternoons are the only times you can pay a combined visit to both houses (keep in mind, too, that the houses are closed Nov–Mar). Because the houses attract many visitors on weekends, it's best to try to visit on Wednesday. Plus, if you want to explore **Lewes,** you should do so in the morning before visiting the houses, when the shops are still open (many close at 5pm).

GETTING THERE
BY TRAIN
The train station closest to the houses is the one in the charming town of Lewes, where you'll want to spend some time before or after your visits. The direct trip from London's Victoria Station to Lewes takes just over an hour, and a day return ticket costs about £18 ($36). The first direct train to Lewes departs at 6:48am and the last direct train returns to London at 10:40pm; trains run about every half-hour. For more information, call **National Rail Enquiries** at ✆ **08457/484950** or go to www.nationalrail.co.uk.

BY CAR
It's useful to have a car here, especially if you want to see both houses in a day. The trip from London takes just over an hour, depending on traffic. Take the M25 to the M23, which becomes the A23; follow that to the A27, which leads east to Lewes. If you're driving directly to Monk's House, at the western edge of Lewes turn off A27 at

Living It Up in Lewes

Lewes goes a bit wild (well, with the good taste typical of a British country town) twice a year. May through August, the stunning **Glyndebourne opera house** (℗ **01273/813-813**; www.glyndebourne.com) mounts six productions and brings the best of the opera world, and many ardent fans, to town. On November 5, Lewes stages one of England's biggest Guy Fawkes Night celebrations, commemorating the events of this evening in 1605—that's when Guy Fawkes and members of the Gunpowder Plot, rebelling against the oppression of Roman Catholicism under King James I, attempted to blow up Parliament but were thwarted when Fawkes was apprehended in the cellars of the House of Lords with 36 kegs of gunpowder. Fireworks, a costumed procession, and an enormous bonfire are part of the show.

the exit for Kingston, and follow the road to Rodmell; from there, turn left at the pub and follow the lane down to Monk's House. For Charleston, follow A27 east of Lewes; about 7 miles (11km) east of Lewes you'll see a turnoff for Charleston on the right side of the road, between the villages of Firle and Selmeston.

GETTING AROUND

From Lewes train station you can continue to Monk's House or Charleston by bus, but service is infrequent and you won't have time to see both houses in one afternoon if you use public transportation. Of the two, Monk's House is the most accessible by bus from Lewes; take bus no. 123, which runs about every hour, get off in the village of Rodmell, and follow the main lane about a quarter of a mile (.4km) down to the house. For Charleston, take bus no. 125, which runs every 1½ to 2 hours. (Ask the driver to let you off at the foot of the lane leading from A27 to the house; the walk is about 1.5 miles/2.4km.) The fare to each house is £1.60 ($3.20). To reach one of the houses from the other, it's necessary to return to Lewes and transfer buses. For additional bus information, call **Traveline** at ℗ **0870/608-2608** or visit www.traveline.org.uk.

If you're not traveling by car, the most feasible way to see both houses is by taxi from Lewes. Fares, however, are a bit steep: For example, expect to pay about £8 ($16) for the trip from Lewes to Monk's House, £17 ($34) from Monk's House to Charleston, and £12 ($24) from Charleston back to Lewes. There's a taxi stand outside the Lewes train station, but to ensure that a taxi will be available when you arrive, arrange a pickup in advance by calling **Meridian Taxis** at ℗ **01273/580-099** or **Newhaven/Seaford Taxis** at ℗ **01273/611-111.** You can easily visit Lewes and the houses from Brighton, just 8 miles (13km) to the southwest (see trip 3). Trains from Brighton to Lewes run about every 20 minutes throughout the day and make the trip in 15 minutes; the ride costs £4 ($8).

2 A Day at Monk's House & Charleston

Your first impression of ❶ **Monk's House** 🟊🟊🟊 may be just how charming the surrounding village is. Then you might be struck by how small and unassuming the white clapboard house is. Clearly, the luxury the Woolfs valued most was not a great amount of creature comfort but the leisure to do what they wanted—she to write, and he to run his small, literary Hogarth Press and to garden. Leonard remained at Monk's House until his death in 1969, and the house has been in the hands of the National Trust ever since—as a result, almost nothing has changed since these two literary giants of the 20th century inhabited its small rooms, Virginia writing such profoundly influential, groundbreaking novels as *Mrs. Dalloway* and *Orlando* and Leonard encouraging such writers as E. M. Forster and T. S. Eliot, and writing his own autobiography.

You can wander through the house at your leisure, and as there are only four rooms to see, you should indulge in the luxury of lingering in each room and soaking up the atmosphere. It's quite easy to imagine the couple in the Sitting Room where, Virginia wrote, "We sit, eat, play the gramophone, prop our feet up on the side of the fire and read endless books." The tile-topped, painted table is the work of the painter Duncan Grant and the painter/designer Vanessa Bell, Virginia's sister, and Vanessa designed the fabric that covers an extraordinarily comfortable-looking reading chair; Duncan and Vanessa also designed the dining room chairs. Another luxury the couple enjoyed was freedom from household duties: The primitive kitchen, where Virginia seldom ventured, was the domain of a series of housekeepers by whom she generally felt intimidated.

"A woman must have money and a room of her own if she is to write fiction," Virginia wrote, and as her novels began earning money she added a rather austere room that didn't suit her as a workroom but became her bedroom. The room's most noticeable attributes are its brightness and the presence of the garden beyond the windows. Virginia wrote in a rustic structure at the far end of the garden known as the Lodge, where apples from the large orchard were stored throughout the winter. The orchard still bears fruit, and if you visit in the autumn, you can get into the spirit of Monk's House by picking some to take away with you.

❷ **Charleston** 🕸🕸🕸 is a different sort of house altogether—it is much larger than Monk's House, and is as much a design statement as it is a home. Entry is by guided, 1-hour tour Wednesday through Saturday (unguided on Sun), and the knowledgeable docents show remarkable restraint in not resorting to back-fence gossip as they lead tours through the dining room, bedrooms, sitting room, and studio and describe the presences in the house of Vanessa Bell, her husband Clive, her sometime lover Duncan Grant, the children Vanessa had with both men, and visitors who included such luminaries as the economist Maynard Keynes and the biographer Lytton Strachey.

Instead, the focus is on the enormous amount of creativity the house seemed to generate: Vanessa and Duncan were both painters and decorative artists, and they created designs for many of the leading fabric and ceramics producers of the time. Their designs appear on upholstery, draperies, and tilework throughout the house. They also brought a personal style to Charleston by painting their distinctive geometric patterns on walls, window frames, mantelpieces, and just about every other surface. The effect can be a bit gloomy, but it is unique and pays tribute to the fact that in this rather extraordinary house, for more than 60 years, Vanessa and Duncan created a distinctive artistic style.

The sense of design extends to the small walled garden just outside Vanessa's bedroom, where the hedges, gravel pathways, pond, and statuary are distinctly Mediterranean in feel.

Impressions

I could fancy a very pleasant walk in the orchard under the apple trees, with the grey extinguisher of the church steeple pointing my boundary.
                                                    —Virginia Woolf, diary entry for July 3, 1919

> (Moments **A Garden of Your Own (Almost)**
>
> The Woolfs and their visitors enjoyed many happy hours in the garden and orchard of Monk's House, and you can, too. Bring a book, stretch out, and enjoy. The only noise you'll hear will be the hum of bees and the tolling of the church bells just beyond the garden wall.

The Fridays-only "Sisters" tour is especially illuminating: A well-informed guide leads groups from room to room discussing the domestic routines in the house as well as the intertwined lives of Vanessa Bell and Virginia Woolf, discussing their Victorian childhoods in Kensington as well as their lives and careers in London and here in Sussex.

MORE THINGS TO SEE & DO

❸ **Lewes** 𝒜𝒜, a handsome county seat of medieval lanes and brick Georgian houses, is far too appealing to be just a jumping-off point for Monk's House and Charleston. Take some time to walk along the High Street past shops selling antiques and rare books. Peaceable as this country town seems, Lewes has a fiery past. When "Bloody" Queen Mary I (reigned 1553–58) tried to reinstate Catholicism to England after her father, Henry VIII, broke from the Church, Protestants in Lewes were persecuted and 17 citizens were burned at the stake. On November 5 the town stages some of England's most boisterous celebrations commemorating the thwarting of Guy Fawkes, the Roman Catholic rebel who tried to blow up Parliament for its unjust treatment of Catholics under James I (reigned 1603–25). Thomas Paine, who argued for American independence in his pamphlet "Common Sense," lived in half-timbered Bull House on High Street and debated politics in the nearby White Hart Hotel. (Step inside to enjoy the excellent selection of British ales in the hotel's atmospheric bar.)

❹ & ❺ **Lewes Castle & the Anne of Cleves House** 𝒜   Lewes's hilltop castle dates to the days of William the Conqueror. Though largely in ruin, it is still a commanding presence, and views over the Sussex Downs from the ramparts seem to extend forever. In the adjoining Barbican House Museum, you can learn more about local history than you may want to during the sound-and-light show, "The Story of Lewes Town." From the castle, a steep downhill walk of about 10 minutes brings you to the Anne of Cleves House, which Henry presented to his queen when he divorced her in 1541 (unlike his first divorce from Catherine of Aragon, this one was so amicable that Anne was still welcomed at Court). The kitchen, bedroom, and Tudor-style garden are touchingly quaint in their simplicity, with rough-hewn floors and rustic furnishings.

Lewes Castle, High St.; Anne of Cleves House, Southover High St. ℂ **01273/405-732. www.sussexpast.co.uk.** The castle is open Tues–Sat 10am–5:30pm, Sun 11am–5:30pm. Anne of Cleeves House is open Mar–Oct Tues–Sat 10am–5pm, Sun 11am–5pm; Nov–Feb Mon–Sat 10am–5pm. Admission to castle: £4.70 ($9.40) adults, £4.20 ($8.40) students and seniors, £2.40 ($4.80) children 5–15, £12.20 ($24) families of 2 adults and 2 children. Admission to house: £3.50 ($7) adults, £3 ($6) students and seniors, £1.60 ($3.20) children 5–15, £8 ($16) families of up to 2 adults and 2 children. Combined admission: £7 ($14) adults, £6 ($12) seniors and students, £3.50 ($7) children, £17 ($34) families of up to 2 adults and 2 children.

3 Shopping

Charleston has an appealing shop (ℂ **01323/811-265**) filled with fabrics, ceramics, prints, and other decorative items based on designs created by Vanessa Bell and Duncan Grant for British design studios, as well as an excellent selection of books. It's open

Impressions

It's most lovely, very solid and simple, with . . . perfectly flat windows and wonderful tiled roofs. The pond is most beautiful, with a willow at one side and a stone or flint wall edging it all round the garden part, and a little lawn sloping down to it, with formal bushes on it.

—Vanessa Bell on Charleston

Wednesday to Sunday from 1 to 4pm. As you poke around Lewes, step into the **Church Hill Antiques Centre** at 6 Station St. (✆ **01273/474-842**), where 60 dealers sell such easily portable wares as jewelry, linen, glass, and decorative items.

4 Where to Dine

The Abergavenny Arms ✿ PUB   This dark, woody pub is the social center of Rodmell and a nice place to enjoy a pint or a meal after visiting Monk's House. The cuisine doesn't get fancier than meat and vegetable pies, ploughman's platters, and other traditional pub fare, but it's quite good.

Rodmell. ✆ **01273/472-416.** Main courses £3.50–£7 ($7–$14). MC, V. Food served Mon–Sat noon–3pm and 6–9:30pm; Sun noon–7pm.

Shelleys ✿✿ CONTINENTAL   The dining room of this country-house hotel, once home to the poet Percy Bysshe Shelley's family, is a gracious place to enjoy lunch or dinner. French doors open to a delightful garden, but your attention may well be riveted on the dishes that highlight local produce, game, and lamb.

High St., Lewes. ✆ **01273/472-361.** Lunch £9.50–£15 ($19–$30); dinner £16–£17 ($32–$34). AE, DC, MC, V. Daily 12:15–2:15pm and 7–9:15pm.

5 Extending Your Trip

Lewes, your base for exploring Monk's House and Charleston, is also a pleasant place to spend the night—especially during the Glyndebourne opera season (see "Living It Up in Lewes," above). You might want to visit one of the houses the first afternoon, spend the evening and following morning in Lewes, then visit the other house the following afternoon before returning to London. Or devote the first afternoon to seeing the two houses, then spend the next morning poking around this pleasant town.

Shelleys ✿✿✿   The chance to spend the night in this charming house, once the home of the family of the poet Percy Bysshe Shelley, is reason enough to extend your stay in Lewes. Guest rooms are traditionally but not fussily appointed with style and comfort in mind, and many overlook a beautiful garden.

High St., Lewes, E. Sussex BN7 1XS. ✆ **01273/472-361.** www.shelleys-hotel.com. £110–£170 ($220–$340) double. Rates include breakfast. AE, DC, MC, V.

Moreton-in-Marsh & the Cotswolds

*T*he Cotswolds hills, known simply as the Cotswolds, present a gentle landscape of woodland; high, open plateaus known as "wolds"; and lovely villages of soft yellow stone and thatched roofs that date from the Middle Ages, when fortunes were made here in the wool trade. This is rural England as you imagined it—a welcome tonic from busy London, and a chance to take a peek at British country life. The pretty village of Moreton-in-Marsh is an excellent base, especially if you're not traveling by car—it's centrally located in the region, is the only major Cotswolds village on a train line, and is also the hub of a bus network you can use to visit other Cotswolds villages. With travel to and from London and time to poke around a village or two, you should expect to spend a full day visiting the Cotswolds, and you may well be so enchanted with the region that you'll want to stay over at least 1 night.

Make sure you allow enough time to venture beyond Moreton-in-Marsh to at least one other village, because much of the appeal of this region is a trip through the green, rolling countryside and the spectacle of the gray villages surrounded by fields and woods. We suggest moving on from Moreton-in-Marsh to Broadway and Chipping Campden, because we consider these to be the most attractive villages and, with their sturdy stone market halls and churches, the places where you are most likely to find an appreciation for the region's prosperous past. However, you might also be tempted to head south to Stow-on-the-Wold and Bourton-on-the-Water (Bourton is a good choice if you have kids with you, as the village is chockablock with child-pleasing amusements; see "More Things to See and Do," below).

Keep in mind, too, that this region, perhaps more than any other in this book, lends itself well to a few days of traveling from village to village to see the sights. For that reason, we've included some good accommodations options at the end of this chapter, and suggested enough activities to last you a few days.

Moreton-in-Marsh & the Cotswolds Highlights

• Seeing Moreton-in-Marsh and other charming villages of mellow stone.

• Taking in the views over the rolling hills and "wolds" (high plateaus).

• Walking from Chipping Campden to Broadway or elsewhere in the countryside.

• Viewing Hidcote Manor Garden, beautiful from spring to fall.

1 Essentials

VISITOR INFORMATION

The **Tourist Information Centre** in Moreton-in-Marsh, Cotswold District Council Offices, High Street (© **01608/650881;** www.moreton-in-marsh.co.uk), is well stocked with maps and information on what to see and do and where to stay and dine throughout the Cotswolds. The center is open Monday to Thursday from 8:45am to 5:15pm, Friday from 8:45am to 4:45pm, and Saturday from 10am to 12:30pm.

SCHEDULING CONSIDERATIONS

The bucolic beauty of the Cotswolds attracts hordes of visitors who can put a pall on your rural reveries. In summer it's difficult to find a quiet patch anywhere in the region, and Broadway and Bourton-on-the-Water may be more crowded than Piccadilly Circus. May and October are ideal times to visit—the crowds are thinner, and the landscape is either budding or in majestic fall color. If you are using public transportation, try to visit the Cotswolds on a day other than Sunday, when bus service between the villages is extremely limited. If you only have 1 day in the Cotswolds, and especially if you're relying on public transportation, you'll need to limit your outings from Moreton-in-Marsh to no more than two other villages—this is relatively easy to do if you visit villages that are near each other and on the same bus lines. For example, from Moreton-in-Marsh you might want to travel north to Chipping Campden and/or Broadway or south to Stow-on-the-Wold and/or Bourton-on-the-Water.

GETTING THERE
BY TRAIN

Trains run about every 1 to 1½ hours from London's Paddington Station to Moreton-in-Marsh; the first direct train departs for Moreton-in-Marsh at 5:52am and the last direct train returns to London at 11:13pm. The direct trip takes about 1 hour and 30 minutes. The saver day return fare is £29 ($58); standard day return fare is £52 ($104). For information, call **National Rail Enquiries** (© **08457/484950**) or visit www.nationalrail.co.uk.

BY CAR

Moreton-in-Marsh is about 90 miles (145km) west of London. The quickest route from London is the M40 to Oxford, and the A40 and A44 from there; the trip usually takes about 2 hours.

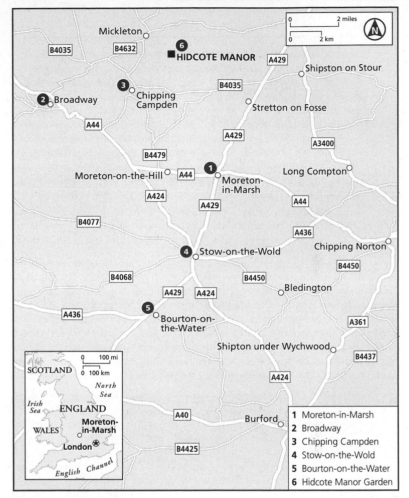

6 ■ HIDCOTE MANOR

1 Moreton-in-Marsh
2 Broadway
3 Chipping Campden
4 Stow-on-the-Wold
5 Bourton-on-the-Water
6 Hidcote Manor Garden

GETTING AROUND

From Moreton-in-Marsh you can reach several other villages by bus Monday through Saturday.

For **Broadway** and **Chipping Campden,** take **bus no. 21,** operated by **First Midland Red** (*©* **01905/763-888**). Buses leave from the train station and the Corn Exchange on High Street and operate roughly every hour during peak morning and evening times and every 2 hours throughout the day, with the first departure at 7:02am and the last departure at 6:50pm. Buses return to Moreton-in-Marsh with the same frequency, with the last bus leaving Chipping Campden at 5:59pm. Travel time between Moreton-in-Marsh and Broadway is 20 minutes, and travel time between Moreton-in-Marsh and Chipping Campden is about 35 minutes. For **Stow-on-the-Wold** and **Bourton-on-the-Water,** take **bus no. 55,** operated by **Beaumont Travel**

Wool & Walls

You'll see telltale signs of Cotswolds history just about everywhere you look. The native sheep that graze on the hillsides yield wool of unusually high quality that was prized throughout Europe in the Middle Ages. The wool trade brought enormous wealth into the region, and traders invested their riches in the churches (known as "wool churches") that still rise above every village. The distinctive stone walls you see crisscrossing the fields are known as "drystone walls" and are built without mortar. They were introduced in the 18th and 19th centuries to enclose sheep runs, making it possible to pro-tect fields for farming. While the sheep and stone enclosures were once economic necessities in these parts—and to a degree still are—today they present irresistible photo ops for countless numbers of Cotswolds visitors.

(© 01452/309-770). Buses leave from the Town Hall on High Street and run about every 1 to 1½ hours throughout the day; the first bus is at 6:30am and the last bus is at 5pm. Buses return from Bourton-on-the-Water and Stow-on-the-Wold with simi-lar frequency throughout the day, with the last bus returning from Bourton-on-the-Water at 7:05pm. The travel time between Moreton-in-Marsh and Stow-on-the-Wold is 10 minutes, and travel time between Moreton-in-Marsh and Bourton-on-the-Water is 20 minutes; fares are about £1.60 ($3.20).

You can also travel between villages, much more expensively, by taxi; the fare from Moreton-in-Marsh to Stow-on-the-Wold is about £8 ($16) each way. Call **Cotswolds Taxis** (© **07710/117-471**) or **Town and Country Taxi** (© **07968/763-379**).

2 A Day (or More) in Moreton-in-Marsh & the Cotswolds

❶ **Moreton-in-Marsh** 🏛️🏛️ straddles the Fosse Way, a Roman road that extends from Leicester to Cirencester—in fact, there's not much more to the village than a mile-long string of handsome 17th- and 18th-century buildings along this wide road, called High Street, as it passes through town. The street has been a major route for Roman legions as well as stagecoach passengers traveling between the west of England and London, and is today thronged with shoppers on Tuesdays, when Moreton-in-Marsh hosts the region's largest and liveliest market. Among the most notable landmarks along High Street is **White Hart Royal,** a manor house in which King Charles I shel-tered during the English Civil War. **Curfew Tower** still sports its original clock and bell, dating from 1633, rung to tell the inhabitants to lock themselves in and cover their fires so they couldn't be seen by invaders. "Marsh," as you will soon discover, does not refer to wetlands—the town is high and dry. Rather, the term is medieval and connotes a boundary, as the town once marked the edge of an administrative district.

Artist-craftsman William Morris supposedly "discovered" ❷ **Broadway** 🏛️🏛️ (about 8 miles/13km northwest of Moreton-in-Marsh on A44 and served by frequent buses) in the 19th century, and the village of mellow honey-colored stone has been a hit with sightseers ever since. Even when the town buzzes with visitors, it's easy to agree with the novelist Henry James, who said it was "delicious to be in Broadway." The width of High Street gave the place its name. This handsome avenue was once lined with inns (some, such as the venerable **Lygon Arms,** remain) and other establishments that did a brisk business providing travelers and horses with rest, in readiness for the steep climb up the hill towering over the village. The escarpment is crowned with the **Broadway Tower** (© **01386/852-390;** www.broadwaytower.co.uk), an 18th-century folly built by the earl of Coventry. You can climb the tower April through October, daily from 10:30am to 5pm; November through March, Saturday and Sunday from 11am to 3pm. The fee is £3.80 ($8) for adults, £2.30 ($4.60) for children, and £10 ($20) for families of up to two adults and three children.

The appealing **Snowshill Manor** (© **01386/852-410;** www.nationaltrust.org.uk) is about 2 miles (3km) southwest of town, and worth the walk (alternatively, find a taxi in front of any of the hotels on High St.). This typical stone Cotswold manor traces its origins to the ninth century and once belonged to Catherine Parr, last wife of Henry VIII, but its most recent occupant made the place the fascinating jumble it is today. Craftsman and architect Charles Paget Wade bought the house in 1919 and filled it with bicycles, toys, suits of armor, tapestries, and the other objects—22,000 pieces in all—he spent his lifetime collecting. The house and its beautiful gardens are open from late March through late October, Wednesday through Sunday, house from noon to 5pm, garden from 11am to 5:30pm. Admission to the house and garden is £7.70 ($15) for adults, £3.90 ($7.80) for children, and £19.60 ($39) for families.

❸ **Chipping Campden** ★★ (about 4 miles/6.4km west of Broadway; www.chipping campden.co.uk) is a beautiful village of 14th- to 17th-century stone buildings that owes its substantial air of prosperity to its centuries-long prominence in the wool trade. Sheep still graze in the Vale of Evesham, which stretches beneath the village. The most photogenic of the proud stone structures are the 17th-century gabled market hall, the 14th-century **Woolstaplers Hall,** and the 15th-century **church of St. James.** All grace High Street, which the British historian G. M. Trevelyan described as "the most beautiful street now left in the island." You may well agree, though the effect can be a bit diminished on a summer weekend when the cobblestones are jammed with visitors.

MORE THINGS TO SEE & DO

If you have more than a day in the Cotswolds, continue your explorations by heading south from Moreton-in-Marsh. You may also want to follow this route instead of the one above if you have little travelers with you, since Bourton-on-the-Water is a paradise for kids, laced with streams they can walk along and home to several attractions geared to young visitors.

Frequent bus service (see "Getting Around," above) connects Moreton-in-Marsh with ❹ **Stow-on-the-Wold** ★★, "where the wind blows cold," as the saying goes (a meteorological reality caused by the fact that Stow is the highest of the Cotswolds towns). Stow, just 4 miles (6.5km) south of Moreton-in-Marsh on A429, is still a place where life goes on somewhat untouched by the tourist fray. The engaging center of

---

⎛*Moments* Basking in the Light

You'll never tire of the mellow, yellow stone of village houses and churches glowing in the sunlight. A good place to appreciate this phenomenon is from one of the bridges in Bourton-on-the-Water, where the sound of the gurgling River Windrush adds another dimension to the scene.

---

town is the market square, a lovely assemblage of stone buildings housing shops selling antiques as well as everyday essentials.

You may decide that ❺ **Bourton-on-the-Water** ☝ (about 5 miles/8km south of
Stow-on-the-Wold on A429 and also served by frequent buses from Moreton-in-
Marsh) is a victim of its own charms. No small part of its appeal is the River Windrush, which gurgles through the center of town beneath five bridges, each of them
presenting another photo op. For visitors not content with rolling hills and sheep,
Bourton offers many amusement park–type attractions. **The Model Village,** on High
Street behind the Old New Inn (© **01451/820-467**), is a ⅑-scale miniature replica of
the village built of Cotswold stone in 1937. It's open every day, 9am to 6pm; admission is £2.75 ($5.50) for adults, £2.50 ($5) for seniors, and £2 ($4) for children. **Bird-
land Park,** on Rissington Road (© **01451/820-480;** www.birdland.co.uk), houses
pelicans, penguins, cranes, toucans, and parrots in some 50 different aviaries. The
park is open daily, April to October from 10am to 6pm, and November to March
from 10am to 4pm; admission is £5.25 ($11) for adults, £4.25 ($8.50) for seniors,
£3.25 ($6.50) for children 4 to 14, free for children under 4, and £15.50 ($31) for families of up to two adults and two children. **Cotswold Motoring Museum** (© **01451/
821-255;** www.cotswold-motor-museum.co.uk), in the Old Mill, displays vintage
cars, motorcycles, and children's pedal cars as well as a small collection of historic toys.
It's open February through October, daily from 10am to 6pm; admission is £3.60
($7.20) for adults, £2.50 ($5) for children 4 to 16, free for children under 4, £11.10
($22) for families of 2 adults and 2 children.

❻ **Hidcote Manor Garden** ☝☝☝   This enchanting garden is the creation of
Lawrence Waterbury Johnston, son of the wealthy American heiress Gertrude
Winthrop. Johnston lived at Hidcote for nearly 40 years, creating a series of outdoor
rooms that incorporate acres of rare plantings, lush borders, pools, lawns, and long vis-
tas. The gardens have inspired generations of landscape designers, and are said to have
influenced Vita Sackville-West and Harold Nicolson in their designing of Sissinghurst; see trip 21); they are also a delight to explore, allowing visitors to wander
from one outdoor space to another. If you're using public transportation, a visit to the
garden entails a pleasant country walk: From Moreton-in-Marsh, take bus no. 55 (see
"Getting Around," above) one stop past Chipping Campden to the village of Mickle-
ton. Then follow the marked footpath from the village church through fields and
parkland to Hidcote Manor; the walk is about 1.5 miles (2.4km) each way.

Hidcote Bartrim, outside Chipping Campden. © **01386/438-333.** www.nationaltrust.org.uk. £8 ($16) adults, £4 ($8)
children 5–15, £20 ($40) families of 2 adults and 2 children. Mid-Mar to June and Sept Sat–Wed 10am–6pm;
July–Aug Fri–Wed 10am–6pm; early Oct to early Nov Sat–Wed 10am–5pm.

OUTDOOR ACTIVITIES

The Cotswolds hills are laced with footpaths, and the country lanes are ideal for cycling.
From Moreton-in-Marsh, for example, footpaths lead through the surrounding wolds to
the charming hillside village of **Bourton-on-the-Hill,** and you can return through **Bats-
ford Arboretum,** founded in the 1880s. The total walk is about 8 miles (13km); for
details on this and other easy walks, purchase the pamphlet "The Complete Footpath
Guide to Moreton-in-Marsh and Surrounding Areas" for £1.20 ($2.40) at the Tourist
Information Centre in Moreton-in-Marsh. If you plan to visit other Cotswolds villages,
consider taking the bus to Chipping Campden, walking along the well-marked
Cotswold Way from there to Broadway, and returning to Moreton-in-Marsh via bus;

the walk is about 4 miles (6.4km). For cycle rental in Moreton-in-Marsh, contact **Country Lanes Cycle Centre,** at the train station (© **01608/650-065**).

3 Shopping

The **Moreton-in-Marsh market,** held on Tuesday from 8am to 2pm, is the largest in the Cotswolds and attracts some 200 vendors who sell everything from antiques to fresh produce.

4 Where to Dine

Eagle and Child Pub ⍟⍟ PUB/BRITISH   While this cozy beamed room is a popular local gathering spot, the fare is many cuts above what you normally find in a pub—venison, wild mushroom tarts, smoked fish chowder, and an innovative and delicious version of fish and chips are on the menu, and several daily specials are usually available.

Royalist Hotel, Digbeth St., Stow-on-the-Wold. © **01451/830-670**. Main courses £7.75–£15 ($16–$30). AE, MC, V. Food served Mon–Sat noon–2:30pm and 6–10pm; Sun noon–3pm and 6–9pm.

Tilly's ⍟ LIGHT FARE/TEA   This bright, airy teashop in the village center serves sandwiches, salads, and pastries throughout the day, and is a handy spot for a quick bite or a cream tea.

18–19 High St., Moreton-in-Marsh. © **01608/650-000**. Most items £4–£7 ($8–$14). MC, V. Mon–Sat 9am–5pm.

5 Extending Your Stay

Cozy inns are about as common as sheep in the Cotswolds, and you may want to settle into one and divide your explorations and wanderings over a couple of days. In fact, if you head out into the inviting countryside for a long walk, you'll probably find it a lot more pleasant to come back and relax in front of a roaring fire than to hop on a train for London.

The Cotswolds House ⍟⍟⍟   Even in London, accommodations don't get much more comfortable and stylish than this elegant manor house with a large garden, centered in one of the most beautiful of the Cotswolds villages. Rooms are equipped with everything you might need, from cushy armchairs to state-of-the-art audio equipment, bathrooms are large and have deep tubs and power showers, meals are excellent, and service is gracious.

The Square, Chipping Campden, Gloucestershire GL55 6AN. © **01386/840-330**. www.cotswoldhouse.com. £150–£275 ($300–$550) double. Rates include full breakfast. AE, MC, V.

The Royalist Hotel ⍟⍟⍟   Exposed beams and handsome furnishings lend warmth and style to unusually comfortable accommodations in this centuries-old inn. Two excellent restaurants and a welcoming fireside lounge occupy the ground floor.

Digbeth St., Stow-on-the-Wold, Gloucestershire GL54 1BN. © **01451/830-670**. www.theroyalisthotel.com. £120 ($240) double. AE, MC, V.

Oxford

*T*his "sweet city with her dreaming spires" (to quote the poet Matthew Arnold) is best known as the seat of one of the world's most respected centers of learning. Oxford also happens to be one of the most appealing cities in England. The chapels, quads, and lecture theatres of Oxford's 39 colleges, the oldest of which date to the 13th century, are spread throughout the city and are a pleasure to come across. Though you'll find that most colleges are hidden away behind thick walls, many open part of their premises to visitors on schedules (posted at the gates) that vary wildly from college to college and at different times of the year—keep in mind that almost all are closed to outsiders during the springtime exams. An excellent way to gain admittance to a selection of colleges without trying to fathom the confusing welter of differing opening times is to tag along on one of the Oxford's Guild of Guides walking tours (see "Organized Tours," later in this chapter). As you explore Oxford, you'll notice that town and gown converge on lively commercial streets. This city is not all about brain power (though there's quite a bit of it in evidence): For every architectural masterpiece by Sir Christopher Wren and medieval cobbled lane, there's a snug pub or a lovely riverside walk to enjoy. In fact, there's so much to see and do that you may wish to spend a night in Oxford; see the last section in this chapter for some nightlife and hotel recommendations.

1 Essentials

VISITOR INFORMATION
The **Oxford Information Centre,** 15/16 Broad St. (© **01865/726-871;** www.visit oxford.org), provides information on what to see and do, where to dine and shop, how to get around, and where to stay. It has a small bookshop where you can purchase photo books on Oxford and other specialized guides. Hours are Monday to Saturday 9:30am to 5pm, and Sunday from 10am to 4pm. The official website of the University of Oxford (www.ox.ac.uk/visitors) lists opening times of the colleges, as well as concerts, exhibitions, and other events at the university.

SCHEDULING CONSIDERATIONS
Most colleges are open daily from 2 to 5pm, but it's wise to check with the university website or the Oxford Information Centre for hours and admission policies, since

Oxford

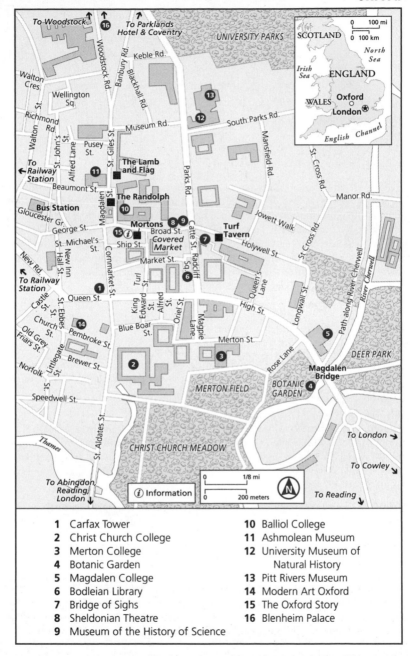

1 Carfax Tower
2 Christ Church College
3 Merton College
4 Botanic Garden
5 Magdalen College
6 Bodleian Library
7 Bridge of Sighs
8 Sheldonian Theatre
9 Museum of the History of Science
10 Balliol College
11 Ashmolean Museum
12 University Museum of Natural History
13 Pitt Rivers Museum
14 Modern Art Oxford
15 The Oxford Story
16 Blenheim Palace

Oxford Highlights

- Walking through the water meadows along the rivers Thames and Cherwell.
- Viewing the paintings and antiquities at the Ashmolean Museum.
- Enjoying the beautiful quad at Christ Church College.
- Strolling through the bustling High and Cornmarket streets and the covered market.

colleges are often closed during exams and at other times. If you're visiting Oxford on a Sunday, you might be able to work a concert into your visit: **Oxford Coffee Concerts** is a chamber music series performed on Sunday mornings in the Holywell Music Room on Holywell Street at 11:15am. Tickets cost £9 ($18) for adults, £8 ($16) for seniors, students, and children under 16; purchase them from the **Oxford Playhouse** box office on Beaumont Street (✆ **01865/305-305**). For schedules and more information, visit **www.coffeeconcerts.com**. Holywell Music Room, built in 1748, is the oldest purpose-built concert hall in Europe.

GETTING THERE
BY TRAIN
Trains run about every 15 to 20 minutes from London's Paddington station to Oxford; the first train departs for Oxford at 5:24am and the last direct train returns from Oxford to London at 12:20am. The fastest trains take about an hour and the standard day return fare is £39 ($78). For information, call **National Rail Enquiries** at ✆ **08457/484950** or go to www.nationalrail.co.uk.

BY CAR
Oxford is 60 miles (97km) west of London. The quickest route from London is the M40, a trip that usually takes a little over an hour. The most convenient places to park are the municipal car parks near the city center, off Beaumont Street, Worcester Street, and Norfolk Street; these charge on average about £2 ($3.20) an hour.

BY BUS
National Express buses (✆ **08705/808080;** www.nationalexpress.com) leave London's Victoria Coach Station for Oxford about every half-hour from about 7am to 9pm, and less frequently outside those times; service is round-the-clock. The trip takes about an hour and 40 minutes and costs £12 ($24) for a day return.

GETTING AROUND
You can probably get anywhere you want to go in Oxford on foot. The train station is about a 10-minute walk west of the city center, off Park End Street, and the bus station is on the north side of the city center at Gloucester Green. The two main shopping and business streets are Cornmarket Street, running north-south through the center, and High Street, running east-west through the center. There's a taxi rank outside the train station; if you want to reserve a taxi, call **001 Taxis** at ✆ **01865/240-000** or **City Taxis** at ✆ **01865/794-000.**

2 A Day in Oxford

An illuminating way to begin a tour of Oxford is with a climb up the spiral staircase of the ❶ **Carfax Tower** ⚔, at the crossroads of the town's busiest thoroughfares (Cornmarket, Queen, St. Aldate's, and High sts.). As you look over the surrounding streets and spires, you'll get a good sense of the layout of the university—the colleges sit behind high walls and are built around inner courtyards called "quads." The tower, which once rose above the 14th-century church of St. Martin (demolished in the late 19th c. to ease traffic flow) is open daily April to October from 10am to 5pm, November to March from 10:30am to 3:30pm; admission is £2 ($4).

Walk south from the tower down Cornmarket Street, which becomes St. Aldate's Street, and step into ❷ **Christ Church College** ⚔⚔ (℡ **01865/286-573**). As you enter, you'll pass beneath Tom Tower, from which a bell tolls 101 times nightly at 9:05 when the college gates are closed. Cardinal Wolsey, King Henry VIII's powerful associate, founded the college in 1525 and graced it with the largest quad in Oxford. Christ Church also claims a Norman church, 800-year-old St. Frideswide (better known as Oxford Cathedral), and a Picture Gallery graced with works by Sir Joshua Reynolds and William Gainsborough. William Penn and John Wesley studied at Christ Church, as did many British prime ministers, and Lewis Carroll, better know for his *Alice in Wonderland,* taught mathematics here for many years. The college is open Monday to Saturday from 9am to 5:30pm, and Sunday from 1 to 5:30pm (last admissions 4:30pm); the Picture Gallery is open Monday to Saturday from 10:30am to 1pm and 2 to 5:30pm, and Sunday from 2 to 5:30pm (closes at 4:30pm Oct–Mar). Admission to the college (including the Picture Gallery) is £4.90 ($10) for adults, £3.90 ($8) for seniors and children.

Now cross Christ Church Meadow and adjoining Merton Field (these two greenswards are on the banks of the River Thames) to ❸ **Merton College** ⚔ (℡ **01865/276-310**). Dating to the 13th century and rich in medieval ambience, this is one of the earliest centers of learning in Oxford; the 14th-century library houses Geoffrey Chaucer's astrolabe. The college is open Monday to Friday from 2 to 4pm, and Saturday and Sunday from 10am to 4pm; there's no admission charge.

Across Rose Lane is the ❹ **Botanic Garden** ⚔ (℡ **01865/276-920**), founded in 1621 for the study of medicinal plants—a rose garden commemorates the Oxford researchers whose work paved the way for the discovery of penicillin. The garden is

Town & Gown

While one of the appeals of modern Oxford is the mix of town and gown, or the way ordinary townsfolk and students mingle (the students wore gowns until fairly recently, and on occasion still do), the relationship has not always been so amicable. On February 10, 1355 (St. Scholastica's Day), widespread rioting broke out when students accused the keeper of an inn near Carfax tower of serving inferior wine—when the hostilities died down several days later, dozens of students had been beaten to death and the colleges ransacked. The moral to be learned from this event, known as the St. Scholastica Day Massacre, is . . . never send back a bottle of wine in Oxford.

open from 9am to 5pm daily (last admission is at 4:15pm); admission is £2.60 ($5.20). At dawn on May Day, undergraduates gather in punts beneath nearby Magdalen (pronounced "maud-lin") Bridge, as hymns ring out from Magdalen bell tower. The tower rises above ❺ **Magdalen College** ☆ (℃ **01865/276-000**), where the grounds encompass a deer park and water meadows (which were once used as a basic irrigation system) along the River Cherwell; you can walk through the meadows on Addisons' Walk. The college's bell tower is the center of Oxford's famous May Day celebrations—at dawn a choir climbs the tower to sing a hymn, and the sound of the voices floating over the city signals pubs to open and a day of raucous behavior to begin. Oscar Wilde studied at Magdalen, and Sir Edward Gibbon, who wrote *The Decline and Fall of the Roman Empire*, described his time here as "the most idle and unprofitable of my whole life." The college is open daily July through September noon to 6pm, and October to May from 1pm to dusk. Admission is £3 ($6) for adults; £2 ($4) for seniors, students, and children.

Follow High Street back toward the town center, and turn right (north) into Radcliff Square to reach the ❻ **Bodleian Library** ☆☆ (℃ **01865/277-224**), established in 1450 and the oldest library in Europe—it's also one of the largest, with more than 5 million volumes tucked away on its 80 miles of shelving. Students using the library still take an oath "not to bring into the library or kindle therein any fire or flame." This tradition stems from the not-so-long-ago days when the library was not lit or heated and scholars resorted to dangerous means of illumination and warmth. The Bodleian's main reading room is the domed and round **Radcliffe Camera.** Although this and other reading rooms are closed to the public, you can see the Divinity School; a 15th-century lecture hall; the Exhibition Room, which mounts rotating displays of rare volumes and prints; Duke Humfrey's Library, a collection of early manuscripts; and other parts of the library on guided tours daily at 10:30, 11:30am, 2, and 3pm. The fee is £6 ($12).

Just north of Radcliffe Square, turn north onto New College Lane, and follow it a few steps to the enclosed bridge known as the ❼ **Bridge of Sighs** ☆ for its resemblance to the Venetian landmark. The bridge connects two parts of Hertford College. The ❽ **Sheldonian Theatre** ☆☆ (℃ **01865/277-299**) on Broad Street was designed in the style of a Roman theatre by the famous architect of St. Paul's Cathedral in London, Sir Christopher Wren. He was a professor of astronomy at Oxford, but his first major commission was for the Pembroke Chapel at Cambridge, which was not begun until the Sheldonian was completed. The university holds its commencement exercises (in Latin) in the richly paneled hall, and the public can step inside for a look Monday to Saturday from 10am to 12:30pm and from 2 to 4:30pm; the admission fee is £2 ($4) for adults and £1 ($2) for children under 15.

Early medical and scientific instruments and such paraphernalia as Albert Einstein's blackboard are on display in the ❾ **Museum of the History of Science** ☆, also on this stretch of Broad Street. The 17th-century premises once housed Elias Ashmole's Cabinet of Curiosities, the forerunner of the Ashmolean Museum (see below). The museum is open Tuesday to Saturday from noon to 4pm, and Sunday from 2 to 5pm; admission is free.

❿ **Balliol College** ☆ (℃ **01865/277-777**), farther west on Broad Street at the intersection of St. Giles Street, was founded in 1263. In the 16th century, bishops Latimer and Ridley and Archbishop Cranmer were burned at the college entrance for heresy on the orders of Bloody Mary; the huge gates still bear scorch marks. The three men are also commemorated with the Martyrs Monument, just across St. Giles Street. The college is open daily from 2 to 6pm. Admission is £1 ($2).

From St. Giles Street, follow Beaumont Street to two other august Oxford landmarks: The Randolph hotel, an ornate hostelry that has accommodated visiting parents for more than a century; and the ⓫ Ashmolean Museum 𝄐𝄐 (ⓒ 01865/278-000; www.ashmolean.org), the university's vast and rather musty collections of art and archaeology; it's the oldest public museum in England. Poke around the galleries and you'll come upon many a treasure. Paolo Uccello's *Hunt in the Forest* will alone reward a visit, and the antiquities and Chinese ceramics reflect the bounty of the expeditions the university has sponsored over the years. The museum is open Tuesday through Saturday 10am to 5pm, and Sunday from noon to 5pm. Admission is free.

MORE THINGS TO SEE & DO

⓬ **University Museum of Natural History** 𝄐 **&** ⓭ **Pitt Rivers Museum** 𝄐
Though somewhat off the main tourist track, these two side-by-side museums have an unexpected charm. The venerable Natural History museum shows off a good collection of dinosaur skeletons and other curiosities in a marvelous glass-roofed Victorian hall. The Pitt Rivers Museum, entered from the Natural History museum, is worth poking your head into for its curiosity value. General Pitt Rivers gave his collection of ethnic artifacts to the university in 1884, and there are now more than half a million objects in old-fashioned cases crammed into a dimly lit room. Arranged by type, rather than geography or date, the exhibits demonstrate how different peoples tackled the same tasks. Most redolent of adventure are the 150 pieces collected during Captain Cook's second voyage, from 1773 to 1774.

Parks Rd. ⓒ **01865/270949**. Free admission. Museum of Natural History daily 10am–5pm. Pitt Rivers Museum Tues–Sun 10am–4:30pm; Sun noon–4:30pm.

⓮ **Modern Art Oxford** 𝄐   This leading center for contemporary visual arts holds ever-changing exhibitions of sculpture, architecture, photography, video, and other media. Café Varvara is a great place for a breakfast, lunch, or tea-time snack. It opens at 9:30am from Tuesday to Saturday, and nothing costs much more than £5 ($10).

Pembroke St. ⓒ **01865/722733**. www.modernartoxford.org.uk. Free admission. Tues–Sat 10am–5pm; Sun noon–5pm.

⓯ **The Oxford Story** 𝄐   This attraction packages Oxford's complexities into a concise, entertaining, and albeit rather silly ride in a vehicle that resembles a school desk and takes you through 800 years of the city's history, reviewing some of the architectural and historical features you might otherwise miss. It also fills you in on the backgrounds of the colleges and those people who've passed through their portals.

6 Broad St. ⓒ **01865/790-055**. £7.25 ($14) adults, £5.25 ($11) children 5–15. Daily July–Aug 9:30am–5pm; Sept–June 10am–4:30pm (from 11am on Sun).

⓰ **Blenheim Palace** 𝄐   This 18th-century baroque palace—one of the largest houses in England, home of the dukes of Marlborough, and birthplace of Sir Winston Churchill, Britain's wartime prime minister—is imposing and a bit overwhelming; it's best to take one of the free tours. Your guide will point out such details as the carvings by Grinling Gibbons in the Great Hall and the portraits by Sir Joshua Reynolds and John Singer Sargent. Just as impressive as the house's considerable treasures are the small room where Sir Winston was born in 1874 and, in an exhibition devoted to him, several of the former prime minister's paintings. The grounds, designed in part by the great Capability Brown, are lavish and extensive.

In Woodstock village, 8 miles (13km) north of Oxford on A44. (No. 20 buses from Oxford train station run every half-hour; £5/$10 round-trip.) Admission £16 ($32) adults, £13.50 ($27) seniors and students, £7.50 ($15) children 5–15, £43 ($86) families. Palace daily mid-Feb to mid-Dec 10:30am–4:45pm (closed Mon–Tues Nov–Dec); grounds daily summer 9am–6pm, winter 9am–4pm.

ORGANIZED TOURS

You can see a lot of the city and several colleges (but not New College or Christ Church) on Oxford's Guild of Guides **2-hour walking tour,** offered daily at 11am and 2pm, with additional Saturday walks at 10:30am and 1pm; the cost is £6.50 ($13) for adults, £3 ($6) children 5 to 15. All tours depart from the **Oxford Information Centre** (see "Visitor Information," earlier in this chapter), where you can purchase tickets. (Buy them from the guide if the center is closed.)

City Sightseeing (© 01708/864340; www.citysightseeing.co.uk) offers a 1-hour **bus tour** (£9.50/$19) with hop-on hop-off service. Buses depart daily from the train station starting at 9:30am and run every 15 to 20 minutes until 5 or 6pm, depending on the season. Oxford is a pleasure to explore on foot, so these tours likely make sense only if walking is difficult for you or if you are pressed for time and want a quick overview of the city and university.

OUTDOOR ACTIVITIES ·

For a quick escape into bucolic settings, take a riverside walk: From St. Aldate's Street you'll find entrances to Christ Church Meadow and a network of paths that follow the rivers Thames and Cherwell. From Walton Road, northwest of the center, you can enter Port Meadow, where you may be joined by grazing livestock. For a leisurely afternoon, follow the Thames-side path north from Port Meadow to two charming pubs: The **Perch** (© 01865/728-891) and the nearby **Trout** (© 01865/302-071); they are about a 2-mile (3.2km) walk from the center of Oxford and have delightful riverside gardens.

You can also enjoy the rivers from a punt, rented by the hour from the **Cherwell Boathouse,** Banbury Road (© 01865/515-978); and from **Old Horse Ford,** off High Street under the Magdalen Bridge (© 01865/202-643). Both are open from mid-March to mid-October and charge £12 to £14 ($24–$28) an hour, plus a damage and theft deposit of £60 ($120) and £70 ($140).

3 Shopping

Not too surprisingly, Oxford is well endowed with bookstores. **Blackwell's** (© 01865/792-792), at 48–52 Broad St., is the largest, with more than 200,000 new and rare books and more than 3 miles (4.8km) of shelving in its cavernous underground Norrington Room. **Oxford University Press Bookshop** (© 10865/242-913), at 116–117 High St., sells dictionaries and a complete inventory of other books published by the university's famous press, founded in the 15th century.

4 Where to Dine

To stock up on provisions for a picnic on the water meadows or simply to grab a quick bite, take a walk through the **covered market** at the intersection of High and Cornmarket streets. Aunt May's is one of many vendors of "fast food"—in this case,

> ## ⌒ *Moments* A Pint in a Pub
>
> Enjoying a pint in a cozy pub is a tradition that goes back centuries in Oxford—the Bear Inn on Alfred Street claims to be the oldest watering hole in town, dating from 1242. At the Head of the River (on the River Thames at the end of St. Aldate St.) and at many other pubs there's an added feature—you can arrive by punt, or at least enjoy a river view from a lovely garden.

authentic Cornish meat or cheese pasties—deliciously heavy combinations of pastry and a generous filling of meat, cheese, and veggies.

Mortons ⑆   If you don't want to spend a lot for lunch, stop in at Mortons. They make delicious sandwiches on fresh baguettes and serve a daily soup. You can eat upstairs, in the back garden, or take your sandwich and picnic elsewhere.

22 Broad St. ⓒ **01865/200860.** Sandwiches £2.50–£4 ($5–$8). MC, V. Daily 8:30am–5pm.

The Turf Tavern ⑆   For inexpensive pub grub (salads, soups, sandwiches, beef pie, chili con carne) or a pint of beer, try this old favorite. Dating to the 13th century, the tavern has served the likes of Thomas Hardy, Richard Burton and Elizabeth Taylor, and Bill Clinton, who was a frequent visitor during his student days at Oxford. You reach the pub using St. Helen's Passage, which stretches between Holywell Street and New College Lane.

4 Bath Place. ⓒ **01865/243-235.** Main courses £4–£9 ($8–$18). MC, V. Food served Mon–Sat noon–8pm.

5 Extending Your Trip

Oxford provides plenty of evening entertainment, and you may wish to stay the night to partake of some. Besides, an overnight will allow you to see the town and university in a leisurely day and visit Blenheim the next morning. Check out the offerings of the **Oxford Playhouse,** opposite the Ashmolean Museum on Beaumont Street (ⓒ **01865/305-305;** www.oxfordplayhouse.com), where Richard Burton, John Gielgud, and Dirk Bogarde have acted. The **Burton-Taylor Theatre** on Gloucester Street was funded by the famous pair and is associated with the Oxford Playhouse. Music venues include the **Apollo Theatre** on George Street (ⓒ **0870/606-3500**), which often hosts big-name acts and touring companies; and the **Jacqueline du Pré Music Room** at St. Hilda's College (ⓒ **01865/276-821**), the city's newest concert hall. **Music at Oxford** mounts concerts from January to July, usually on Friday and Saturday evenings, at the Sheldonian Theatre; for more information, call ⓒ **01865/242-865** or visit www.musicatoxford.com.

Parklands Hotel ⑆   This large Victorian home, built for an Oxford don in a leafy residential neighborhood about a mile from the city center, now offers pleasant and quiet accommodations. Newly refurbished bathrooms, some with tubs, adjoin all of the guest rooms.

100 Banbury Rd., Oxford, Oxfordshire OX2 6JU. ⓒ **01865/554-374.** www.oxfordcity.co.uk/hotels/parklands. £98 ($196) double. Rates include full breakfast. MC, V.

The Randolph ⑆⑆⑆   This grand old Victorian hostelry is the best address in town and a favorite with parents checking on their young scholars. The most atmospheric rooms are the high-ceilinged ones in the front of the house. That said, all of the hotel's guest rooms—recently refurbished—are smartly and comfortably furnished, and all have large marble bathrooms with large tubs. The Morse Bar and Oyster Bar and Restaurant are popular gathering spots.

Beaumont St., Oxford, Oxfordshire OX1 2UN. © 0870/400-8200. www.macdonaldhotels.co.uk. £180–£250 ($360–$500) double. Rate includes buffet breakfast. AE, MC, V.

Rye

"*R*ye is like an old beautifully jewelled brooch worn at South-England's throat." So wrote Patric Dickinson, one of the many writers who have fallen under the spell of this remarkably beautiful coastal town in East Sussex, 62 miles (100km) southeast of London. Novelist Henry James spent the last years of his life here, and E. F. Benson, author of *Mapp and Lucia,* was mayor of Rye in the 1920s. (In his novels, Benson called the town "Tilling.") Rye's official title, "The Ancient Town of Rye," was bestowed upon it nearly a millennia ago when Rye joined the medieval federation of coastal defense towns known as the Cinque Ports—membership brought with it an obligation to supply the king with ships and men to ward off pirates and invading navies, along with freedom from taxes and the assurance of considerable wealth. A powerful seaport, Rye carried on a lively business in smuggling, and occasionally fell prey to invasions, usually from the French, who pillaged and burned the town in 1377. In one notable skirmish, though, Edward III and the Black Prince repelled a fleet of 40 Spanish warships attempting to invade Rye.

That old maritime history still clings to the cobblestone lanes threading through Rye, even though the port began silting up in the 15th century, leaving Rye in a kind of drydock about 2 miles (3.2km) inland from the English Channel, rising above the flat green expanse of Romney Marsh. While Rye lost its prominence as a seaport, this turn of events ensured the town has grown little since medieval times and has retained its historic boundaries and appearance.

Few English towns are more picturesque or pleasurable to explore. Rye claims to have more historic buildings than any other town in England, and is jampacked with half-timbered Tudor and Elizabethan houses, one of its 14th-century entrance gates (Land Gate), a 12th-century defensive tower (Ypres Tower), handsome Georgian town houses, secret passageways, quaint corners, cobbled lanes, windy viewpoints, enticing shops, and wonderful restaurants. All this charm has not been lost on an impressive roster of late 19th- and early-20th-century writers who chose to reside in Rye. They include the Anglo-American novelist Henry James, the humorist E. F. Benson (whose *Mapp and Lucia* series is set in Rye), the novelist Radclyffe Hall, and the American poet Conrad Aiken (the home of the latter is now a guesthouse, and one of our recommendations). The town is small enough to see in about 3 hours, but you'll probably want to stay the better part of a day and wander out to the surrounding salt

Rye Highlights

- Strolling along the winding warren of cobblestone streets lined with ancient stone and half-timbered buildings.
- Climbing the tower of St. Mary's Church for a stunning view over Rye and the Romney Marsh.
- Visiting Lamb House, last residence of Henry James.

marshes or over to seaside Winchelsea (see "Outdoor Activities," below). Rye is a great choice for a day trip when you feel you need a break from London and need a dose of fresh sea air and small town-life. In fact, Rye is so appealing that you may want to spend the night—see our hotel recommendations at the end of this chapter.

1 Essentials

VISITOR INFORMATION

The Rye Heritage Centre on Strand Quay is also the **Tourist Information Centre** (© **01797/226-696;** www.visitrye.co.uk). You can obtain a free town map and rent an excellent audio walking tour (£3/$6) that guides you around the streets. The center can also help you find a room should you wish to extend your stay. The center is open daily from 10am to 5pm (Mar and Nov–Dec until 4pm; Jan–Feb until 3pm).

SCHEDULING CONSIDERATIONS

Lamb House, the home of Henry James, is open April through October on Thursday and Saturday only from 2 to 5:30pm. **Ypres Tower,** which houses collections of Rye's local history museum, is open April through October, Thursday to Monday, 10:30am to 1pm and 2 to 5pm; November through March, it's open Saturday and Sunday only, 10:30am to 3:30pm.

You might want to consider visiting Rye during one of its town celebrations. During late July, the **Siege of Rye** features a weekend of medieval-themed attractions, including demonstrations by the Order of Rye Longbowmen. In September, the town hosts the **Rye Arts Festival,** which features concerts, lectures, performances and exhibitions. On **Rye Bonfire Weekend,** celebrated around Guy Fawkes Night (Nov 5; see p. 200 for more on Guy Fawkes), bonfire societies from all over Sussex participate in a parade and torchlight procession through the darkened streets before the ceremonial bonfire is lit and fireworks set off. Contact the Tourist Information Centre at the number above for more information on all of these events.

GETTING THERE
BY TRAIN

By train, Rye is an easy day trip if you take one of the trains that require only one change and take about 2 hours; other trains require three to four changes and may take up to 6 hours, so do pay attention to the schedules. Trains requiring only one change (at Ashford International) depart hourly starting as early as 7am from London's Charing Cross Station. Trains with only one change return to London until 9:57pm. The standard day return fare from London is about £24 ($48). For train

Rye

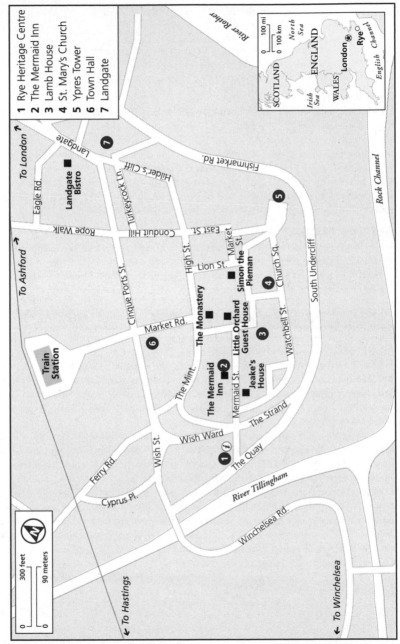

1 Rye Heritage Centre
2 The Mermaid Inn
3 Lamb House
4 St. Mary's Church
5 Ypres Tower
6 Town Hall
7 Landgate

To London
To Ashford
To Hastings
To Winchelsea

Landgate
Eagle Rd.
Landgate Bistro
Hilder's Cliff
Turkeycock Ln.
Fishmarket Rd.
Rope Walk
Conduit Hill
East St.
High St.
Lion St.
Market St.
Simon the Pieman
Church Sq.
South Undercliff
The Monastery
Little Orchard Guest House
Watchbell St.
Cinque Ports St.
Market Rd.
The Mint.
The Mermaid Inn
Mermaid St.
Jeake's House
Wish Ward
The Strand
The Quay
Wish St.
Ferry Rd.
Cyprus Pl.
River Tillingham
Winchelsea Rd.
Train Station
Rock Channel
River Rother

SCOTLAND
North Sea
Irish Sea
ENGLAND
WALES
London
Rye
English Channel
100 mi
100 km

300 feet
90 meters

schedules call **National Rail Enquiries** at ℭ **08457/484950,** or visit www.national rail.co.uk. The easy walk from Rye train station on Cinque Ports Street to Strand Quay, a good place to start your explorations, takes about 10 minutes.

BY BUS

Currently, no regular daily bus service is available from London to Rye.

BY CAR

By car, Rye is 10 miles (16km) northeast of Hastings on A259. From London, take the M25, M26, and M20 to Maidstone, going southeast along the A20 to Ashford. At Ashford, continue south on the A2070. The trip usually takes just over an hour, but allow more time if traveling on weekends, when many Londoners venture down to the Kent coast. Cars aren't allowed into the historic center, so you need to park in one of the many lots on the north side of town and near the train station; you can walk from there. If you drive, you can easily combine a trip to Rye with a trip to Battle, scene of the momentous Battle of Hastings in 1066. (See trip 2.)

GETTING AROUND

Cars are not permitted in Rye's historic center, and the town is small enough to make a complete circuit on foot in a couple of hours. This is one place where good walking shoes come in handy: Getting into the center requires a bit of a climb, though nothing too strenuous, and you'll encounter many uneven cobblestone streets.

2 A Day in Rye

A good place to start your walk is the ❶ **Rye Heritage Centre** on Strand Quay (ℭ **01797/226-696;** www.ryeheritage.co.uk). The center occupies one of Rye's old sail lofts, where ships' sails were repaired. Take 20 minutes to watch "The Story of Rye," which uses an elaborate scale model of the town for a miniature sound-and-light show detailing highlights in Rye's long and sometimes bloody history. The show runs continuously from 10am to 3pm. Admission is £3 ($6) for adults, £1.50 ($3) for seniors, and £1 ($2) for children 5 to 15.

Walk up Mermaid Street, which begins just south of the Heritage Centre. On your left you'll pass ❷ **The Mermaid Inn** (ℭ **01787/223-065**), a half-timbered building that houses one of the oldest inns in England (and a favorite of smugglers from Tudor times until the 19th c.). (See "Extending Your Stay," below.)

Continue south on West Street and you'll come to ❸ **Lamb House** (ℭ **01892/ 890-651**), a dignified, redbrick Georgian house that served as the last residence of the American writer Henry James, who became a British citizen and lived here from 1898 to 1916. The writer E. F. Benson acquired the house after James's death and, watching the coming and goings of town from his windows, used his neighbors and scenes of everyday life in Rye in his humorous *Mapp and Lucia* novels, set in the fictional town of Tilling. You can see some of the rooms and personal possessions of James and Benson and step into the charming walled garden. Lamb House is open April through October on Thursday and Saturday from 2 to 5:30pm. Admission is £3.30 ($6.60) for adults, £1.70 ($3.40) for children 5 to 15.

Turn left on Watchbell Street and follow it to Church Street, site of ❹ **St. Mary's Church** (ℭ **01797/222-430**), which has stood on the highest point in Rye for almost 900 years. Step inside for a look at the turret clock, the oldest in the country, dating from 1561 and with an 18-foot (5.4m) long pendulum; it is said to have inspired the nursery rhyme "Hickory Dickory Dock." The beautiful stained-glass window by Sir Edward Burne-Jones, the pre-Raphaelite painter, dates from 1891. French raiders set Rye on fire in 1377 and carried the bells of St. Mary's across the Channel, but a party from Rye retrieved them, along with other stolen loot, the next year. You can climb the church tower for a magnificent view over the rooftops of Rye to Romney Marsh. The church and tower are open daily from 9am to 6pm (to 4pm in winter). Admission to the tower is £1.50 ($3).

Just south of the church, on Pump Street, you'll find the 12th-century ❺ **Ypres Tower** (© **01797/226-728**), one of Rye's oldest buildings (locals pronounce it "eepers"). Originally built as part of the town's defenses in the 12th century, the tower was later used as a prison and a mortuary. Today it houses a small local history museum displaying medieval pottery, ironwork, and items having to do with smuggling. From the terrace, you can view what was once Rye's busy harbor. The tower/museum is open April through October Thursday through Monday from 10:30am to 1pm and 2 to 5pm; November through March, Saturday and Sunday only from 10:30am to 3:30pm. Combined admission ticket for the tower and nearby East Street Gallery (containing an 18th-c. fire engine, paintings of Rye, and maritime memorabilia) is £5 ($10) for adults, £4 ($8) for seniors and students, and free for children under 16.

From Ypres Tower, take Pump Street north to Market Street and have a look at the arcaded ❻ **Town Hall,** dating from 1742 (not open to the public), then continue north on East Street, turning right on East Cliffe. At the end of it you'll see the ❼ **Landgate,** a fortified stone gate—one of three such entrances erected in the 14th century and the only one remaining. Backtrack along East Cliffe and follow High Street, full of shops and galleries, to The Mint, which will bring you back to the Heritage Centre.

ORGANIZED TOURS

On Wednesday and the first and third Saturdays of the month, from the last week in May to September, the secretary of the E. F. Benson Society leads a 90-minute **"Mapp and Lucia's Rye" walking tour** that highlights Rye as it appears as Benson's fictional town of Tilling and past the characters' houses to the Benson memorials in St. Mary's Church, ending at Lamb House. Cost is £4.95 ($10) per person. You do not need to reserve; just show up at The Belvedere, the viewpoint at the eastern end of High Street, at 2pm. For more information, call © **01797/223-114.**

OUTDOOR ACTIVITIES

Rye Harbor, with its fishing fleet and pleasure boats, runs along the inlet of the River Rother. Its focal point, the **Rye Harbour Nature Preserve,** can easily be reached on foot or bicycle by taking Harbour Road, a small road off the A259 on the Hastings side of the town. (You have to pass some industrial buildings on the road.) The distance is about 2 miles (3km). The road leads to the 209-acre (84-hectare) preserve, a tract of shingle ridges formed over hundreds of years as the sea receded. The varied

---

Moments **Ghost Walk**

You might see a strange shadow or two as you stroll through Rye's old, winding streets on a dark night with the "Ghost Walks" audio tour (available from the Tourist Information Centre). Spooky fun!

habitat of grazing marsh, arable fields, and intertidal salt marsh is known for its birdlife, particularly for its 50 or so breeding species of terns, oystercatchers, and plovers. **Rye Hire,** 1 Cyprus Place (© **01797/223-033**), close to the train station and Tourist Information Centre, rents bicycles for £12 ($24) per day plus a deposit of about £12 ($24).

Winchelsea, the smallest town in England, stands 2 miles (3km) west of Rye on A259 and is also a pleasant bike ride or walk. In 1277, a charter fortified Winchelsea against French invaders and resulted in the town being rebuilt and laid out in grid form, the first such example of town planning in England. At that time, Winchelsea had a harbor and, like Rye, was one of the "Ancient Towns" affiliated with the Cinque Ports defense network. Today Winchelsea is a quiet, unspoiled town with fine old buildings and great views toward the coast. **The Tea Tree,** 12 High St. (© **01797/226-102**), serves sandwiches and teas.

3 Shopping

The Rye **Farmers Market,** held on Wednesday from 10am to 1pm on Strand Quay, has stalls selling fish and local organic produce, plus cakes and breads. On Friday, the **Rye Market** is held in the Rye Community Center, Conduit Hill, starting at 10am; here you'll find more local products, including crafts. The **Rye Chocolate Shop,** 5A Market Rd. (© **01797/222-522**), sells Charbonnel & Walker chocolates and gifts. **David Sharp Pottery,** 55 The Mint (© **01797/222-620**), sells handmade pottery.

4 Where to Dine

Landgate Bistro ⚘ MODERN BRITISH   This highly regarded bistro, set in interconnected Georgian buildings close to the old town gate, is known for the quality of its local produce, fish, and lamb. The cooking is sophisticated but not fussy. For starters, you may have chard and Roquefort tart or butternut squash risotto. Main courses may include free-range chicken, wild rabbit, or "very fishy stew," which uses fresh, locally caught fish.

Landgate. © **01797/222-829.** Main courses £8–£15 ($16–$30). AE, MC, V. Tues–Sat 7–9:30pm.

The Monastery MODERN BRITISH/ITALIAN   The Monastery on busy High Street is one of Rye's top restaurants and serves good food at reasonable prices. The menu features a mix of Italian and British cuisine and might feature chicken breast stuffed with prawns, poached salmon in white wine and dill, or tagliatelle with porcini mushrooms. In the summer, reserving a table in advance is a good idea.

6 High St. © **01797/223-272.** Main courses £10–£16 ($20–$32); fixed-price lunch £12–£15 ($24–$30). MC, V. Tues–Sun noon–2pm and 7–9:45pm.

Simon the Pieman LIGHT FARE/AFTERNOON TEA   At this charming old tearoom in the shadow of St. Mary's Church, you can get a light lunch, homemade cakes and pastries, or an afternoon cream tea. Check out the original 16th-century fireplace as you dine.

3 Lion St. © **01797/222-207.** Lunch £4–£8 ($8–$16). Cream tea £4.75 ($9.50). No credit cards. Mon–Sat 9:30am–5pm; Sun 1:30–5:30pm.

5 Extending Your Stay

Jeake's House 🎭🎭   Widely recognized as one of the top bed-and-breakfasts in England, this quirky old house and connected outbuildings, the former home of the American poet Conrad Aiken, is comfortable, attractive, and welcoming. Guest rooms are large and charmingly furnished, and a fire warms the beamed, book-lined public rooms.

Mermaid St., Rye, E. Sussex TN31 7EU. ℂ **01797/222-828.** Fax 01797/222-623. www.jeakeshouse.com. £90–£156 ($180–$312) double. Rates include English breakfast. AE, DC, MC, V.

Little Orchard House 🎭   This charming, Georgian-era B&B is named for the romantic little orchard garden tucked behind the house. Period antiques and paintings decorate the two guest rooms; both have private bathrooms. The rate includes a generous country breakfast with many local and organic products.

West St., Rye, E. Sussex TN31 7ES. ℂ/fax **01797/223-831.** www.littleorchardhouse.com. £80–£110 ($160–$220) double. Rates include English breakfast. V.

The Mermaid Inn 🎭   When you enter this famous half-timbered inn, one of the oldest in England (the current structure dates back to the 15th c.), you're instantly wafted back to the "olde England" of your dreams. Full of ancient oak timbers, creaking floors, huge fireplaces with log fires, plus a resident ghost or two, the inn has 31 rooms (each one individually sized and decorated), all equipped with modern bathrooms.

Mermaid St., Rye, E. Sussex TN31 7EU. ℂ **01797/223-065.** Fax 01797/225-069. www.mermaidinn.com. £80–£110 ($160–$220) double. Rates include English breakfast. AE, DC, MC, V.

St. Albans

St. Albans, Hertfordshire's oldest town, first appeared as a Celtic Iron Age settlement called Verlamion ("settlement above the marsh"). After the Roman conquest of Britain in A.D. 43, the name changed to Verulamium and the settlement became the third-largest town in Roman Britain. Encircled by gated walls, it was filled with impressive town houses and public buildings, including a large theatre.

After the departure of the Roman army in A.D. 410, the Roman city fell into decay and its ruined buildings provided building materials for the new Saxon settlement of St. Albans, which grew up around a monastery founded A.D. 900 to 950 near the site of St. Alban's execution. (Alban was a Roman soldier martyred for his Christian faith.) It developed into a town of significance with a powerful abbot and was one of five venues chosen by the barons and clergy in 1213 for the drafting of the Magna Carta, the charter of liberties to which King John gave his (forced) approval at Runnymede in 1215 (for Runnymede, see trip 24). The town prospered during the Middle Ages, catering to travelers and pilgrims who flocked to St. Alban's shrine in the Abbey Church. In 1877, St. Albans received a Royal Charter giving it city status and the Abbey Church was elevated to cathedral status. Today St. Albans is a commuter town that, with the presence of these ancient monuments and a medieval appearance, has enough character and history to make for a very pleasant day trip. St. Albans is close enough to London that you can easily make this visit in half a day.

1 Essentials

VISITOR INFORMATION
The **Tourist & Information Centre,** located in the Town Hall on Market Place (*©* **01727/864-511;** www.stalbans.gov.uk), is open Monday to Saturday from 10am to 5pm.

SCHEDULING CONSIDERATIONS
If you want to maximize your day trip to St. Albans by visiting the **Royal National Rose Garden** and **Hatfield House** (see "More Things to See & Do," below), schedule your visit between Easter and September; late May through June are the best times to view the roses, and Hatfield House is closed October through Easter. **St. Albans**

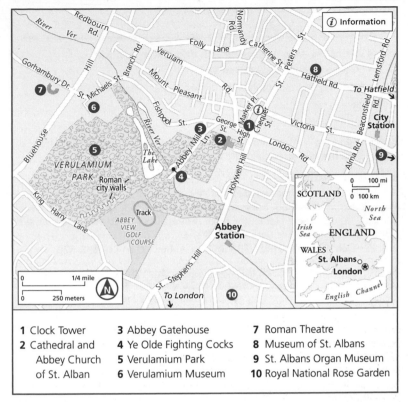

(i) Information

River Ver

Redbourn Rd.

Folly Lane

Normandy Rd.

Catherine St.

St. Peters St.

Lemsford Rd.

Gorhambury Dr.

Hill

St. Michaels St.

Branch Rd.

Verulam

Mount Pleasant

Rd.

Hatfield Rd.

8

To Hatfield →

Beaconsfield Rd.

7

6

Fishpool St.

River Ver

Abbey Mill Ln.

George St.

Market Pl.

(i)

Cheque St.

Victoria St.

London Rd.

Alma Rd.

City Station

Bluehouse

5

The Lake

3

2

1

St.

High St.

Holywell Hill

9 →

VERULAMIUM PARK

Roman city walls

4

Track

0 ——— 100 mi

0 ——— 100 km

King Harry Lane

ABBEY VIEW GOLF COURSE

Abbey Station

SCOTLAND

North Sea

Irish Sea

ENGLAND

WALES

St. Stephen's Hill

0 ——— 1/4 mile

N

0 ——— 250 meters

To London ↓

10

St. Albans ○

London ✷

English Channel

1 Clock Tower	**3** Abbey Gatehouse	**7** Roman Theatre
2 Cathedral and Abbey Church of St. Alban	**4** Ye Olde Fighting Cocks	**8** Museum of St. Albans
	5 Verulamium Park	**9** St. Albans Organ Museum
	6 Verulamium Museum	**10** Royal National Rose Garden

market, one of the best in southern England, is held on Wednesday and Sunday (see "Shopping," below).

GETTING THERE
BY TRAIN
St. Albans is only 40 minutes from London, and the easiest way to reach it is by train. **Thameslink** trains (**www.thameslink.co.uk**) run half-hourly throughout the day from London's King's Cross Station and arrive at **City Station** (© **08457/484950**) on Victoria Street; trains depart St. Albans just as frequently, until 1:18am. A day return costs £16.40 ($33). For train schedules and information, call **National Rail Enquiries** at © **08457/484950,** or visit www.nationalrail.co.uk.

BY BUS
National Express buses from London go only as far as Luton, where you must change to a local carrier. Take the train; it's easier.

BY CAR
From London, take the M1 or M25 motorways north to the St. Albans turnoff. St. Albans is a historic city with many narrow and residential streets, and street parking is difficult. You'll find parking lots on Victoria Street, London Road, and St. Peter's

St. Albans Highlights

- Visiting the ancient cathedral with its shrine to St. Alban.
- Strolling through Verulamium Park.
- Exploring the ruins of Britain's largest Roman amphitheatre.

Street, and at the Verulamium Museum. The trip from central London takes about 45 minutes, but can be much longer when traffic is heavy.

GETTING AROUND

The center of town is small enough that you can explore it all on foot. There is a useful bus service (Intalink) from the station to the town center, the Verulamium Museum, and Hatfield House; for more information call **Traveline** (© **0870/608-2608**). Taxis are available outside City Station, but not Abbey Station. To reserve a cab, call **Gold Line** (© **01727/833-333**) or **Abbey** (© **01727/832-822**).

2 A Day in St. Albans

Begin your day in St. Albans at the city's famous ❶ **Clock Tower** (© **01727/751-826**), located in the marketplace at the intersection of Chequer Street and London Road. Built between 1403 and 1412, it is one of only two medieval belfries in England. Its construction, during a time of growing tension between the church and the townspeople, became a political statement because the tower enabled the town (as opposed to the Abbey) to sound its own hours and curfew. On Saturday and Sunday from Easter to October you can climb the tower for fine views of the Abbey, the Roman Verulamium, and the city; the tower is open Easter through October on Saturday and Sunday only from 10:30am to 5pm.

Cross High Street and enter the passageway (called Waxhouse Gate) directly across from the Clock Tower to reach the ❷ **Cathedral and Abbey Church of St. Alban** ✦✦ (© **01727/860-780**; www.stalbanscathedral.org.uk). For centuries (it was built in 1077) the church has dominated the city's skyline. A Norman church replaced the original Saxon monastery, and St. Albans, with its attached Benedictine Monastery, became the premier abbey of medieval England. The architecture is a blend of many different periods, and the great tower includes Roman bricks salvaged from the ruins of the Roman city of Verulamium. The cathedral is best known for the ornate shrine of St. Alban (restored in 1993), Britain's first Christian martyr, which from about 950 attracted pilgrims from far and wide and contributed to the growth of the city well into the Middle Ages. Monastic life at St. Albans ended in 1539 when Henry VIII dissolved England's monasteries, and everything but the Abbey Church and Gatehouse was destroyed; the marble shrine to St. Alban was shattered (and later painstaking reassembled piece by piece). The cathedral is open daily from 8:30am to 5:45pm.

Walk around the church to look at the ❸ **Abbey Gatehouse,** the only other building that remains of the Abbey of St. Albans. Built in 1365, it was used as a prison until 1868 and now forms part of St. Albans school.

From the Gatehouse, follow Abbey Mill Lane, a delightful country-like lane, south. You'll pass ❹ **Ye Olde Fighting Cocks,** one of the oldest pubs in England and an

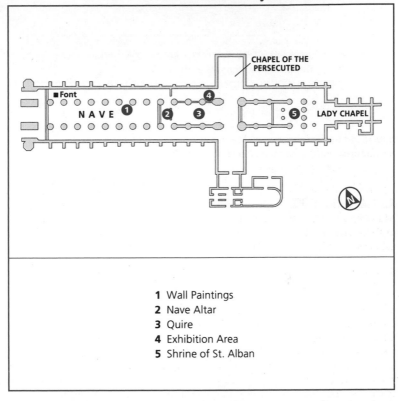

1 Wall Paintings
2 Nave Altar
3 Quire
4 Exhibition Area
5 Shrine of St. Alban

excellent spot for lunch or a drink. (See "Where to Dine," below.) A pathway just beyond the pub brings you into ❺ **Verulamium Park** 🕊, set in more than 100 acres (40 hectares) of beautiful parkland alongside the River Ver. Named after the Roman city of Verulamium on which it stands, the park contains the remains of the Roman city walls and the main London Gate. From the park you have a wonderful view of the Cathedral and Abbey Church to the east. The park's large ornamental lake is home to a variety of water birds.

Signposts on the pathway will direct you to the ❻ **Verulamium Museum** 🕊 (📞 **01727/751-810;** www.stalbansmuseums.org.uk). The museum tells the story of everyday life in Roman Britain with displays that include re-created Roman rooms and some of the best Roman mosaics and wall frescoes outside Italy. The museum is open Monday through Saturday from 10am to 5:30pm and on Sunday from 2 to 5:30pm. Admission is £3.30 ($6.60) for adults, £2 ($4) for seniors and children 5 to 16, free for children under 5, and £8 ($16) for families of two adults and two children.

From the museum, cross Bluehouse Hill Road to the ❼ **Roman Theatre** 🕊 (📞 **01727/854-051;** www.romantheatre.co.uk), the best preserved example of a Roman theatre in Britain. Used originally for bear baiting and cock fighting, its fine acoustics were also perfectly suited to musical and dramatic performances. Within the site are the foundations of a row of Roman shops and the remains of a 3rd-century

---

Moments **A Pleasant Stroll**

Strolling from the Abbey Gatehouse down Abbey Mill Lane is pure English pleasure. The quiet, leafy lane has a few old cottages and an ancient pub, Ye Olde Fighting Cocks, waiting for you at the end.

---

town house with an underground shrine. The site is open daily year-round from 10am to 5pm (until 4pm Nov–Feb). Admission is £2 ($4) adults, £1.50 ($3) seniors and students, £1 ($2) children 5 to 16, and free for children under 5. Free tours are given on Saturday and Sunday in summer at 11am and 3pm.

If you don't want to walk back into the city center, you can catch bus no. 30 to the train station from the St. Michael's Village stop beside the Verulamium Museum.

ORGANIZED TOURS

Guided city walks start from the Tourist Information Centre, usually at 11:15am and/or 3pm on Saturday and Sunday, and take from 1 to 1½ hours. Tickets (£3/$6 for adults, £1.50/$3 for children 5–16) can be obtained from the Tourist Information Centre or from the guide. You'll find the current schedule at the tourist center or online at **www.stalbans.gov.uk**.

Every Sunday at 3pm in July and August, a free, guided **Verulamium Walk** covers the remains of Verulamium, Roman Britain's third-largest town. The walk starts from outside the Verulamium Museum.

MORE THINGS TO SEE & DO

❽ **Museum of St. Albans**   The museum tells the story of historic St. Albans, from the departure of the Romans to the present day.

Hatfield Rd. Ⓒ **01727/819-340.** www.stalbansmuseums.org.uk. Free admission. Mon–Sat 10am–5pm; Sun 2–5pm.

❾ **St. Albans Organ Museum** *(Kids*   This specialty museum gives live performances of the various mechanical musical instruments in its permanent collection, everything from music boxes to theatre organs, on Sunday from 2 to 4:30pm (the only day it's open). Kids enjoy these performances, as do ardent music buffs, but for the general visitor it's probably not worth the trek. From City Station or the city center, take bus no. S2 or C2.

320 Camp Rd. (about 2 miles/3.2km east of city center). Ⓒ **01727/873-896.** Admission £3.50 ($7). Sun 2–4:30pm.

❿ **Royal National Rose Garden** *⟨⟩*   This is the flagship rose garden of the Royal National Rose Society, with more than 30,000 roses on display (as well as clematis, iris, and other flowers). From St. Albans, take a taxi, or take bus no. 727 or 320 and ask the driver for the stop nearest the gardens; it's about a 10-minute walk from the bus stop to the garden entrance.

Chiswell Green Lane (2 miles/3.2km south of city center). Ⓒ **01727/850-461.** Admission £5 ($10) adults, free for children under 16 accompanied by an adult. June–Sept daily 10am–5pm.

Hatfield House *⟨⟨⟩⟩*   Located 6 miles (9.5km) east of St. Albans, this famous Jacobean house (home to the seventh Marquess of Salisbury) has staterooms loaded with paintings, furniture, and armor. Within the lovely gardens is the Old Palace (built in 1485 by the Bishop of Ely), childhood home of Queen Elizabeth I and the site of her first Council of State in 1558 (once she'd learned of her succession to the throne following the death of her half-sister, "Bloody Mary" Tudor). From St. Albans, take a taxi or bus no. 30 from City Station; by car, take A414 east.

Hatfield, Hertfordshire. (✆ 01707/262-823. www.hatfield-house.co.uk. Admission £10 ($20) adults, £9 ($18) seniors and students, £4.50 ($9) children under 16, £26 ($52) families of 2 adults and up to 4 children. Easter to Sept Sat–Wed, house noon–4pm, gardens 11am–5:30pm.

3 Shopping

With over 170 stalls, **St. Albans market** is one of the most colorful and vibrant street markets in the south of England. Held on Wednesday and Saturday in the city center along the length of St. Peters Street, it offers everything from fish to fancy goods. The market was granted a special Royal Charter in 1553 but dates as far back as the 9th century.

4 Where to Dine

Ye Olde Fighting Cocks PUB   Situated on a quiet, leafy pathway close to the River Ver and Verulamium Park, this is one of the oldest pubs in England. The food is nothing fancy, but the atmosphere is great. You can get a club sandwich, hot soup, sausage, and mash, or a ploughman's lunch of cheese, ham, bread, pickles, apple, and salad. If the weather is nice you can eat at a table outside.

16 Abbey Mill Lane. (✆ 01727/869-152. Main courses £5.50–£7.50 ($11–$15). MC, V. Daily 11am–11pm.

Salisbury & Stonehenge

*I*n this beautiful cathedral city dating from the 13th century, half-timbered inns and houses line medieval lanes that surround a still-lively marketplace. Salisbury is actually two cities—Old Sarum, the Iron Age fortification that the Romans took over and that later flourished as a Saxon, Danish, and Norman town well into the Middle Ages, when New Sarum, the city we know as Salisbury, began to grow up around the huge cathedral. William the Conqueror disbanded his troops in Old Sarum in 1070, when the Norman invasion of England was finally complete, and the remains of his castle can still be seen.

Its long history aside, what will strike you most about Salisbury is the beauty of the place—it's one of England's most pleasant and unspoiled cities. The tall spire of a graceful Gothic cathedral pierces the sky, and the Rivers Avon and Nadder course through water meadows. Little wonder that John Constable captured Salisbury in his paintings, and that Thomas Hardy and Anthony Trollope set novels here. Walk its medieval streets and lanes, or mingle with the crowds in the marketplace. You may find yourself wishing you didn't have to rush away from Salisbury—you can spend a full day enjoying the city sights, walk through the Water Meadows and Cathedral Close on a warm evening, and visit Stonehenge and/or Wilton the next day. Add a side trip to nearby **Winchester** (see trip 23) and you may want to stay even longer.

1 Essentials

VISITOR INFORMATION

The **Salisbury Information Centre,** in the marketplace on Fish Row (✆ **01722/334-956;** www.visitwiltshire.co.uk/salisbury), provides maps and information on major attractions, shops, restaurants, and local events. The center is open Monday through Saturday from 9:30am to 5:30pm, and on Sunday, May through September, from 10:30am to 4:30pm.

Salisbury

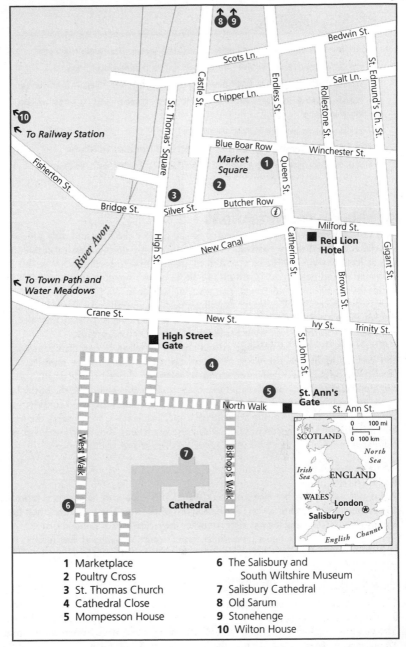

1 Marketplace
2 Poultry Cross
3 St. Thomas Church
4 Cathedral Close
5 Mompesson House

6 The Salisbury and
  South Wiltshire Museum
7 Salisbury Cathedral
8 Old Sarum
9 Stonehenge
10 Wilton House

Salisbury Highlights

• Visiting the medieval marketplace, still the scene of a lively market.

• Strolling down High Street, lined with half-timbered buildings.

• Seeing Cathedral Close, Mompesson House, and other elegant landmarks.

• Viewing Salisbury Cathedral, a Gothic masterpiece, and its copy of the Magna Carta.

• Walking through the Water Meadows.

• Touring Old Sarum, the ruins of Roman and Norman Salisbury.

• Visiting Stonehenge, the world's most famous prehistoric landmark.

SCHEDULING CONSIDERATIONS

This usually sedate city is quite animated for 10 days in late May and early June during the annual **Salisbury Festival,** when you can enjoy drama, classical music, and jazz at locations around the city, as well as architectural tours and other walks. For information and tickets, call ℂ **0845/241-9651** or visit www.salisburyfestival.co.uk.

In late July of alternating years (the next one will be in 2009), the choirs of Salisbury, Chichester, and Winchester cathedrals perform in Salisbury Cathedral during the **Southern Cathedrals Festival.** For information and tickets, contact the Salisbury Information Centre or visit **www.southerncathedralsfestival.org.uk**.

If you want to visit **Stonehenge** as well and are traveling by car, plan your trip so you can get to Stonehenge when the gates open first thing in the morning—the crowds will be thinner—then continue to Salisbury for the rest of the day. If you are using public transport, you'll only be able to get to Stonehenge during the busier late-morning, midafternoon hours. In fact, if you can't beat 'em, join 'em—consider joining one of the City Sightseeing Stonehenge Tours (see below), which takes the hassle out of travel, includes a stop in Old Sarum, and works out about the same cost-wise compared to what you'd pay for independent transport and admission fees.

GETTING THERE
BY TRAIN

Trains run half-hourly between London's Waterloo Station and Salisbury at morning and evening peak travel times and hourly the rest of the day. The first direct train from London is at 7:10am and the last direct train for the return trip to London is at 9:25pm. The trip takes about 1½ hours (non-direct trains require a change at Bassingstoke and take about an hour longer); the standard day return fare is about £26 ($52). For information, call **National Rail Enquiries** at ℂ **08457/484950** or visit www.national rail.co.uk. The train station is at the western edge of the city center, off Fisherton Street, and within easy walking distance of Salisbury Cathedral and other sights.

BY CAR

The quickest route from London is the M3, then the A30. The trip takes about 1½ hours. Convenient car parks near the city center are **Central Car Park,** north of the marketplace on the west side of the River Avon; and **Culver Street Car Park,** a few blocks northeast of the Cathedral Close. Fees at most car parks near the center are £3 ($6) per day.

BY BUS

National Express buses (© **08705/808-080;** www.nationalexpress.com) leave London's Victoria Coach Station for Salisbury about every 2 to 3 hours. The bus ride takes at least 3 hours and sometimes requires a change at Southampton or Bristol, making the train a much faster alternative. The bus trip costs about £15 ($30) return. The bus station is at the east end of the marketplace.

GETTING AROUND

Salisbury is compact and easy to get around, all the more so because much of the marketplace and surrounding streets, High Street, and the Cathedral Close are closed to traffic. The marketplace is at the north end of the center; from there, High Street leads south to the Cathedral Close.

If you need a taxi, call **City Cabs** (© **01722/423-000).** The company will take you on excursions to Stonehenge and other nearby sites—the trip to Stonehenge is about £25 ($50). **Wilts and Dorset buses** (© **01722/336855;** www.wdbus.co.uk) provide daily service between Salisbury and Winchester, with several buses leaving each city for the other between 8 and 9:30am as well as in the early evening; fare is about £5 ($10) and the trip takes about 1 hour and 45 minutes. If you're driving, follow A30 and A272 between the two cities; the trip by car takes only about 45 minutes.

2 A Day in Salisbury

The best place to begin a walk around Salisbury is the heart of town—the ❶ **marketplace** ✿✿, where vendors have congregated since 1227 and continue to do so every Tuesday and Saturday. The medieval ❷ **Poultry Cross,** so called because it once marked the poultry section of the market, still rises above the stalls, and the names of the narrow medieval lanes—Fish Street, Silver Street, Butcher Row—represent the trades that once transpired on them.

Just to the west of the marketplace, off Silver Street, is 700-year-old ❸ **St. Thomas Church** ✿. Step inside (the church is open daily 8am–6pm) to see the terrifying painting called Doom, probably the gift of a medieval pilgrim to the cathedral; it hangs over the chancel arch and depicts ordinary folk rising from their graves and marching toward heaven or hell. High Street leads south toward Salisbury Cathedral, past many half-timbered buildings. The Old George (near the corner of New St.) is a former inn that was already 300 years old when the diarist Samuel Pepys stayed here in 1668. Just across New Street is the Old Bookshop, also dating to the 14th century.

The ❹ **Cathedral Close** ✿✿ is a small city, protected by walls constructed of stone taken from the Norman cathedral at Old Sarum and entered through four gates. (Raucous citizens who preyed upon the wealthy clergy rendered these precautions necessary.) From High Street you'll pass through High Street Gate, with elaborate stonework above its archway. The entrance from Queen Street, to the east, is through St. Anne's Gate, where George Frederick Handel is said to have given his first recital in England in a room over the gatehouse. Some of Salisbury's finest houses are in the large Close, which includes some 75 buildings. When the cathedral was built in the 13th century, the close was planned as a sort of medieval housing development in which persons attached to the cathedral would live, and over the following centuries various deacons and officers were allocated an acre and a half on which to build a home. You can tour one of the best of the remaining houses: ❺ **Mompesson House** 🎭🎭 (© **01722/335-659;** www.nationaltrust.org.uk) was built in 1701 and retains its original plasterwork, paneling, and furnishing, including an astonishing collection of 18th-century glassware; the house evokes the Queen Anne period so richly that period dramas are often filmed here. (You might recognize the house from director Ang Lee's 1995 *Sense and Sensibility*.) The house is open late March through October, Saturday to Wednesday from 11am to 5pm, and admission is £4.70 ($9.40) for adults and £2.30 ($4.60) for children, half price if you show a train ticket. Mompesson House is on the west side of the Close, at the top of West Walk, the most desirable part of the Close, since houses here back onto the River Avon. As you walk through the Water Meadows (see "Outdoor Activities," below) you can enjoy a view of the backs and gardens of these fine homes.

If you follow West Walk south from Mompesson House, you'll notice that many houses are much older—the Medieval Hall and Old Deanery were built in 1277; much of Braybrooke House dates from the same period, and gained a licentious reputation later, when records show that 15th-century resident William Osgodby was reprimanded by the constable of the Close for entertaining a woman of loose morals.

❻ **The Salisbury and South Wiltshire Museum** 🎭, 65 The Close (© **01722/ 332-151;** www.salisburymuseum.org.uk), occupies a magnificent house on West Walk dating from the end of the 11th century and known as King's House. This regal name derives from royal visits that James I and the Prince of Wales paid in 1610 and 1612. The occasions are commemorated in a stained-glass window on the second floor depicting the hostess, Lady Elihonor, clad in a black Tudor dress. A few flints and other artifacts from the Stonehenge site are on display, but most interesting are the displays showing how the monument was constructed, as well as Stone Age and Roman finds from around Salisbury. The museum is open Monday to Saturday from 10am to 5pm; in July and August it's also open Sunday from 2 to 5pm. Admission is £5 ($10) adults, £3.50 ($7) seniors and students, £2 ($4) children 5 to 16, and £11 ($22) families of up to two adults and three children.

❼ **Salisbury Cathedral** 🎭🎭🎭 (© **01722/555-120;** www.salisburycathedral.org. uk) was built in just 38 years, from 1220 to 1258, and because the graceful and soaring structure doesn't bear the influence of other centuries, it is thoroughly Gothic. Join one of the free, highly informative guided tours offered throughout the day. You'll learn that the cloisters are the largest in England; the spire, at 404 feet (123m), is the tallest in the land; and a mechanical clock in the north aisle is one of the oldest pieces of working machinery in the world, telling time since 1386. In the octagonal Chapter House, remarkable stone friezes from the 13th century tell Old Testament stories, and one of four copies of the Magna Carta has been housed here since 1225. The

---

Moments **A Picture-Perfect View**

Walk into the Water Meadows, find a bench, and look back toward the cathedral. Does the scene look familiar? The sight of the tall spire piercing the blue sky has remained unspoiled since John Constable painted the scene 200 years ago. You may have seen his canvases in the National Gallery in London and in other museums.

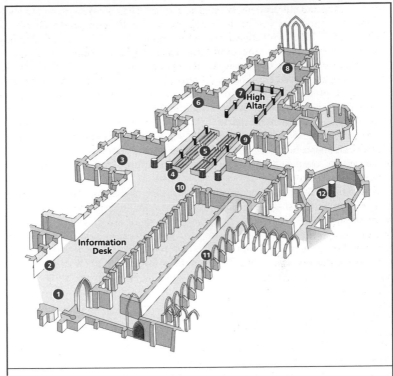

1 West End
2 Medieval Clock
3 North Transept
4 Spire Crossing
5 Quire
6 Morning Chapel
7 Chantry Chapel of Edmund Audley
8 Trinity Chapel
9 Mompesson Tomb
10 William Longespee
11 Cloisters
12 Chapter House & Magna Carta

cathedral is open daily from 7:15am to 6:15pm (to 7:15pm Mon–Sat June 9–Aug 30); the Chapter House is open Monday to Saturday from 9:30am to 5:30pm (until 6:45pm June 9–Aug 30) and Sunday from noon to 5:30pm. Admission to the cathedral is £5 ($10) for adults, £4.50 ($9) for seniors and students, and £4 ($8) for children. On Tower Tours, you can climb into the tower via 332 winding steps past medieval scaffolding to enjoy airy views. The tours last 1½ hours and are held January to February and November to December at 2:15pm, March through October at 11:15am, 2:15, and 3:15pm. Tower Tour fees are £5.50 ($11) for adults and £4.50 ($9) for seniors and children.

ORGANIZED TOURS

The highly informative 1½-hour **Salisbury City Walk** (© **01725/518-658**) begins at the Tourist Information Centre in Fish Row at 11am daily from April to October, on

The Magna Carta

The light-filled, octagonal Chapter House of Salisbury Cathedral, built in the second half of the 13th century as a meeting hall for the cathedral's governing body, houses one of England's most treasured documents, the Magna Carta. The manuscript here is one of four originals known to exist—one of the others is in Lincoln Cathedral and two are in the British Library in London.

King John granted the charter largely as a concession to meet demands from his barons to ensure their privileges. Drafted and sealed at Runnymede (see trip 24) in June 1215, the document protects land rights, guarantees freedoms for the Church, ensures legal reforms, makes the monarchy accountable, and addresses other basic tenets of civil liberties. Portions of the Magna Carta have been incorporated into the U.S. Constitution and many other documents.

Saturday and Sunday from November to March. You'll get an earful of tidbits about commerce in the bustling medieval city, the building of the cathedral, and life within the Cathedral Close. The cost is £3.50 ($7) for adults and £1.50 ($3) for children.

MORE THINGS TO SEE & DO

❽ Old Sarum (Old Salisbury) 𝒶𝒶   The Romans built a town on a desolate plain a mile north of the present-day center of Salisbury, atop a settlement dating from the Iron Age. Old Sarum was a flourishing city by the 13th century, having become one of the most important centers in England when William the Conqueror took up residence here around 1070. Old Sarum was abandoned less than 2 centuries later, though, when Salisbury Cathedral was constructed and a new town took root around the walls of its Close. The moody ruins of the Norman castle, cathedral, and Bishop's Palace attest to what an important place this once was. You can reach the site on a well-marked footpath off Husle Road. Bus no. 3 runs from the bus station and elsewhere in the city center every 15 minutes; the fare is about £1 ($2).

Castle Rd. ☎ **01722/335-398.** www.English-heritage.org.uk. Admission £2.90 ($5.80) adults, £2.20 ($4.40) seniors and students, £1.50 ($3) children 5–15. Daily Apr–June and Sept 10am–5pm; July–Aug 9am–6pm; Oct and Mar 10am–4pm; Nov–Feb 10am–3pm.

❾ Stonehenge 𝒶𝒶𝒶   The world's most renowned prehistoric site, a stone circle of pillars and lintels, has risen above the Salisbury Plain for almost 4,000 years. Why these stones are here or what they signify is not known, but obviously the complex was a meeting place and a ceremonial center of great significance. Given the stones' alignment with the summer equinox, the monument may have been intended in part as an astronomical observatory. Stonehenge also seems to have served at times as a burial ground. Whatever the reason for the presence of these great slabs, the task of getting them to this site must have been herculean. The stones in the Inner Circle, the oldest part of the monument, are from the Prescelly Mountains in southwestern Wales, 240 miles (385km) away, and theories hold that they were dragged overland on roller and sledge and floated over the sea and down rivers. Stones in the Outer Circle are from Marlborough Downs, 20 miles (32km) north, but weigh 50 tons and their transport, too, must have required extensive manpower and complex logistics.

Stonehenge is, today, a victim of its allure, and parking lots and concession stands are what greet you as you approach the site. Matters improve as you turn your back on these modern incursions and follow an excellent self-guided audio tour to view the stones from a well-designed encircling walkway that does not intrude upon the majesty of the haunting monoliths. If you can turn your back on the crowds, you might be able to get into the spirit of this evocative place and get swept away by its mysteries.

If you're traveling by public transportation, which will get you to Stonehenge only in the busy late-morning and midafternoon hours, resign yourself to seeing the stones in the company of tour groups and crowds of other visitors. Just pay attention to the excellent audio guide and try to block out the hubbub around you; the trick is to position yourself at the edge of the railings of the walkways that encircle the stones so you will have an unblocked view. If you're traveling by car or taxi, try to be at the site when the gates open or arrive an hour or so before closing—it's likely the tour groups, at least, will be gone, and you can enjoy the spectacle of soft light playing over the mysterious stones in relative peace and quiet. You can see the stones from the road, but the experience is much better when the stones are viewed from the walkway inside the gates, no matter how dense the crowds.

Wilts and Dorset bus no. 3 (C 01722/336-855; www.wdbus.co.uk) departs from Salisbury bus station for Stonehenge about every hour beginning at 9:45am, and depart from Stonehenge for Salisbury every 2 hours from 10:30am, with the last return to Salisbury at 5:30pm. The trip takes 40 minutes and the fare is £7.50 ($15) return if you buy an Explorer pass good for an entire day. *Note:* For maximum convenience, consider taking the **City Sightseeing Stonehenge Tour.** From mid-May through September, City Sightseeing buses depart from the Salisbury train station daily at 9:55 and 11:55am and 1:55pm (the rest of the year, on Sat–Sun only). Visitors ride a double-decker bus to Old Sarum and on to Stonehenge, where a guide explains the site. This is an excellent and easy way to explore the region's lengthy history, and the cost is about what you'll pay if you choose to visit these sights independently via public transportation. The cost is £16.50 ($33) for adults, £13.50 ($27) for seniors and students, and £8 ($16) for children 5 to 15; admission to Stonehenge is included in the price.

8 miles (13km) north of Salisbury off A360. C 01980/624-715. www.english-heritage.org.uk. £6.30 ($13) adults, £4.70 ($9.40) seniors and students, £3.20 ($6.40) children 5–15, £15.50 ($31) families of up to 2 adults and 3 children. Daily Mar 16–May 9:30am–6pm; June–Aug 9am–7pm; Sept–Oct 15 9:30am–6pm; Oct 16–Mar 15 9:30am–5pm.

🔟 Wilton House 🍳🍳   The 17th-century architect Inigo Jones (whose other works include Queen's House in Greenwich; see trip 8) designed this house, home to the earls of Pembroke. His use of classicism is most in evidence in the Double Cube Room, a harmonious 60-feet-long×30-feet-wide×30-feet-high (18m×9m×9m). General Dwight D. Eisenhower planned the logistical support for the D-day Landings in 1944 in this room, when Wilton was a top-secret operations center. Paintings by Anthony van Dyck line the walls, and paintings by Peter Paul Rubens, Pieter Bruegel, Sir Joshua Reynolds, and other masters hang throughout the other staterooms. One of the most striking treasures is not a painting, but the elegant Chippendale bookcase in the Large Smoking Room. The River Avon flows through the lawns and gardens (home to giant cedars of Lebanon, planted here in 1630), and is spanned by a Palladian bridge. You can reach Wilton House on bus no. 60 or 61 from the bus station and elsewhere in the city center; the fare is £1.75 ($3.50).

3 miles (5km) northwest of Salisbury on A30, in Wilton village. C 01722/746-720. www.wiltonhouse.co.uk. Admission £12 ($24) adults, £9.75 ($20) seniors and students, £6.50 ($13) children 5–15, £29.50 ($59) families. Mid-Mar to Oct daily 11:30am–4:30pm.

OUTDOOR ACTIVITIES

A well-maintained footpath traverses the **Water Meadows** 👣👣 between Mill Road and the old Harnham Mill, crossing the River Avon and affording wonderful views toward the cathedral. A walk through the meadows and back to the city center covers a little less than 2 miles (3km). For a longer excursion, rent a bike from **Stonehenge Cycles,** 86–88 Fisherton St. (© **01722/334-915;** www.stonehengecycles.com), for a spin around town and onto a series of public footpaths that wind through the countryside. For advice on routes, call the **Walking and Cycling Helpline** at © **01980/623-255.**

3 Shopping

Watsons, 8/9 Queen St. (© **01722/320-311**), sells a huge selection of British crystal and fine china. The wares are not the only draw, though—the shop occupies two of Salisbury's oldest buildings, dating back to 1306 and 1425. The **National Trust Shop,** 41 High St. (© **01722/331-884**), carries needlepoint kits, tea towels, and other souvenir-type items.

4 Where to Dine

You can equip yourself with sandwiches, quiches, and delicious pastries at **Reeve the Baker,** 2 Butcher Row (© **01722/320-367**), and enjoy a picnic in the Water Meadows. For cheeses, fruit, and other local produce, stroll through the marketplace Tuesday and Saturday mornings.

Harper's Restaurant 👣 BRITISH/INTERNATIONAL   "Real food is our specialty" is the motto in this pleasantly old-fashioned second-floor room overlooking the marketplace. Excellent meals, including vegetarian dishes, are served a la carte and on reasonably priced prix-fixe menus.

6–7 Ox Row. © **01722/333-118.** Main courses £7.50–£14 ($15–$28); fixed-price lunch £8.50 ($17); fixed-price dinner £11 ($22). MC, V. Mon–Sat noon–2pm and 6–9:30pm; Sun 6–10pm.

One Minster Street 👣 BRITISH   Locals may refer to this place as the Haunch of Venison, which is Salisbury's oldest pub, dating from 1320. One Minster occupies a series of small, heavily beamed rooms above the pub and caters to modern tastes with such fare as burgers and sea bass filets. It's still the town's most atmospheric place to dine.

1 Minster St. © **01722/411-313.** Main courses £7.50–£15 ($15–$30). AE, MC, V. Daily noon–2:30pm and 7–10pm.

5 Extending Your Stay

Red Lion Hotel 👣 Atmosphere fills every nook and cranny of this 750-year-old inn (now owned by Best Western), from which the express stagecoach used to depart for London every night at 10pm. The cozy lounge is a popular spot for tea, and drinks are served in the vine-covered courtyard in good weather. Each guest room is uniquely furnished, some with fireplaces and four-poster beds.

Milford St., Salisbury, Wiltshire SP1 2AN. © **01722/323-334.** www.the-redlion.co.uk. £134–£154 ($268–$308) double. AE, DC, MC, V.

Sissinghurst Castle Garden

W hat has become one of England's favorite gardens is the creation of the poet, novelist, and gardening writer Vita Sackville-West and of her husband, the diplomat and writer Harold Nicolson. Vita's childhood home was Knole, one of the largest houses in England (see trip 13), and as the only heir of her father, Lionel, the 3rd Lord Sackville, she would have inherited the estate had she been male. At Sissinghurst, and in the gardens especially, she and Harold sought to re-create the feeling of a grand English house like Knole.

In 1930, the couple bought the nearly ruined remains of a grand Elizabethan house and restored the gatehouse, stables, tower, and other buildings, but most notably turned their attention to the gardens. They were inspired by Britain's best-known garden designers of the early 20th century, Sir Edwin Lutyens and Gertrude Jekyll, in stressing color, texture, and the overall experience of being in a garden, and by Lawrence Johnston, the American-born heir who created a series of roomlike gardens at Hidcote Manor, his estate in the Cotswolds (see trip 16).

At Sissinghurst, Harold and Vita laid out 10 outdoor rooms, each with a distinct look and feel, separated by hedges and walls, and each planted with plants of different appearance and color. In these gardens Vita found inspiration for the gardening essays she wrote for the *Observer,* and in turn her vast knowledge of gardening and commitment to creating a beautiful garden became manifest at Sissinghurst. Walking through the gardens, you make a discovery around every corner and through every archway. The experience is delightful, and it's little wonder that Sissinghurst has become the model of gardens around the world. None, however, is quite as enticing as the original.

Of course, the charms of Sissinghurst are well known and the garden is one of England's most popular attractions. You'll have the most pleasant experience if you try to visit when the garden is not crowded—Sissinghurst is spectacular at any time, and you will enjoy a visit even during early spring or late fall. Because the trip down from London is relatively quick, Sissinghurst is an excellent choice for a half-day excursion.

Sissinghurst Highlights

- Seeing Vita Sackville-West's study in the Tower.
- Exploring the Rose Garden, especially when it is in bloom in June.
- Viewing the White Garden, at its best in early July when the central rose blooms form a huge canopy.
- Touring the Cottage Garden, at any time of the year.
- Taking in the Lime Walk, just after the limes have come into leaf and the spring flowers are in bloom.

1 Essentials

VISITOR INFORMATION

Sissinghurst is beautifully situated in the rolling lands known as the Weald of Kent, about 50 miles (80km) southwest of London and 7 miles (11km) south of the town of Staplehurst. The garden is open from mid-March to late October Friday through Tuesday from 11am to 6:30pm. Admission is £7.90 ($16) for adults, £4 ($8) for children under 16, and £22 ($44) for families of up to two adults and two children. For more information, call © 01580/710-700 or visit www.nationaltrust.org.uk/places/sissinghurst.

SCHEDULING CONSIDERATIONS

You'll want to linger in these gardens, and there is very little to do indoors at Sissinghurst, so try to arrange your visit on a day when it is not raining. Only a certain number of visitors are allowed into the garden at a time, so expect a wait on weekends (when the gardens are especially crowded) and at any time in the late spring and early summer, when the plants are in their fullest bloom. It's best to visit during the week if you can. Like most English gardens, Sissinghurst is at its prime in June, but it is colorful from early spring well into the fall.

GETTING THERE
BY TRAIN

The train station closest to Sissinghurst is the one in the village of Staplehurst, about 7 miles (11km) away. The direct trip from London's Charing Cross Station to Staplehurst takes just over an hour and the standard day return fare is £13.40 ($27). There are some 35 trains a day from London, running about every half-hour. The first train to Staplehurst is at 5:30am and the last train returns to London at 10:51pm; a few trains return to London Bridge Station, so be sure to check the destination before boarding. For more information, call **National Rail Enquiries** (© 08457/484950) or go to www.nationalrail.co.uk.

From the Staplehurst train station, you can continue to Sissinghurst by bus no. 4/5. Buses run roughly every half-hour throughout the day (less frequently before 9:30am and after 7pm), and the fare is £1.80 ($3.60). Tell the driver you want to get off at the gates to Sissinghurst. (You'll have to walk a quarter mile or so up the drive.) Or get off in Sissinghurst village and follow the well-marked footpath through surrounding woods and hops fields to the garden; the walk is delightful and less than a mile. (As

Sissinghurst Castle Garden

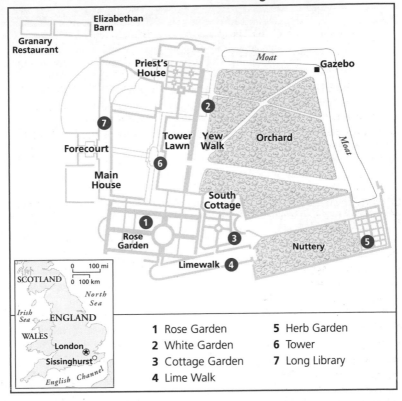

you near the grounds of Sissinghurst, the path passes beneath a magnificent spreading beech.) For additional bus information, call **Traveline** at ℂ **0870/608-2608** or visit www.traveline.org.uk.

Alternatively, you can take a taxi from Staplehurst right to the garden entrance for about £10 ($20). If you wish to return via taxi, arrange to have the driver pick you up at a set time, because public phones are scarce at the garden. There's a taxi stand outside the Staplehurst train station, but to ensure that a taxi will be available when you arrive, arrange a pickup in advance by calling the **Maidstone Taxi Company** at ℂ **01580/890-003.**

BY CAR

The trip from London takes just over an hour, depending on traffic. Take the M25 to Maidstone, where you will get on A229 and travel south through Staplehurst to A262; Sissinghurst is about 3 miles (4.8km) west of the junction. Parking is free.

GETTING AROUND

Travelers with disabilities will want to consider the fact that a visit to the garden involves quite a bit of walking when using public transportation—you will have to walk about a quarter of a mile up the drive from the bus stop on the main road. A taxi from Staplehurst (see "By Train," above) may be a better option.

2 A Day at Sissinghurst Castle Garden

If you're a royalist at heart, you'll be pleased to know that you enter **Sissinghurst Castle Garden** *✹✹✹*—through an arch in the stable and servants' block into the courtyard and past the base of a tall tower of pale pink brick—the same way that Queen Elizabeth I did when she paid a visit to then-owner Sir Richard Baker in 1573; Baker built a grand Elizabethan manor at Sissinghurst on the foundations of a medieval house surrounded by a moat. The estate served as a prisoner of war camp during the Anglo-French Wars of the mid–18th century, and was later used as a workhouse for the indigent. Only parts of the house still stood when Harold and Vita bought Sissinghurst in 1930, and they fashioned living quarters out of the remains of the manor, tower, and different buildings across the estate. The two rooms of the home you can visit, the Long Library and Vita's study in the Tower, are reached off the courtyard, but save them for later; instead, focus on the gardens that lie just on the other side of the Tower.

There's no best route through the garden; in fact, it's best just to wander across these 6 acres (2.4 hectares) wherever your curiosity takes you. The garden is designed so that you rarely see one section from another, so each time you come through a gap in a hedge or wall, you're in for a surprise.

As you move from outdoor room to outdoor room, take note of the way the garden incorporates classical symmetry and romantic abandon—in this way, the garden is said to capture the personalities of the couple who created it. In the ➊ **Rose Garden** *✹✹✹*, to your right as you pass through the arch at the base of the Tower, Harold designed the disk of mown lawn surrounded by yew hedges; and Vita, whose preference was for colorful beds and flowers straying over paths, planted the luxuriant, old-fashioned varieties that bloom in June. In the ➋ **White Garden** *✹✹✹*, Vita planted white flowers that bloom throughout the season among the paths and hedges laid out by Harold. The ➌ **Cottage Garden** *✹✹✹* also combines formality and a sense of abundance, and in it grows the white rose the couple planted the day they bought Sissinghurst. The classically oriented Harold planted the formal, Italian-style ➍ **Lime Walk** *✹✹*, and Vita lavished care on the ➎ **Herb Garden** *✹✹*; supposedly, she could identify every herb in it with her eyes closed, by smell alone.

Once you've seen the gardens, return to the ➏ **Tower** *✹✹✹*, where you can look into Vita's study (an extremely romantic room). Just across the courtyard is the ➐ **Long Library** *✹✹*, a handsome room dating from 1490 and filled with centuries-old family furniture. Don't turn your back on the gardens yet, though—you might want to return for another walk around and to find a spot in which to sit and do what Harold and Vita did for many years—simply enjoy this splendid creation.

Moments A Bird's-Eye View

After you've toured the garden, climb to the top of the Tower for one more look. From this vantage point, you can clearly see the separate outdoor rooms and appreciate just what an accomplishment the garden is. You'll also see why Vita Sackville-West enjoyed spending her days here in the Tower.

Portrait of a Marriage

Vita Sackville-West (1892–1962) and her husband, the diplomat Harold Nicolson (1886–1968), are famous for the gardens they cultivated at Sissinghurst and for their literary achievements—Vita's poem "The Land" is one of many works in which she pays homage to her beloved Kent, and Harold's books include biographies of Tennyson and Byron, and studies of politics and diplomacy. The couple is also notable for a long and unconventional marriage that began in 1913 and came to an end with Vita's death from cancer in 1962. Both were bisexual, and Vita's extramarital affairs included a rather scandalous and much-publicized liaison with Violet Keppel Trefusis in 1920 (Violet was the daughter of Alice Keppel, mistress of King Edward VII) and a love affair with the novelist Virginia Woolf. Vita often visited Monk's House, the country home that Virginia and Leonard Woolf bought near Lewes in 1920. (See trip 15.) She was the model for the gender-bending hero/heroine of *Orlando,* Woolf's brilliant novel set in part at Knole, Vita's family estate in nearby Sevenoaks and one of the greatest houses in England. (See trip 13.) The couple had two children, the art critic Benedict Nicolson, and the writer and publisher Nigel Nicolson. Nigel wrote about his parents' enduring union in *Portrait of a Marriage,* published in 1973.

3 Where to Dine

Granary Restaurant CAFETERIA/LIGHT FARE   An airy outbuilding on the estate near the garden entrance is an unusually pleasant setting for a cafeteria-style restaurant that overlooks fields through a wall of glass. Sandwiches, salads, and a few hot dish specials are on offer, as are tea and other beverages, including wine and beer.

℃ **01580/710-704.** Most items £3–£7 ($6–$14). DC, MC, V. Late Mar to Oct Sun–Tues 11am–5:30pm.

Stratford-upon-Avon

*T*his market town on the River Avon, 91 miles (146km) northwest of London, is a shrine to the world's greatest playwright, William Shakespeare, who was born, lived much of his life, and is buried here. Stratford boasts many fine and beautifully preserved Tudor, Elizabethan, and Jacobean buildings, but it's not really a quaint village anymore. If you arrive by train, your first glimpse will be of a vast parking lot across from the station. Don't let this put you off. The charms of Stratford's formerly bucolic setting haven't been completely lost, and you'll find plenty of quaint corners as you explore. If the weather is cooperative, you can escape the crowds and float along the River Avon in the company of swans (see "Outdoor Activities," later in this chapter). Besides the literary pilgrimage sights, the top draw in Stratford is the Royal Shakespeare Theatre, where Britain's foremost actors perform. Nearby Warwick Castle is also worth visiting, but you'll be hard-pressed to do so unless you spend the night in Stratford. Actually, with all there is to see and do in Stratford and the surrounding area, you may well want to spend more than 1 day here, and an overnight will allow you time to see a performance at the Royal Shakespeare Theatre. See the last section in this chapter for hotel recommendations.

1 Essentials

VISITOR INFORMATION

Stratford's **Tourist Information Centre,** Bridgefoot (© **0870/160-7930;** www. shakespeare-country.co.uk), provides information and maps of the town and its principal sights. The center has a currency exchange and a room-booking service. It's open Easter through October, Monday through Saturday from 9am to 6pm (until 5pm Nov–Easter), and Sunday 11am to 5pm (10:30am–4:30pm Nov–Easter).

SCHEDULING CONSIDERATIONS

All of the Shakespeare properties keep basically the same hours, opening daily between 10 and 11am and closing at 5pm. They open slightly earlier in the summer and close an hour earlier in the winter. All of them are closed December 24 through December 26; some are also closed January 1 and Good Friday. Crowds are heaviest from June through mid-September; if you are visiting during those times, you'll find the town

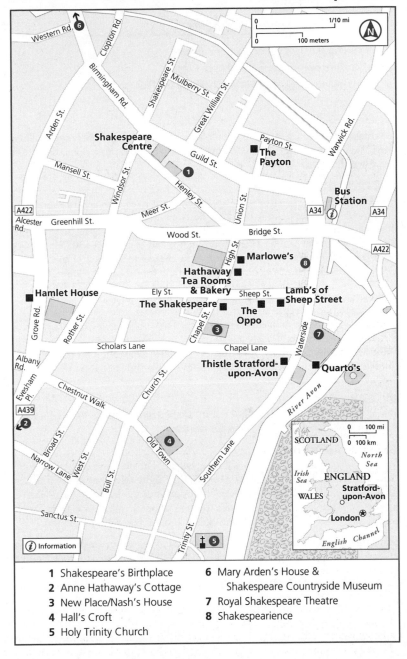

1 Shakespeare's Birthplace
2 Anne Hathaway's Cottage
3 New Place/Nash's House
4 Hall's Croft
5 Holy Trinity Church
6 Mary Arden's House &
  Shakespeare Countryside Museum
7 Royal Shakespeare Theatre
8 Shakespearience

Stratford-upon-Avon Highlights

- Visiting the Bard's birthplace and grave.
- Strolling over to Anne Hathaway's Cottage.
- Attending a play at the Royal Shakespeare Theatre.

less congested on weekdays. If you want to see a play at the **Royal Shakespeare Theatre** (see "More Things to See & Do," below), book ahead and don't come during October, when the theatre is closed.

GETTING THERE

BY TRAIN

Fast, direct trains leave from London's Marylebone Station weekdays at 8:54 and 10:54am (later on weekends, and requiring one change) and depart Stratford-upon-Avon at 7:43pm; the journey takes about 2 hours and costs about £30 ($60) for a day return ticket. Note that on this route, it may be cheaper to buy two "single" (one-way) tickets than a day return. You can also catch a train from London Paddington, but all the trains require one, two, or three changes and the fare is higher (£33.50/$67). Contact **National Rail Enquiries** (**© 08457/484950**) or visit www.nationalrail.co.uk for information and schedules.

BY BUS

National Express (**© 0990/808080;** www.nationalexpress.com) offers daily express bus service from London's Victoria Coach Station; the trip takes just over 3 hours and costs about £17 ($34) return.

BY CAR

By car from London, take the M40 toward Oxford and continue to Stratford-upon-Avon on A34. Allow about 2½ hours for the trip.

GETTING AROUND

Stratford is compact, and you can walk everywhere. The train and bus stations are less than a 15-minute walk from the town center. **City Sightseeing** (see under "Organized Tours," below) runs a convenient hop-on/hop-off bus service to all the Shakespeare properties, including Anne Hathaway's Cottage (about 1 mile/1.6km from Stratford town center) and Mary Arden's House (about 2 miles/3km from the center).

2 A Day in Stratford-upon-Avon

One money-saving ticket gets you into the five sites administered by the **Shakespeare Birthplace Trust** (**© 01789/201-807;** www.shakespeare.org.uk): Shakespeare's Birthplace, Anne Hathaway's Cottage, New Place/Nash's House, Hall's Croft, and Mary Arden's House, all of which are described below. You can pick up the ticket at your first stop; it costs £14 ($28) for adults, £12 ($24) for seniors and students. If you only want to visit the three Shakespeare sites in Stratford (not Mary Arden's Cottage or Anne Hathaway's Cottage), you can buy a special combination ticket for £11 ($22).

Start your walking tour of Stratford at ❶ **Shakespeare's Birthplace** ★★★ on Henley Street (**© 01789/204-016;** www.shakespeare.org.uk), where the Bard, son of a glover and wool merchant, first saw the light of day on April 23, 1564. You enter through the modern **Shakespeare Centre,** where exhibits illustrate his life and times. The house, filled with Shakespeare memorabilia, is actually composed of two 16th-century half-timbered houses joined together. You can visit the bedroom where Shakespeare was born, the living room, and a fully restored Tudor-style kitchen. The house and gardens are open daily from 10am to 5pm (from 10:30am on Sun; June–Aug from 9am weekdays and from 9:30am Sun; Nov–Mar until 4pm). Admission is £7 ($14) adults, £6 ($12) seniors and students.

Make ❷ **Anne Hathaway's Cottage** ★★★ (✆ **01789/204-016;** www.shakespeare. org.uk) your next stop. It's located on Cottage Lane in Shottery, about 1 mile (1.6km) south of Stratford. To get there, walk along the well-marked country path from Evesham Place or hop on a bus from Bridge Street. Anne Hathaway, who came from a family of yeomen farmers, lived in this thatched cottage until 1582, the year she married 18-year-old Shakespeare. (Anne was 7 years older.) Many original 16th-century furnishings are preserved inside the house, which was occupied by Anne's family until 1892. Before leaving, be sure to stroll through the beautiful garden and orchard. The hours are the same as for Shakespeare's Birthplace. Admission is £5.50 ($11) adults, £4.50 ($9) seniors and students.

From Anne Hathaway's Cottage, retrace your steps to Shakespeare's Birthplace and then walk east on Henley Street and south on High Street, which becomes Chapel Street. Here you'll find the gardens of ❸ **New Place** (✆ **01789/204-016;** www. shakespeare.org.uk), all that remains of the Stratford house where a relatively prosperous Shakespeare retired in 1610 and died in 1616. The Bard bought the house for the then-astronomical sum of £60 ($120). Reverend Francis Gastrill, a mid-18th-century owner, allegedly tore the house down rather than continue paying taxes on the property, where he couldn't live peaceably because of the legions of visitors coming to see where the famous past resident had lived. You enter the garden through Nash's House, which belonged to Thomas Nash, husband of Shakespeare's granddaughter. The house contains 16th-century period rooms and an exhibit illustrating the history of Stratford. New Place/Nash's House is open daily from 11am to 5pm (June–Aug from 9:30am weekdays and from 10am Sun; Nov–Mar until 4pm; opens at 1:30pm Jan 1 and Good Friday). Admission is £3.75 ($7.50) adults, £3 ($6) seniors and students.

From New Place, walk south on Chapel and Church streets and turn east on Old Town to reach ❹ **Hall's Croft** ★★ (✆ **01789/204-016;** www.shakespeare.org.uk), a magnificent Tudor house once lived in by Shakespeare's daughter Susanna and her husband, Dr. John Hall. The house is furnished in the style of a middle-class 17th-century home and also has exhibits illustrating the theory and practice of medicine in Dr. Hall's time. It has the same opening hours and admission as New Place/Nash's House.

From Hall's Croft, walk south to Southern Lane, which runs beside the River Avon, and follow it south to Trinity Street and the path to ❺ **Holy Trinity Church** ★ (✆ **01789/266-316**), where Shakespeare is buried. (He died on his birthday, Apr 23, 1616, at age 52.) A bust of the immortal Bard looks down on his gravesite in front of the altar. Holy Trinity is open Monday through Saturday from 8:30am to 6pm (Nov–Feb 9am–4pm, Mar and Oct 9am–5pm), and Sunday year-round from 2 to 5pm. You can get into the church for free, but to see Shakespeare's grave costs £1.50 ($3). Holy Trinity, by the way, is in urgent need of structural repairs and is raising funds for that purpose.

The last Shakespeare site, ❻ **Mary Arden's House & the Shakespeare Country-side Museum** ⟨⟨ (ℂ **01789/204-016;** www.shakespeare.org.uk), is located in Wilmcote, about 3½ miles (5.5km) north of Stratford on A34. To reach it, you'll probably want to drive or take the City Sightseeing bus (see "Organized Tours," below). For more than 200 years, Palmers Farm, a Tudor farmstead with an old stone dovecote and outbuildings, was identified as the girlhood home of Mary Arden, Shakespeare's mother. Recent evidence revealed, however, that Mary Arden actually lived in the house next door, at Glebe Farm. In 2000, the house at Glebe Farm was officially designated as the Mary Arden House. Dating from 1514, the house contains country furniture and domestic utensils; the extensive collection of farm implements in the barns and outbuildings illustrate life and work in the local countryside from Shakespeare's time to the present. The house and museum are open daily from 10am to 5pm (Nov–Mar and Sept–Oct until 4pm; Sun from 10:30am). Admission is £6 ($12) adults, £5 ($10) seniors and students.

The ❼ **Royal Shakespeare Theatre,** Waterside (ℂ **01789/403-403;** www.rsc.org.uk), is the home of the Royal Shakespeare Company, which stages Shakespeare plays from November to September. The company features some of the finest actors in Britain. Note, however, that the theatre is closed from 2007 to 2010 for a complete refurb. In the meantime, all performances take place in the nearby Swan Theatre and the Courtyard Theatre. It's a good idea to order your tickets 2 to 3 weeks in advance, even earlier if you can. (A few tickets are always held for sale on the day of a performance, and you can queue for returns starting 2 hr. before a performance.) The box office is open Monday through Saturday from 9:30am to 8pm, but closes at 6pm on days when there are no performances. Ticket prices are £8 to £50 ($16–$100).

MORE THINGS TO SEE & DO

❽ **Shakespearience**   Stratford's newest attraction presents the life and works of Shakespeare in a unique way, using cinematic technology and special effects. The show, projected on specially designed screens that present actors with lifelike verisimilitude, includes information about the Bard of Stratford and dramatic highlights from nine of his best-loved plays.

Waterside Theatre, Waterside. (ℂ 01789/290-111. Tickets £7.25 ($15) adults, £6.25 ($13) seniors, students, and children under 12, £24 ($48) families (2 adults and 2 children).

Warwick Castle ⟨⟨⟨   Mighty Warwick Castle, one of the most popular tourist attractions in England, is located 8 miles (13km) northeast of Stratford in the town of Warwick. Dramatically sited above the River Avon, the castle is a splendid example of a medieval fortress that's been adapted over the centuries to reflect the tastes and ambitions of its inhabitants. Though the first fortifications were built on this site in 914, much of the external structure dates to the 14th century; the interiors, however, were renovated in the 17th century when the fortress was converted into a mansion for the Earl of Warwick. Scattered through the castle apartments (restored to the way they appeared in the late 19th c.) are lifelike wax figures created by Madame Tussaud's to represent famous figures who visited the castle and the servants who kept the place running. There's also a dungeon to visit, an exhibition on the warlords who built the place, battlements to walk on, and towers to explore. If you're going to visit the castle and the lovely gardens and parkland around it, you need at least 2 hours.

Chiltern Railways (ℂ **08705/165-165**) runs direct trains to Warwick from Stratford-upon-Avon; the trip takes 20 to 30 minutes and the cheap return fare is £3.50

> ### Moments Shakespeare's Grave
>
> He wrote some of the world's most immortal lines, but the epitaph you see scratched on Shakespeare's grave in Holy Trinity Church is little more than doggerel: "Good frend for Jesus sake forbeare/to digg the dust encloased heare/bleste be ye man yt [that] spares the stones/and curst be he yt moves my bones."

($7). **National Express** (℃ **0990/808080;** www.nationalexpress.com) runs buses to Warwick from Riverside bus station in Stratford-upon-Avon; the 15-minute journey costs about £4 ($8) return. By car from Stratford, take Junction 15 of the M40 and continue on for 2 miles (3km). Bus tours of Warwick Castle from Stratford-upon-Avon are available through City Sightseeing (see below).

Warwick Castle. ℃ 0870/442-2000. www.warwick-castle.co.uk. Admission (price is slightly less in low season and if you book online) £16 ($32) adults, £12 ($24) seniors and students, £10 ($20) children ages 5–15, £48 ($96) family tickets (2 adults and 2 children). Daily 10am–6pm (Oct–Mar until 5pm, Aug until 7pm).

ORGANIZED TOURS

The **Stratford Town Walk** ℛ (℃ **01789/292-478**) departs daily (Mon–Wed at 11am, Thurs–Sun at 2pm) from the Swan Fountain near the Royal Shakespeare Theatre, year-round. This is a 90-minute "insider's tour" of Shakespeare's Stratford. All the Shakespeare sights are visited, and you're given a lively commentary on the Bard's life. No need to reserve; just show up. The tour costs £5 ($10) for adults, £2 ($4) for children under 16.

City Sightseeing, 14 Rother St. (℃ **01708/866-000;** www.citysightseeing.co.uk), offers guided tours of Stratford that leave from outside the tourist office. Open-top, double-decker buses depart every 15 to 30 minutes daily between 9:30am and 5:30pm (until 3:30pm in winter). You can take the 1-hour ride without stops or get off and on at any or all the town's five Shakespeare properties, including Mary Arden's House in Wilmcote. The tour ticket is valid all day but doesn't include admission into any of the houses. The bus tour cost is £9 ($18) for adults, £7 ($14) for seniors and students, £4 ($8) for children under 12. You can buy your ticket on the bus.

OUTDOOR ACTIVITIES

Avon Boating (℃ **01789/267-073**) offers half-hour cruises on the River Avon in traditional Edwardian launches, with regular departures Easter through October (10am–dusk) from Swan's Nest Boatyard near the Royal Shakespeare Theatre. The cost is £4 ($8) for adults, £2.50 ($5) for children. Rowboats, punts, and canoes can be rented for £3 ($6) per hour.

3 Shopping

Stratford's weekly **Market,** held on Friday, dates back over 800 years. The **Shakespeare Bookshop,** in the Shakespeare Centre, Henley Street (℃ **01789/201-819**), is the region's best bookshop for Shakespeare-related material.

The nearby **Pickwick Gallery,** 32 Henley St. (℃ **01789/294-861**), carries a wide variety of old and new engravings. Elaine Rippon Craft Gallery, Shakespeare Craft Yard off Henley Street (℃ **01789/415-481**), designs, creates, and sells sumptuous silk and velvet accessories and carries fine British contemporary crafts.

4 Where to Dine

Hathaway Tea Rooms & Bakery TEAROOM   For afternoon tea in atmospheric surroundings, try this tearoom on the second floor of a building that dates from 1610. Cream tea comes with homemade fruit scones, clotted cream, and jam, and high tea includes a variety of sandwiches. You can also get an English breakfast and light meals throughout the day.

19 High St. ⓒ **01789/292-404.** Main courses £5.50–£7.50 ($11–$15); cream tea £5.25 ($11); high tea £6.95 ($14). No credit cards. Daily 9am–5:30pm.

Lamb's of Sheep Street ⓐ MODERN BRITISH   Housed in one of Stratford's oldest buildings (it dates back to 1547), with low ceilings and an oak-beamed dining room, Lamb's serves up modern British cooking with flair. It's especially good for a pre-theatre dinner. Typical menu offerings include roasted saddle of lamb, duck breast with cabbage and potatoes, and non-meat choices such as open ravioli with sautéed wild mushrooms.

12 Sheep St. ⓒ **01789/292-554.** Reservations recommended. Main courses £11–£19 ($22–$36); fixed-price lunch £10–£15 ($20–$30); fixed-price dinner £15–£20 ($30–$40). AE, MC, V. Mon–Sat noon–2pm and 5:30–10pm; Sun noon–2pm and 6–9:30pm.

The Oppo ⓐ BRITISH/INTERNATIONAL   Good bistro fare is served up in this cozy, oak-beamed restaurant, housed in a 16th-century building in the heart of Stratford. Lunch and dinner choices are a mix of traditional and Modern British cuisine with some pasta dishes and Cajun breast of chicken. For dessert, you may want to try sticky toffee pudding, a traditional favorite.

13 Sheep St. ⓒ **01789/269-980.** Reservations recommended. Main courses £9–£17 ($18–$34). MC, V. Daily noon–2pm and 5–11pm.

Quarto's ⓐⓐ BRITISH/CONTINENTAL   This lovely restaurant and cafe-bar in the Royal Shakespeare Theatre looks out on the River Avon's gliding white swans. On the daily changing (and wide-ranging) menu you might find pot roast guinea fowl, roast cod, loin of pork, rib of beef, and stuffed baby peppers. A fixed-price lunch special is offered on matinee days.

In the Royal Shakespeare Theatre. ⓒ **01789/799-9217.** Reservations required. Main courses £9–£18 ($18–$36); fixed-price matinee lunch £16 ($32). AE, MC, V. Noon–2:30pm on matinee days (call for schedule) and Mon–Sat 5:45pm–midnight.

5 Extending Your Stay

Hamlet House *(Kids*   This unpretentious, well-maintained B&B in a Victorian town house is a convenient 3-minute walk from the train station and close to everything else in Stratford. Two of its five guest rooms have private bathrooms; the others share a toilet and shower. Yvonne and Paul, the owners, are helpful and hospitable, and welcome children. The breakfast is hearty.

52 Grove Rd., Stratford-upon-Avon, Warwickshire CV37 6PB. ⓒ **01789/204-386.** www.hamlethouse.com. £47–£56 ($94–$112) double. Rates include English breakfast. No credit cards.

The Payton ⓐ   The five en-suite guest rooms in this Georgian-era town house are larger and furnished with more style than those at Hamlet House. The B&B is both charming and quiet, located on a side street that's just a 3-minute walk from the town center.

6 St. John St., Stratford-upon-Avon, Warwickshire CV37 6UB. ℂ/fax **01789/266-442.** www.payton.co.uk. £70–£75 ($140–$150) double. Rates include English breakfast. MC, V.

The Shakespeare Hotel Stratford 𝒦𝒦   The Shakespeare successfully blends old and new: Parts of this centrally located hotel date from 1635 and preserve the original Tudor-era beams and stone floor, but all 76 rooms were completely refurbished in 2005 in a comfortably elegant and traditional style. The rooms come with a host of modern amenities, and all the bathrooms have bathtubs with showers.

Chapel St., Stratford-upon-Avon, Warwickshire CV37 6ER. ℂ **0870/400-8182.** Fax 01789/415-411. www. mercure.com. £90–£190 ($180–$380) double. Rates include English breakfast. AE, DC, MC, V.

Thistle Stratford-upon-Avon   If this hotel were any closer to the Royal Shakespeare Festival theatres, the guests would be onstage. Thistle is a British chain of upscale full-service hotels, offering well-decorated rooms (63 of them in this hotel) with an abundance of amenities. The building dates back to 1791 and has been decorated to look like a traditional Georgian town house.

Waterside, Stratford-upon-Avon, Warwickshire CV37 6BA. ℂ **800/847-4358** in U.S. and Canada, or 01789/294-949. Fax 01789/415-874. www.thistlehotels.com. £125–£170 ($250–$340) double. AE, DC, MC, V.

Winchester

One of the best-kept and prettiest small cities in England, Winchester evokes its ancient heritage with pride. An important Roman military headquarters, it became capital of the ancient kingdom of Wessex after the Romans withdrew from Britain, and remained the most important city in England up until the time of the Norman Conquest. Winchester Cathedral, the town's chief glory, was founded by William the Conqueror, who came to Winchester to claim his throne after the Battle of Hastings in 1066. It was in Winchester that William compiled his inventory of England, the famous *Domesday Book*.

Winchester retained its power until the 13th century, when London, with its strategic position on the Thames, became the capital and most important city in the land. Winchester continued to thrive, though, and became an important center of the medieval wool trade.

The ancient cathedral, which, throughout much of the Middle Ages, was the seat of a powerful diocese that stretched from London to the English Channel, is alone worth a trip, but there are many other charms to be discovered in what is, these days, an attractive county town (Winchester is the county seat of Hampshire). Jane Austen fans can visit the great novelist's home in the nearby village of Chawton, and her grave in Winchester Cathedral. You'll also enjoy walking Winchester's attractive streets, strolling through the water meadows that extend behind the cathedral to the banks of the River Itchen, and just soaking in the vibe of a well-preserved English cathedral city.

If you're really ambitious and can't get your fill of cathedrals and medieval charm, you can spend the morning in Winchester and the afternoon in nearby **Salisbury,** only 20 miles (32km) west (see trip 20), or vice versa. Likewise, you might decide to spend a day in Winchester, take the time to venture out to Chawton, and spend the night (see our recommendations in the last section) before heading the next morning to Salisbury. See "Getting Around," below, for information on travel between Winchester and Salisbury.

1 Essentials

VISITOR INFORMATION

The **Tourist Information Centre,** in the Guildhall on Broadway (© **01962/ 840-500;** www.visitwinchester.co.uk), is open year-round Monday through Saturday

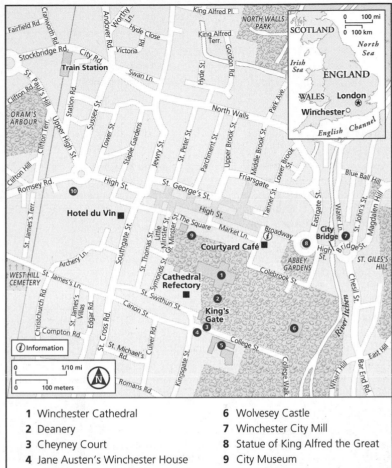

1 Winchester Cathedral
2 Deanery
3 Cheyney Court
4 Jane Austen's Winchester House
5 Winchester College

6 Wolvesey Castle
7 Winchester City Mill
8 Statue of King Alfred the Great
9 City Museum
10 The Great Hall

from 9:30am to 5:30pm (10am–5pm Oct–Mar), and also 11am to 4pm on Sundays from May through September. They distribute free maps of the town and provide information on all local attractions.

SCHEDULING CONSIDERATIONS

Though Winchester is a busy country town, crowds are never a problem and you can enjoy a visit any time of year. The world-famous Winchester Cathedral Choir sings at all main services, including **Evensong,** held Monday though Saturday at 5:30pm and Sunday at 3:30pm. Visitors are welcome to attend. In late July of alternating years (the next one will be in 2008), the choirs of Winchester, Salisbury, and Chichester cathedrals perform in Winchester Cathedral during the **Southern Cathedrals Festival.** For information and tickets, contact the Winchester Tourist Information Centre or visit www.southerncathedralsfestival.org.uk.

Winchester Highlights

• Visiting ancient Winchester Cathedral.

• Jane Austen associations in Winchester and nearby Chawton.

• Exploring the charming streets and byways of Winchester.

GETTING THERE

BY TRAIN

Frequent, direct train service from London's Waterloo Station makes getting to Winchester fast and easy. Service begins at 5:30am; trains return to London until 11:24pm. The trip takes just over 1 hour; a day return ticket costs about £24 ($48). For train schedules and information, call **National Rail Enquiries** at © 08457/ 484-950 or visit www.nationalrail.co.uk.

BY BUS

National Express (© 0990/808-080; www.nationalexpress.com) runs several buses a day from London's Victoria Coach Station. The fastest trip takes 2 hours (the longest, over 4 hr.); a ticket costs £13 ($26) return. The bus lets you off on Broadway, in the center of town.

BY CAR

If you're driving from London, take the M3 to Junction 9; the trip takes about an hour and a half, depending on traffic in and around London. You can't drive in the town center, but there are 29 car parks, including two on the east side of the cathedral. Convenient, long-term car parks are located on Friarsgate, Chesil Street, Cattle Market, Durngate, Gladstone Street, St. Peters, and Worthy Lane.

GETTING AROUND

The center of town is about a half-mile from the train station. To get there, you can easily walk (10 min.), hop on a Park and Ride bus (40p/80¢), or take a taxi (about £4/$8) from the rank outside the station. If you want to reserve a taxi, call **Wessex** (© 01962/877-749) or **Wintax** (© 01962/878-727). Anyone can use Park and Ride buses around town for the 20p (40¢) rate along the circuit of stops: Broadway, Brooks, Jewry Street, Castle, Station, City Road, North Walls, and Broadway. **Wilts and Dorset buses** (© 01722/336855; www.wdbus.co.uk) provide daily service between Winchester and Salisbury, with several buses leaving each city for the other between 8 and 9:30am as well as in the early evening; the fare is £5 ($10) and the trip takes about 1 hour and 45 minutes. If you're driving, follow A30 and A272 between the two cities; the trip by car takes only about 45 minutes.

2 A Day in Winchester

Winchester is a walking city par excellence, with all sorts of fascinating corners. The following tour hits the main sights and takes about 2 hours—longer, if you linger.

Begin your tour at ❶ **Winchester Cathedral** ✹✹✹ (© 01962/857-200), in the center of town. One of Europe's greatest cathedrals, the 900-year-old structure, begun in 1079, is graced with the longest nave (central aisle) of any church in Europe, and, as befits a cathedral that was for so long a symbol of power and might, is the repository of many historic treasures. Mortuary chests containing the remains of Saxon kings and bishops sit atop the 15th-century **Great Screen.** In all, 12 English kings lie here, indicative of Winchester's long reign as capital of Wessex and England after the Norman Conquest. **Jane Austen's grave** is a simple, stone-floor marker in the north aisle, near a 12th-century font made of Tournai marble carved with stories of St. Nicholas, the patron saint of pawnbrokers long before he became known as Old Saint Nick. Winchester's own saint, Swithin, is also honored with a shrine. This ninth-century bishop requested a simple burial and was laid to rest outside the city walls. A century later, though, on July 15, 971, his bones were removed and given what was thought to be proper burial in the cathedral that stood on the site of the present church. The skies opened and it rained for 40 days. (It is still local legend that rain on July 15 is a warning that it will rain for the next 40 days.) The beautiful choir stalls were carved in about 1308, and two of the cathedral's prize possessions are simple benches that date from the reigns of the Norman kings; these humble pieces are some of the oldest examples of wooden furniture in the world. The **Winchester Bible,** an extraordinary illuminated manuscript, is displayed in the library. Admission to the cathedral is £5 ($10), £4 ($8) for students and seniors; the price includes a free 1-hour tour (available hourly, Mon–Sat 10am–3pm). The cathedral is open daily from 8:30am to 6pm (on Sun it closes at 5:30pm).

Adjacent to the cathedral is the ❷ **Deanery,** formed from 13th-century buildings that belonged to the Priory of St. Swithin (which stood here before Henry VIII dissolved all the monasteries in 1539). ❸ **Cheyney Court,** the picturesque half-timbered porter's lodge beside the ancient priory gate (King's Gate), was formerly the bishop of Winchester's courthouse. The long line of powerful Winchester bishops includes William of Wykeham (1324–1404), who also served as Chancellor of England. Having accrued considerable wealth, Wykeham devoted himself to public works and founded New College at Oxford and Winchester College, part of the cathedral compound; students here are still called Wykehamists. The Deanery and Cheyney Court buildings are not open to the public.

Walk through King's Gate and turn left onto College Street. Almost immediately you come to ❹ **Jane Austen's House,** with a plaque on it. (The house is not open to the public.) This is where Jane Austen died on July 18, 1817, at the age of 42. The ailing writer came to Winchester from the nearby village of Chawton (see "More Things to See & Do," below) so she could be close to her doctor. She is buried in Winchester Cathedral. Another famous resident of the Close was Izaac Walton, author of the *Compleat Angler,* who died here in 1683. Farther down Queen Street are the buildings of ❺ **Winchester College,** the oldest public school in England, founded by William of Wykeham, bishop of Winchester and chancellor of England, in 1382. There's no public access to the college.

Follow College Street to the end, turn left, and take the short, lovely walk along the narrow River Itchen, which served as part of the Roman defense system when the Empire still held England, and through the Water Meadows. Ambles along the river and across these green meadows inspired the poet John Keats to write his poem, "To Autumn"; the path is aptly called "Keats Walk." To your left are the remains of ❻ **Wolvesey Castle,** a 12th-century palace that was home to many bishops of Winchester and was destroyed during the Civil War of 1642 to 1649; Queen Mary I ("Bloody Mary") and Philip of Spain held their wedding breakfast here in the East Hall in 1554. You can roam through the evocative ruins from April through the end of September,

> ⌒ *Moments* **Evensong**
>
> Sitting in the choir of Winchester Cathedral and listening to Evensong (5:30pm Mon–Sat, 3:30pm Sun) is nothing less than sublime.

daily, 10am to 5pm; admission is free. Enough walls, arches, and foundations remain to give an idea of the enormous size and grandeur of the immense palace.

The **Hospital of Saint Cross** ⍟, just down the walk, is an almshouse founded by William de Blois, a grandson of William the Conqueror, in 1132. The hospital was a resting place for pilgrims who once made their way to the cathedral to honor Saint Swithin, and also housed and fed crusaders on their way to Southampton to set sail for the Holy Land. The 25 resident brothers still do their duty and, along with showing you the kitchen brethren's hall and garden, will serve you a small chunk of bread. The hospital is open 9:30am to 5pm in summer and 10:30am to 3:30pm in winter; admission is £2.50 ($5) for adults, £2 ($4) for seniors and students, and 50p ($1) for children.

At the end of Bridge Street, you come to the City Bridge, an 1813 reconstruction of a Saxon span built 1,000 years earlier. On the opposite side of the bridge is the ❼ **Winchester City Mill** (🕾 **01962/870-057**). You can stop in to have a look at the mill's 18th-century machinery (still operational), an exhibition on the history and surroundings, and a pretty island garden that's home to kingfishers, otters, and water voles. From March through Christmas the mill is open Wednesday through Sunday 11am to 5pm. Admission is £3.40 ($6.80).

Turn left on Bridge Street and you come to the famous bronze ❽ **statue of King Alfred the Great** holding his sword aloft. What made Alfred so "great"? Probably that he was an enlightened man in the Dark Ages, and drove off the marauding Danes. A soldier, statesman, and scholar, he made Winchester capital of his southern England kingdom, called Wessex. Winchester remained as powerful and prosperous as London up to and beyond the Norman Conquest of 1066.

Walk down Broadway to The Square, where you find the small, attractive ❾ **City Museum** (🕾 **01962/863-064**). A room devoted to Roman Winchester contains a fine Roman mosaic centerpiece. Admission is free. Hours are Monday through Saturday 10am to 5pm, Sunday noon to 5pm (Nov–Mar until 4pm and closed Mon).

Continue down High Street and turn left (south) through the Westgate, a fortified medieval gateway. All that remains of once-mighty Winchester Castle is ❿ **The Great Hall** ⍟ (🕾 **01962/846-476**) on Castle Avenue. The stone hall is famous for displaying what has for centuries been called the "Round Table" of King Arthur and his knights. Looking like a giant Wheel of Fortune, the painted wooden table is indeed old, but not old enough to have served sixth-century Arthur (himself probably legendary) and his knights, and has hung here for some 600 years. The hall is open daily 10am to 5pm (until 4pm on winter weekends), and admission is by donation.

ORGANIZED TOURS

Guided walking tours of Winchester leave from the Tourist Information Centre and make a 1½-hour circuit around the city. This is a good way to gain an overall introduction to the history and main sites in historic Winchester. Tours take place at the following times: November through March, Saturday only at 11am; April, Monday through Friday at 2:30pm and Saturday at 11am; May and June, daily at 11am, Saturday at

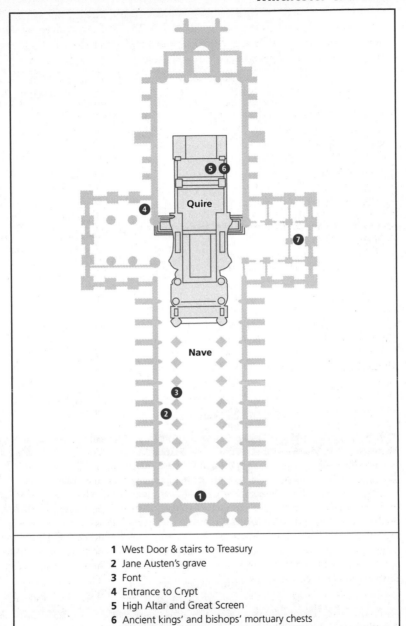

1 West Door & stairs to Treasury
2 Jane Austen's grave
3 Font
4 Entrance to Crypt
5 High Altar and Great Screen
6 Ancient kings' and bishops' mortuary chests
7 Stairs to Cathedral Library & Triforium Gallery

11am and 2:30pm, and Sunday at 2:30pm; July and August, Monday through Saturday at 11am and 2:30pm, and Sunday at 2:30pm; October, Monday through Saturday at 11am and 2:30pm. Tour price is £4 ($8).

MORE THINGS TO SEE & DO

If you're a Jane Austen fan, you might enjoy a visit to **Jane Austen's House** 👾👾 (ⓒ **01420/83262**) in Chawton, about 17 miles (28km) northeast of Winchester. The witty novelist lived in this sturdy redbrick Georgian house with her mother and sister, Casandra, from 1809 until 1817, revising her novels *Pride and Prejudice* and *Sense and Sensibility*, and writing *Mansfield Park* and *Emma*. Creatively, this was where she spent the most productive years of her life. Austen family memorabilia is spread throughout the house, which is open March through December daily 11am to 4pm (Sat–Sun only Dec–Feb). Admission is £5 ($10) adults, £4 ($8) seniors and students.

Stagecoach Hampshire Bus (ⓒ **01256/464-501**) no. X64 runs from Winchester bus station to Chawton at 10 past each hour Monday to Saturday and takes about 30 minutes; Sunday and public holidays, bus no. 64 leaves at 20 past the hour starting at 10:20am and every 2 hours thereafter. Ask the driver to drop you at the Alton Butts stop, the one closest to the Austen house. From the bus stop, walk toward the railway bridge, cross the very busy road, and continue straight on, passing a brown tourist sign and following the road beneath the underpass; the walk from the bus stop to Jane Austen's House in Chawton takes about 15 minutes. For more information, inquire at the Tourist Information Centre in Winchester. If you drive from Winchester, take A31 northeast; you'll see a signed turnoff to the house from the roundabout junction with A32.

> **Impressions**
>
> . . . they were wise enough to be contented with the house as it was, and each of them was busy in arranging their particular concerns and endeavoring, by placing around them their books and other possessions, to form themselves a home.
>
> —Jane Austen, *Sense and Sensibility*

3 Shopping

Carol Darby Jewellery, 23 Little Minster St. (ⓒ **01962/867-671**), is owned by designer Carol Spring, who designed and made the engagement and wedding rings for Princess Anne and Commander Laurence. She can design specialty pieces and make them to your specifications. **Cadogan & James,** 30–31 The Square (ⓒ **01962/877-399**), sells clothes from around the British Isles, including colorful cashmeres and waistcoats. The **Clock-Work Shop,** 6a Parchment St. (ⓒ **01962/842-331**), stocks a large selection of restored antique clocks and barometers. Food, flowers, and crafts are found at **Winchester Street Market** (ⓒ **01962/848-325**), held Wednesday through Saturday on Middle Brook Street.

4 Where to Dine

Cathedral Refectory LIGHT MEALS   Located behind a medieval wall next to the cathedral, this appealing spot specializes in desserts, Hampshire cream teas, and meals made from fresh local ingredients.

Inner Close, Cathedral. ⓒ **01962/853-224**. Main courses £6–£10 ($12–$20). No credit cards. Mon–Sat 9:30am–5pm; Sun 10am–5pm (until 4:30pm Nov–Feb).

Courtyard Café ⟡ LIGHT MEALS   This pleasant cafe right behind the Tourist Information Centre is a great, informal spot for a morning cappuccino; homemade soups, salads, and sandwiches at lunchtime; or an afternoon tea.

Winchester Guildhall, Broadway. ℂ **01962/622-177.** Main courses £5–£7 ($10–$14). MC, V. Daily 9:30am–5pm.

5 Extending Your Stay

Hotel du Vin ⟡⟡   A converted Georgian house at the edge of the city center is the setting for this stylish and lively hotel, part of a small British chain. Rooms are handsomely painted in deep tones and decorated with a mix of contemporary and antique pieces; the most pleasant rooms are those entered directly from the garden. The hotel has an excellent bistro serving hearty French fare and, naturally, a splendid selection of wines.

Southgate St., Winchester, Hampshire SO23 9EF. ℂ **01962/841-414.** www.hotelduvin.com. £130–£200 ($260–$400) double. Rates include English breakfast. AE, MC, V.

Windsor & Eton

*L*ocated in Windsor, Berkshire, 20 miles (32km) from the center of London, **Windsor Castle** is the second-most-visited historic building in England (just behind the Tower of London) and one of the queen's official residences. Constructed some 900 years ago by William the Conqueror, the imposing castle, with its skyline of towers and battlements, rises from the center of the 4,800-acre (1,920-hectare) Great Park. **Eton,** a town right across the Thames from Windsor, is the site of Eton College, one of the most exclusive boys' schools in the world.

You may want to round out your visit to historic Windsor by adding on a short trip to nearby **Runnymede,** a hallowed site in the annals of English history, as it was there, in 1215, that King John signed the Magna Carta. If you're traveling with children, you may want to combine your trip to the castle with a visit to nearby **Legoland.** In fact, that attraction, along with Queen Mary's Dollhouse, the spectacle of the Changing of the Guard, and just the sight of the mighty castle on its hilltop, make Windsor a good choice for kids. If you're planning on visiting only the castle, with a quick walk through the town and Eton, allow half a day for your trip. A full day, however, will give you time to see more attractions, including Runnymede, and to enjoy this pleasant town at your leisure.

1 Essentials

VISITOR INFORMATION
The **Royal Windsor Information Centre,** Old Booking Hall, Royal Windsor Station, Thames St. (© **01753/743-900;** www.windsor.gov.uk), can provide detailed information about Windsor, Eton, and nearby attractions such as Legoland and Runnymede. The center is open Monday through Saturday from 10am to 5pm (May–Sept 9:30am–5:30pm); Sunday 11am to 4pm (May–Sept 10am–4pm).

SCHEDULING CONSIDERATIONS
Windsor Castle is open year-round, but visiting hours are subject to change at short notice; be sure to verify that the castle and State Apartments are open, especially in June when there are many official engagements. The crowds can be daunting from June through mid-September; if you visit then, be sure to go early. Unless you love the madding crowd, avoid Windsor during Ascot, which is generally held from June 20

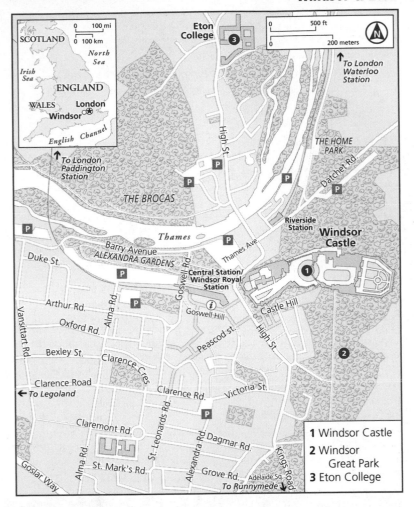

to 24. If you want to watch the 11am **Changing of the Guard** from outside the castle, you need to be on High Street by 10:50am; keep in mind that the ceremony takes place on alternate days August through March and never on Sunday. **Eton College** is open to visitors from late March until early October (closed May 28–June 17), with daily guided tours offered at 2:15 and 3:15pm. **Legoland** is closed November through March.

GETTING THERE
BY TRAIN
Windsor has two train stations, Windsor Central Station and Windsor and Eton Riverside Station, both of them about a 10-minute walk from Windsor Castle. Trains run hourly or more often from London's Paddington Station to Windsor Central Station with a change at Slough. Direct 55-minute trains leave from London's Waterloo

Windsor & Eton Highlights

- Touring 900-year-old Windsor Castle.
- Strolling through Windsor Great Park and alongside the Thames.
- Visiting Eton, England's most prestigious public school.

Station to Windsor & Eton Riverside Station. Hourly service begins at 5:58am on weekdays from Waterloo, with direct trains departing Windsor for London until 10:53pm. The cheapest day return fare is about £14 ($28). For train information and schedules, call **National Rail Enquiries** (© **08457/484950**) or visit www.nationalrail.co.uk.

BY BUS

Greenline (© **0870/6087261;** www.greenline.co.uk) has frequent direct bus service starting at 7:50am from London's Victoria Coach Station to Windsor (and Legoland). Buses depart as often as every 15 minutes for the journey, which takes from 55 minutes to 1 hour and 15 minutes. A return ticket costs £8 ($16) for adults, £4 ($8) for children.

BY CAR

If you're driving from London, take M4 west. Windsor is a historic town, and parking is carefully managed. The trip takes about an hour, depending on traffic. You'll find outdoor and indoor car parks as you approach the town center. Follow the long stay signs for cheaper all-day parking. Windsor's Park and Ride, based at Legoland, provides daily bus service into the town center every 30 minutes, more frequently from June through September.

GETTING AROUND

Walking is the best way to see Windsor and the town of Eton. A hop-on/hop-off bus service makes a circuit of all the main sights in town. (See "Organized Tours," below.) There are taxi ranks outside both train stations. If you want to reserve a cab, call **Windsor Radio** (© **01753/677-677**) or **5 Star** (© **01753/858-888**).

2 A Day in Windsor & Eton

Start your day in Windsor at the town's main attraction, ❶ **Windsor Castle** ✶✶✶ (© **01753/831-118**), one of three official residences of the queen and reputedly her favorite. When the queen is in residence, the Royal Standard flies from the Round Tower. At all other times you will see the Union Flag. The castle (visible and signposted from both train stations) is the largest inhabited castle in the world and the oldest in continuous occupation. It's been home to the British monarchs for over 900 years, and no other royal residence has played such an important role in the nation's history.

On a self-guided tour you can visit the **State Apartments** ✶✶✶, from the intimate chambers of Charles II to the enormous Waterloo Chamber, built to commemorate the victory over Napoleon in 1815. All are furnished with important works of art from the Royal Collection and are open year-round. Open from October until late March,

Royal Remains at Windsor

St. George's Chapel 𝒢𝒢𝒢 (www.stgeorges-windsor.org) in Windsor Castle is one of the finest ecclesiastical buildings in England and the final resting place of 10 English monarchs, including Edward IV; Henry VIII and his third (and favorite) wife, Jane Seymour (who died in childbirth in 1537); Charles I; George V and his wife, Queen Mary; and George VI. Elizabeth, the Queen Mother, and Princess Margaret are also buried here.

Construction of the chapel—one of the finest examples of medieval architecture in Europe—began in 1475 and took 50 years to complete. St. George's is the Chapel of the Most Noble Order of the Garter, Britain's highest order of chivalry, founded by Edward III in 1348. In 2005, the chapel was the scene of the marriage blessing of Prince Charles and Camilla Parker Bowles following their civil ceremony in Windsor Guildhall. The Albert Memorial Chapel, just beyond St. George's Chapel, was converted by Queen Victoria into a memorial to her husband, Prince Albert, who died in 1861.

the **semi-staterooms** 𝒢𝒢 were created by George IV in the 1820s as part of a new series of Royal Apartments for his personal occupation, and they continue to be used by the queen for official entertaining. Damaged in a 1992 fire, they have been restored to their original flamboyant appearance and contain furniture and works of art chosen by George IV. The semi-staterooms include the Green Drawing Room, Crimson Drawing Room, State Dining Room, and Octagon Dining Room. In a separate area of the castle, you'll find **Queen Mary's Dollhouse** 𝒢𝒢, a marvelous miniature palace designed by the architect Sir Edwin Lutyens as a present for Queen Mary (wife of King George V) in 1924. It took nearly 1,500 artists and craftsmen 3 years to create this extraordinary work, full of incredible detailing—note the moving elevators and running water in the bathrooms. Windsor Castle opens daily at 9:45am; November through February, it closes at 4:15pm (last entry 3pm); March through October, it closes at 5:30pm (last entry 4pm). It's closed March 28, June 16, and December 25 and 26. Admission is £14.20 ($28) for adults, £12.70 ($25) for seniors and students, and £8 ($16) for children under 17.

The **Changing of the Guard** 𝒢𝒢𝒢 is as much of an event at Windsor as it is at Buckingham Palace, and the guards here are usually accompanied by a band, although this is subject to weather conditions. April through July, the ceremony takes place at 11am Monday through Saturday (on alternate days the rest of the year). You can watch the guards as they march up High Street and into the castle, but to see the actual ceremony, you need to be inside the castle (admission required).

From the castle, walk down Castle Hill and follow High Street south to Park Street, which takes you to Long Walk, a pedestrian walkway through 4,800-acre (1,920-hectare) ❷ **Windsor Great Park** 𝒢𝒢𝒢 (© 01753/743-900), open year-round from dawn to dusk. The current contours of the park, once a favored hunting spot for Saxon kings, were established in the 1360s. The park today is a perfect place for picnics, walking, and cycling. A footpath map of the park is available from the Royal Windsor Information Centre.

Fun Fact **Dress Code**

Strolling down Eton High Street, you may see some boys wearing black tail-coats and waistcoats and pinstriped trousers. They're Eton boys, and they're wearing the School Dress, a uniform policy started in the 1850s and still in effect today.

To explore the town of Eton and its famous school (it's known as a public school in Britain, though North Americans would consider it private), stroll north on Windsor High Street and follow it as it becomes Thames Street, crosses the river, and becomes Eton High Street. Eton High Street leads you to the entrance of ❸ **Eton College** ⊛ (✆ **01753 671177;** www.etoncollege.com), founded in 1440 by the 18-year-old King Henry VI to provide free education to poor scholars who would go on to study at King's College, Cambridge. Over the centuries, the student body has expanded to about 1,280 boys, ages 13 to 18, who are admitted by competitive examination. One of the most exclusive schools in the world, it's graduated 18 former British prime ministers (including the duke of Wellington), numerous heirs to the throne (Prince William studied here), and leading literary figures (from George Orwell to Ian Fleming). The cloisters, the chapel (note the 15th-c. artwork and reconstructed fan vaulting), the oldest classroom in the college, and the Museum of Eton Life (check out the canes the senior boys once used to dole out punishment to their juniors) are all open to visitors daily: late-March to mid-April and June to September from 10:30am to 4:30pm; mid-April to June and September to late March from 2 to 4:30pm. Admission is £4 ($8) for adults, £3.25 ($6.50) for children. With a 1-hour guided tour (at 2:15 and 3:15pm), the cost is £5 ($10) for adults and £4.20 ($8.40) for children.

ORGANIZED TOURS

City Sightseeing (✆ **01708/865-656;** www.city-sightseeing.com) offers guided bus tours through Windsor, Old Windsor, and Eton. Buses depart year-round (every 15–60 min., depending on the season) from outside Windsor Castle beside the statue of Queen Victoria. The complete loop tour lasts an hour but tickets are valid all day, and you can hop on and off along the route as often as you wish. The tickets, available at the Information Centre or on the bus, cost £9.50 ($19) for adults, £8.50 ($17) for seniors and students, £4.50 ($9) for children, and £25 ($50) for a family (two adults, two children).

Orchard Poyle Carriage Rides (✆ **01784/435-983**) are a fun and elegant way to tour Windsor in a horse-drawn carriage. You're taken along High Street, into Park Street, then down the Long Walk into Windsor Great Park. Carriage rides are available year-round from 12:30 to 5:30pm (later in summer), subject to weather conditions. The cost is £19 ($38) per carriage for a 30-minute ride, £38 ($76) per carriage for a 1-hour ride. The carriage collects visitors from High Street, opposite the Harte and Garter Hotel in front of the castle wall, to the left of the statue of Queen Victoria. In high season, it's a good idea to book in advance.

French Brothers Boats Ltd (✆ **01735/851-900;** www.boat-trips.co.uk) offers 35-minute and 2-hour boat rides from the promenade, next to the bridge over to Eton. River trips are subject to weather conditions, but they generally operate daily from the third week in February through October and into November. The 35-minute trips

(£4.80/$9.60) run every half-hour between 11am and 5pm from Easter onward; 2-hour trips (£7.60/$15) are also available at 1:30 and 2:30pm (Apr–May and Sept–Oct at 2pm only).

MORE THINGS TO SEE & DO

Legoland Windsor *Ⓡ Ⓚids*   Few theme parks are as impressive as the 150-acre (61-hectare) Legoland Windsor, or as expensive. It took 20 million of the famous Danish toy company's little plastic building bricks just to create Miniland (an extremely detailed re-creation of several European villages and cities), one of seven different zones offering over 50 attractions and rides (wet ones, high ones, fast ones, scaled-down ones for little kids). It's a good idea to buy your ticket in advance, because the lines can be extremely long, especially during school holidays. You can buy tickets by phone, online (reduced-price), and at all train stations from Waterloo to Windsor.

Winkfield Rd. Ⓒ **08705/040-404.** www.legoland.co.uk. 1-day admission £33 ($66) adults, £25 ($50) kids under 16 (free for kids under 3). These are peak, at-the-gate prices; you can save several pounds by going off-peak (weekdays, no school holidays). Daily Apr–Oct 10am–6pm (to 5pm Tues–Thurs). A shuttle bus from both Windsor train stations is free with a pre-booked Legoland ticket or by booking a ticket with South West Trains. If you're driving from Windsor, follow Legoland signs from M4 (Junction 6), M3 (Junction 3), and M25 (Junction 13).

Runnymede *Ⓡ*   Located 3 miles (4km) southeast of Windsor on the banks of the Thames, Runnymede is the famous meadow where King John sealed the Magna Carta in 1215 (after enormous pressure was put on him by his feudal barons and lords), establishing the principle of the constitutional monarchy and affirming the individual's right to justice and liberty. In 1957 the American Bar Association erected a memorial to commemorate the fact that the American Constitution is based on the Magna Carta. Nearby, on an acre of ground given to the U.S. by Queen Elizabeth II, is a stone memorial erected in 1965 to the memory of former U.S. president John F. Kennedy. High on the hill is a memorial to the men and women of the Air Forces of the British Commonwealth who lost their lives in World War II. Runnymede is a peaceful place with magnificent views across the Thames Valley.

A boat trip to Runnymede makes a fun excursion: **French Brothers** (Ⓒ **01735/ 851-900;** www.boat-trips.co.uk) provides service from Windsor to Runnymede on Wednesday and Friday through Sunday at 4pm, from the last week in April to the third week in September. The fare is £9 ($18) return.

On the A308, 3 miles (4km) southeast of Windsor. Free admission. Daily dawn–dusk. By car, take the A308 from Windsor toward Staines.

OUTDOOR ACTIVITIES

The splendid 180-mile (288km) **Thames Path National Trail,** which begins at Thames Head near Kemble in the Cotswolds and runs all the way to the Thames Barrier, east of London, passes through Windsor. You'll find flat, paved paths, suitable for walking or biking, on both sides of the river around Windsor. The views here are gently bucolic, at times almost suburban, pretty and pleasant rather than spectacular.

With its Great Park and paved riverside paths, Windsor is a great place for biking. You can rent bicycles for a half or full day at **Windsor Roller Rink & Cycle Hire,** Alexander Gardens (Ⓒ **01753/830-220**).

3 Shopping

Windsor Royal Station is a compact shopping area with designer-name shops. High Street/Thames Street in Windsor has many small shops. Peascod Street has larger stores, and boutiques line St. Leonard's Road. Eton's historic half-mile High Street has a diverse range of small family businesses, including clothing boutiques, jewelers, bookshops, art galleries, and gift shops.

4 Where to Dine

Gilbey's Bar & Restaurant WINE BAR   This specialist importer sells its French wines at shop prices alongside bottles from its own English vineyard. The bar menu is delicious and reasonable. Try a starter of soup with crusty bread, followed by smoked haddock fishcakes. In the summer, you can eat out in the garden.

82–83 High St., Eton. ℰ **01753/854-921.** Bar main courses £8 ($16); 2-course set menu £11 ($22). AE, DC, MC, V. Daily noon–2:30pm and 5:30–11pm.

York

*Y*ork, 195 miles (314km) north of London, is close enough for a day trip by fast train but worlds apart in character, one of the most historic cities in England and one of the best-preserved medieval cities in Europe. York began life as a Roman fort and settlement known as Eboracum, then became the Saxon Eofowic, capital of Northumbria, and then a thriving Viking settlement called Jorvik. Finally, after the Norman Conquest under William the Conqueror, the city became known as York, Queen of the North, a thriving port and trade center, and one of the most important cities of Europe in the Middle Ages.

Enormous York Minster, the largest Gothic structure north of the Alps, dominates the city, and, amazingly, 800-year-old walls and fortified gateways, incorporating parts of the Roman fortifications, still girdle the old town center. You can soak up the city's history while exploring its maze of ancient streets and hidden alleyways, known as snickelways. York is a thriving modern city, too, with a vibrant street life and good-natured attitude toward the two-million-plus visitors who come to town every year. Most of York's attractions can be visited in a day, but there's plenty here to induce an overnight stay. (See our hotel recommendations at the end of this chapter.) You may want to combine your trip to York with a visit to Castle Howard, one of Yorkshire's stateliest of stately homes, located just a few miles east.

1 Essentials

VISITOR INFORMATION

A convenient branch of the **Tourist Information Centre** (no phone), located right in the train station, is open Monday through Saturday from 9am to 5pm (to 6pm in summer), and Sunday from 10am to 4pm (to 5pm in summer). The main **Tourist Information Centre**, De Grey Rooms, Exhibition Square (© **01904/550-099;** www.visityork.org), near York Minster, is open the same hours.

SCHEDULING CONSIDERATIONS

York is a popular place and draws visitors year-round, especially on weekends and from Easter through the summer months. If you want the city more to yourself, visit from mid-October to mid-March, but be aware of reduced hours at many attractions. If you're visiting on Sundays, be aware that the cathedral doesn't open for visitors until 12:30pm. You might want to arrive in time to take one of the free guided walks offered daily at 10:15am; later tours at 2:15 and 6:45pm are offered in summer (see "Organized Tours," below). And you may want to linger longer in York in order to attend Evensong in York Minster at 5pm Monday through Saturday and 4pm on Sunday.

GETTING THERE
BY TRAIN
The only way to make York a viable day trip is to take one of the super-fast Intercity trains that leaves every half-hour from 8:30am onward out of London's King's Cross Station for the 2-hour trip to York's Rougier Street Station; returning trains depart York hourly until 9:28pm. There is always a variety of price options on this fast train; at press time, an advance-purchase day return cost £75.10 ($150). For train schedules and information, call **National Rail Enquiries** (© **08457/484950**) or visit www.nationalrail.co.uk.

BY BUS
National Express buses (© **0990/808080**) to York are cheaper than the train (£31.50/$63 return) but take a minimum of 5 hours, making them impracticable for a day trip.

BY CAR
If you're driving from London, take the M1 expressway north to Junction 45, east of Leeds, and from there continue northeast on A64 to York. The trip takes about 3½ to 4 hours but can be longer with traffic snags.

York Pass

The York Pass, available online at www.yorkpass.com or at either of the city's Tourist Information Centres, is a discount card that offers admission to 30 attractions, public transport around the city, and discounts on dining and entertainment. Many of the attractions it covers are of secondary importance and probably not worth your time, but the pass does include admission to York Minster, the Merchant Adventurers' Hall, Treasurer's House, York Castle Museum, and nearby Castle Howard, plus discounts on City Sightseeing buses and Jorvik. Cost for a 1-day pass is £21 ($42) for adults, £10 ($20) for children 5 to 15, and £58 ($116) for a family of two adults and two children. There are also 2- and 3-day passes available.

York

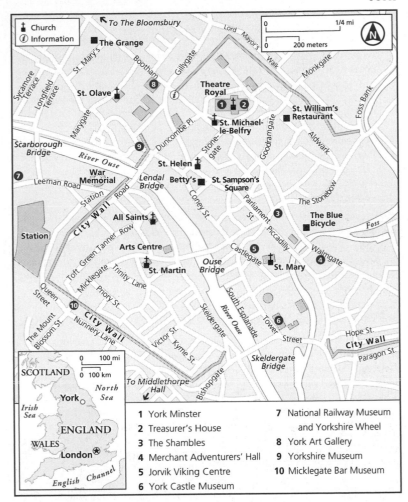

Church
ⓘ Information
The Grange
To The Bloomsbury

1 York Minster
2 Treasurer's House
3 The Shambles
4 Merchant Adventurers' Hall
5 Jorvik Viking Centre
6 York Castle Museum
7 National Railway Museum and Yorkshire Wheel
8 York Art Gallery
9 Yorkshire Museum
10 Micklegate Bar Museum

GETTING AROUND

The train station is a 5-minute walk from York's pedestrian-friendly historic city center, which is where you will want to spend your time, and is easily traversed on foot. If you need a taxi, contact **Station Taxis** (🕿 **01904/623-332**).

2 A Day in York

Begin your explorations at ❶ **York Minster** 𝕬𝕬𝕬, Minster Yard (🕿 **01904/557-216**). The largest Gothic cathedral in Northern Europe was begun in 1220, when Archbishop Walter de Grey set out to build a cathedral to rival the one in Canterbury (see trip 5), and was finally completed in 1472. Before entering, walk around the exterior to take in the massive size of the structure—534 feet (160m) long, 249 feet (75m) at its widest point, 90 feet (27m) high. The north and south transepts are the oldest

(*Fun Fact*   **Guy Fawkes: York's Infamous Son**

Who, you may ask, was Guy Fawkes (1570–1606), and what does he have to do with the fireworks set off throughout England on November 5? Guy, born in York, was the most famous guy behind the Gunpowder Plot, a conspiracy of Catholic extremists to blow up Protestant King James and the Houses of Parliament. On November 5, 1605, poor Guy was caught red-handed in the Palace of Westminster. The treasonous plot, and Guy Fawkes's subsequent execution, gave rise to a popular rhyme:

Please to remember / The 5th November:
Gunpowder, Treason and Plot.
We know of no reason / Why Gunpowder Treason
Should ever be forgot.

Every year since 1605, on November 5, towns, villages, and cities throughout England light bonfires, toss firecrackers, and parade or burn an effigy of Guy Fawkes to celebrate his failure to blow up the king and the parliament. Guy Fawkes Night is perhaps the longest-running tradition in England, even though the religious and royalist sentiments that inspired it have long vanished.

parts of the cathedral, and the east end and west tower were the last sections to be completed. Light in the cavernous interior is diffused by half of all the medieval stained glass in England; the Great West Window, with stained glass dating from 1338, is called the "Heart of Yorkshire." A 15th-century choir screen decorated with statues of 15 kings of England, from William I (the Conqueror) to Henry VI, separates the nave from the choir. In the south transept, you can descend into the undercroft, where excavations have revealed the Roman basilica that stood here nearly 2,000 years ago, as well as portions of a Roman street and an earlier Norman cathedral. From the nave, a separate entrance leads to the 13th-century octagonal chapter house, filled with superlative stone carvings and medieval glass. You can ascend the mighty tower for a fabulous view of York and the surrounding countryside. A combined-admission to the church, chapter house, undercroft, crypt, treasury, and tower is £9 ($18) for adults, £7.50 ($15) for seniors, £3 ($6) for children under 16; admission to the crypt, undercroft, and treasury is £3.50 ($7) for adults, £2 ($4) for children 5 to 15. The minster is open Monday to Saturday from 9am to 5pm, and Sunday noon to 3:45pm.

Next to the cathedral, in Minster Yard, stands an elegant stone house known as ❷ **Treasurer's House** (€ (✆ **01904/624-247**). Built in 1620 to house the treasurers of York Minster, the house and its gardens were extensively remodeled during the Victorian era by an eccentric collector. Inside are beautiful period rooms with collections of 17th- and 18th-century furniture, glass, and china. The house is open mid-March through November, Saturday through Thursday from 11am to 4:30pm (until 3pm in Nov). Admission to the house and a tour of its reputedly haunted (by Roman soldiers) basement is £7 ($14) for adults, £4.50 ($9) for children 5 to 15. A cozy cafe in the basement is a perfect spot for a light lunch or tea; the lovely walled garden is free to the public.

From the cathedral, walk southeast on High Petergate and Low Petergate, and you'll come to one of England's most famous medieval streets, ❸ **The Shambles** 𝆕. Up until 150 years ago, The Shambles was a street where butchers displayed their finest cuts in open windows on wide shelves called shammels. Today, this narrow winding lane, lined with buildings so close they shut out the light, is filled with gift shops.

Follow The Shambles to Pavement, turn south, and then turn east on Piccadilly to reach the ❹ **Merchant Adventurers' Hall** 𝆕 (𝄐 **01904/654-818; www.theyork company.co.uk**), one of England's largest and best-preserved guildhalls. This 14th-century stone and half-timbered structure, with a great hall on the main floor and a hospital and a chapel below, belonged to York's most powerful guild, the Merchant Adventurers. (Adventurers, in this context, means investors, and members profited from trade into and out of the city.) The hall is open Monday through Thursday 9am to 5pm, Friday and Saturday 9am to 3:30pm, and Sunday noon to 4pm. (Oct–Mar, it's open Mon–Sat 9am–3pm.) Admission is £2.50 ($5) for adults, £2 ($4) for seniors and students, and £1 ($2) for children.

Backtrack on Piccadilly to Coppergate, where you turn south and then turn east on Castlegate to the ❺ **Jorvik Viking Centre** 𝆕 (𝄐 **01904/643-211**). There you can hop a "time car" and be transported back to A.D. 948, when Eric Bloodaxe was king and York was Jorvik, a thriving Viking port and trading town. The scenes you pass—of village life, market stalls, crowded houses, and the wharf—are meticulous re-creations based on archaeological finds in this area; even the heads and faces of the animatronic characters were modeled on Viking skulls. It's fun and educational at the same time, but you might find it overpriced for the short spin you get. Jorvik is open daily from 10am to 5pm (Nov–Mar until 4pm). Admission is £7.95 ($16) for adults, £6.60 ($13) for seniors and students, and £5.50 ($11) for children 5 to 15.

Continue on Castlegate to ❻ **York Castle Museum** 𝆕 (𝄐 **01904/653-611; www.yorkcastlemuseum.org.uk**), housed in a former castle and debtors prison and today the most popular folk museum in the country. Using a treasure-trove of now-vanished everyday objects, the exhibitions re-create slices of life from the last 400 years. The major collections are divided into Social History (objects in everyday use), Military History (arms and armor), and Costume History (what people wore). The cells of the Debtors Prison paint a grim picture of the fate reserved for those unfortunates who could not pay their bills. (Dick Turpin, the famous highwayman robber, spent the last year of his life here before being executed in 1739.) Half Moon Court, in the half-moon-shaped prison yard, is a re-created Yorkshire street from the Edwardian era (1901–10). The museum is open daily 9:30am to 5pm. Admission is £6.50 ($13) for adults, £4 ($8) for children 5 to 15.

ORGANIZED TOURS

The **York Association of Voluntary Guides** (𝄐 **01904/640-780**) offers free, 2-hour guided tours of the city. The tours depart daily, year-round, at 10:15am from the front of the York Art Gallery, across from the Tourist Information Centre in Exhibition Square. Additional tours are offered at 2:15 and 6:45pm in summer. You don't need to make a reservation; just show up. **Yorkwalk** (𝄐 **01904/622-303**) leads 2-hour guided walks that focus on Roman York, hidden alleyways, the walls, and other elements of the city. Guides are extremely well informed and provide fascinating commentary; £5 ($10) for adults, £4.50 ($9) for students. Tours depart at 10:30am and 2:15pm from the gates to Museum Gardens, just north of Lendal Bridge. You don't need to reserve in advance.

City Sightseeing (𝒞 01904/625-618; www.city-sightseeing.com) runs open-top, double-decker tour buses on a circuit of all the main sights in York (1 hr. total). The ticket, valid all day so you can hop on and off as you wish, costs £9 ($18) for adults, £7 ($14) for senior and students, and £4 ($8) for children 5 to 15. The buses run year-round from about 9:30am to 5pm; you can board at the train station and buy your ticket from the driver.

Departing from the pier below Lendal Bridge, **York Boat** (𝒞 **01904/647-204;** www.yorkboat.co.uk) provides a 45-minute tour with live commentary that nicely complements a walking tour. At least four boats depart each day from early February through most of November; you can buy your ticket on board. The cost is £7 ($14) for adults, £6 ($12) for seniors, and £3.30 ($6.60) for children.

MORE THINGS TO SEE & DO

❼ National Railway Museum & Yorkshire Wheel ⭐⭐   This museum devoted to Britain's railroads is a bit of a hike from the city center, but it's well worth the effort and an absolute must for train buffs. The superlative collection includes dozens of vintage locomotives and railway cars, the earliest of them dating from the 1840s and looking like stagecoaches on tracks. You can peek into the windows of private royal coaches, ranging from Queen Victoria's 1869 coach to Queen Elizabeth's streamlined carriage, used until 1977. York's newest attraction, a giant Ferris wheel called the Yorkshire Wheel, is located next to the Railway Museum. Rising 114 feet (54m), the wheel offers great views of the city center, York Minster, and the river Ouse from enclosed, air-conditioned pods.

Leeman Rd. 𝒞 **01904/621-261.** www.nrm.org.uk. Free admission to museum; Yorkshire Wheel £6 ($12) adults, £4 ($8) children. Museum daily 10am–6pm; Yorkshire Wheel daily 10am–6pm (until 8pm in summer).

❽ York Art Gallery   Seven centuries of western European painting and a collection of 20th-century studio pottery are displayed in newly refurbished galleries. It's a pleasant way to spend half an hour, but none of the works on display are of major importance; the 17th- and 18th-century portraits by Sir Peter Lely and Joshua Reynolds are perhaps the most interesting. There's a cafe on the premises.

Exhibition Sq. 𝒞 **01904/551-861.** www.yorkartgallery.org.uk. Free admission. Daily 10am–5pm.

❾ Yorkshire Museum   Set on 10 acres (4 hectares) of landscaped gardens amid the ruins of St. Mary's Abbey, this museum gives a solid presentation of Yorkshire's history from 2 millennia ago up through the 16th century, with displays of elegant Roman jewelry, mosaics, Viking swords and battleaxes, and Anglo-Saxon silver. It relies heavily on text panels, so bring your reading glasses.

Museum Gardens in the center of York. 𝒞 **01904/551-800.** £5 ($10) adults, £3.50 ($7) children 5–15. Daily 10am–5pm.

❿ Micklegate Bar Museum   Housed in an 800-year-old fortified tower, this tiny museum looks at the social history of the city's southern entry gate (used by royalty, back in the day) in a quirky, humorous light.

Micklegate Bar. 𝒞 **01904/634-436.** £1.50 ($3) adults, £1 ($2) seniors and students. Feb–Oct daily 9am–5pm; Nov–Dec Sat–Sun only; closed Jan.

OUTDOOR ACTIVITIES

Fortified gateways (or "bars") that still serve as entrances into the old part of town are found along the almost 3 miles (4km) of **medieval walls** ⭐⭐ enclosing the center of York. A path (open daily 8am–dusk) runs along the top of the walls, with plenty of

Fun Fact **How the Other Half Rides**

Take a peek through the windows of Queen Victoria's ornate private railway carriage, on display in the National Railway Museum. When the queen wished to move from one car to the next, or use the toilet, the driver had to stop the train. What a hoot!

great views along the way. You find stairways up to the top of the walls at the four gates. A good place to start a wall walk is Micklegate, the southern entry used by royalty.

3 Shopping

High-end shops, including designer clothes boutiques and fine jewelry, are found on **Swinegate,** a street that was once a hog market. **The Quarter** area around Swinegate is known for its independent, one-of-a-kind shops. **Newgate Market,** between Parliament Street and The Shambles (© **01904/551-355**), is York's biggest open-air market, open daily with over 100 stalls selling crafts, clothes, candles, you name it. If you're looking for antiques, head over to **The Red House Antiques Centre,** 1 Duncombe Place (the street runs south from York Minster; © **01904/637-000**), where over 60 dealers sell quality merchandise in a beautiful Georgian building. Dollhouses and a complete inventory of miniature furnishings are sold at **Miniature Scene,** 42 Fossgate (© **01904/638-265**).

4 Where to Dine

Betty's ✿✿ TRADITIONAL ENGLISH/SWISS/TEAS   Founded in 1919, Betty's is a wonderfully old-fashioned Art Nouveau tearoom/patisserie restaurant. A dozen or so hot dishes, both fish and meat, are available. The pastries, all made according to secret recipes, are superb. At the shop in front, you can buy specialties such as Yorkshire fat rascals: warm scones with citrus peel, almonds, and cherries.

6–8 St. Helen's Sq. © 01904/659-142. Main courses £6.50–£10 ($13–$20); cream tea £7.25–£15 ($14–$30). AE, MC, V. Daily 9am–9pm.

The Blue Bicycle ✿ MODERN BRITISH   If you're looking for atmosphere and good food, try this appealing restaurant overlooking the canal-like River Ouse. It has a brasserie-style menu with a few standard menu items, daily specials, and a chargrill for meat and fish dishes. The Blue Bicycle also rents out two self-contained luxury rooms in the center of York for £150 ($300) per night.

34 Fossgate. © 01904/673-990. www.thebluebicycle.com. Reservations recommended. Main courses £11–£20 ($22–$40). AE, MC, V. Daily noon–2:30pm and 6–9pm.

St. William's Restaurant TRADITIONAL/MODERN BRITISH   For a reasonably priced lunch, dinner, or tea, check out this small, attractive restaurant in front of St. William's College at the east end of York Minster. The menu changes daily but always has some delicious choices, such as wild mushroom and leek risotto, pork loin wrapped in Cumbrian ham, or roast loin of venison. This is also a good spot for a simple cappuccino or an afternoon cream tea with scones and cakes.

3 College St. © 01904/634-830. Main courses £7–£16 ($14–$32). AE, DC, MC, V. Daily 10am–5pm and 6–9:30pm.

5 Extending Your Stay

The Bloomsbury   A pleasant house just a 10-minute walk from the Minster provides unusually comfortable and handsomely furnished rooms, accompanied by attentive service. Amenities include high-speed Internet access and free parking, and the hosts happily dispense information and make recommendations to enhance a visit to York.

127 Clifton, York YO30 6BL. © **01904/620-769.** Fax 01904/634-031. www.bloomsburyhotel.co.uk. £60–£90 ($120–$180) double. Rates include English breakfast. AE, MC, V.

The Grange 🦯🦯   Created from two classical Regency brick town houses, The Grange is a small, elegant hotel close to the city walls and a few minutes' walk from York Minster. The 30 individually designed rooms use antique furniture and convey a comfortable English charm.

1 Clifton, York YO30 6AA. © **01904/644-744.** Fax 01904/612-453. www.grangehotel.co.uk. £125–£220 ($250–$440) double. Rates include English breakfast. AE, MC, V.

Middlethorpe Hall 🦯🦯🦯   One of the country's finest hotels, Middlethorpe Hall is set in a 26-acre (10-hectare) park, 1½ miles (2.4km) south of York. Built in 1699, this stately redbrick country manor house was the residence of Lady Mary Wortley Montagu, a famous diarist of the early 18th century. The hotel offers a high standard of personal service and comfort and features beautifully restored rooms, lovely gardens, a health spa, and a fine restaurant.

Bishopthorpe Rd., York YO23 2GB. © **800/260-8338** in the U.S., or 01904/641-241. Fax 01904/620-176. www.middlethorpe.com. £185–£330 ($370–$660) double. AE, MC, V.

Appendix A:
England in Depth

by Darwin Porter & Danforth Prince

*T*he history of England is an inexhaustible subject. Huge tomes have been written on individual monarchs, colorful personalities, architectural styles, and historical epochs. This overview of England covers the bare essentials and should help put into context some of the historical landmarks you'll be visiting.

1 History 101

FROM MURKY BEGINNINGS TO ROMAN OCCUPATION Britain was probably split off from the continent of Europe some 8 millennia ago by continental drift and other natural forces. The early inhabitants, the Iberians, were later to be identified with stories of fairies, brownies, and "little people." These are the people whose ingenuity and enterprise are believed to have created Stonehenge, but despite that great and mysterious monument, little is known about them.

The Iberians were replaced by the iron-wielding Celts, whose massive invasions around 500 B.C. drove the Iberians back to the Scottish Highlands and Welsh mountains, where some of their descendants still live today.

In 54 B.C., Julius Caesar invaded England, but the Romans did not become established there until A.D. 43. They went as far as Caledonia (now Scotland), where

they gave up, leaving that land to "the painted ones," or the warring Picts. The wall built by Emperor Hadrian across the north of England marked the northernmost reaches of the Roman Empire. During almost 4 centuries of occupation, the Romans built roads, villas, towns, walls, and fortresses; they farmed the land and introduced first their pagan religions, then Christianity. Agriculture and trade flourished.

FROM ANGLO-SAXON RULE TO THE NORMAN CONQUEST When the Roman legions withdrew, around A.D. 410, they left the country open to waves of invasions by Jutes, Angles, and Saxons, who established themselves in small kingdoms throughout the former Roman colony. From the 8th to the 11th centuries, the Anglo-Saxons contended with Danish raiders for control of the land.

By the time of the Norman Conquest, the Saxon kingdoms were united under an elected king, Edward the Confessor. His successor was to rule less than a year before the Norman invasion.

The date 1066 is familiar to every English schoolchild. It marked an epic event, the only successful military invasion of Britain in history, and one of England's great turning points: King Harold, the last Anglo-Saxon king, was defeated at the Battle of Hastings; and William of Normandy was crowned William I.

One of William's first acts was to order a survey of the land he had conquered, assessing all property in the nation for tax purposes. This survey was called the *Domesday Book,* or "Book of Doom," as some pegged it. The resulting document was completed around 1086 and has been a fertile sourcebook for British historians ever since.

Norman rule had an enormous impact on English society. All high offices were held by Normans, and the Norman barons were given great grants of lands; they built Norman-style castles and strongholds throughout the country. French was the language of the court for centuries—few people realize that heroes such as Richard the Lionheart probably spoke little or no English.

FROM THE RULE OF HENRY II TO THE MAGNA CARTA In 1154, Henry II, the first of the Plantagenets, was crowned (reigned 1154–89). This remarkable character in English history ruled a vast empire—not only most of Britain but Normandy, Anjou, Brittany, and Aquitaine in France.

Henry was a man of powerful physique, both charming and terrifying. He reformed the courts and introduced the system of common law, which still operates in moderated form in England today and also influenced the American legal system. But Henry is best remembered for ordering the infamous murder of Thomas Becket, archbishop of Canterbury. Henry, at odds with his archbishop, exclaimed, "Who will rid me of this turbulent priest?" His knights, overhearing and taking him at his word, murdered Thomas in front of the high altar in Canterbury Cathedral.

Henry's wife, Eleanor of Aquitaine, the most famous woman of her time, was no less of a colorful character. She accompanied her first husband, Louis VII of France, on the Second Crusade, and it was rumored that she had a romantic affair at that time with the Saracen leader, Saladin. Domestic and political life did not run smoothly, however, and Henry and Eleanor and their sons were often at odds. The pair has been the subject of many plays and films, including *The Lion in Winter, Becket,* and T. S. Eliot's *Murder in the Cathedral.*

Dateline

- **54 B.C.** Julius Caesar invades England.
- **A.D. 43** Romans conquer England.
- **410** Jutes, Angles, and Saxons form small kingdoms in England.
- **500–1066** Anglo-Saxon kingdoms fight off Viking warriors.
- **1066** William, duke of Normandy, invades England, defeats Harold II at the Battle of Hastings.
- **1154** Henry II, first of the Plantagenets, launches their rule (which lasts until 1399).
- **1215** King John signs the Magna Carta at Runnymede.
- **1337** Hundred Years' War between France and England begins.
- **1485** Battle of Bosworth Field ends the War of the Roses between the Houses of York and Lancaster; Henry VII launches the Tudor dynasty.
- **1534** Henry VIII brings the Reformation to England and dissolves the monasteries.
- **1558** The accession of Elizabeth I ushers in an era of exploration and a renaissance in science and learning.
- **1588** Spanish Armada defeated.

Two of their sons were crowned kings of England. Richard the Lionheart actually spent most of his life outside England, on crusades, or in France. John was forced by his nobles to sign the Magna Carta at Runnymede, in 1215—another date well known to English schoolchildren.

The Magna Carta guaranteed that the king was subject to the rule of law and gave certain rights to the king's subjects, beginning a process that eventually led to the development of parliamentary democracy as it is known in Britain today. This process would have enormous influence on the American colonies many years later. The Magna Carta became known as the cornerstone of English liberties, though it only granted liberties to the barons. It took the rebellion of Simon de Montfort half a century later to introduce the notion that the boroughs and burghers should also have a voice and representation.

THE BLACK DEATH & THE WARS OF THE ROSES In 1348, half the population died as the Black Death ravaged England. By the end of the century, the population of Britain had fallen from four million to two million.

England also suffered in the Hundred Years' War, which went on intermittently for more than a century. By 1371, England had lost much of its land on French soil. Henry V, immortalized by Shakespeare, revived England's claims to France,

and his victory at Agincourt was notable for making obsolete the forms of medieval chivalry and warfare.

After Henry's death in 1422, disputes arose among successors to the crown that resulted in a long period of civil strife, the Wars of the Roses, between the Yorkists, who used a white rose as their symbol, and the Lancastrians with their red rose. The last Yorkist king was Richard III, who got bad press from Shakespeare, but who is defended to this day as a hero by the people of the city of York. Richard was defeated at Bosworth Field, and the victory introduced England to the first Tudor, the shrewd and wily Henry VII.

THE TUDORS TAKE THE THRONE
The Tudors were unlike the kings who had ruled before them. They introduced into England a strong central monarchy with far-reaching powers. The system worked well under the three strong and capable Tudor monarchs, but it began to break down later when the Stuarts came to the throne.

Henry VIII is surely the most notorious Tudor. Imperious and flamboyant, a colossus among English royalty, he slammed shut the door on the Middle Ages and introduced the Renaissance to England. He is best known, of course, for his treatment of his six wives and the unfortunate fates that befell five of them.

- **1603** James VI of Scotland becomes James I of England, thus uniting the crowns of England and Scotland.
- **1620** Pilgrims sail from Plymouth on the *Mayflower* to found a colony in the New World.
- **1629** Charles I dissolves Parliament, ruling alone.
- **1642–49** Civil War between Royalists and Parliamentarians; the Parliamentarians win.

- **1649** Charles I beheaded, and England is a republic.
- **1653** Oliver Cromwell becomes Lord Protector.
- **1660** Charles II restored to the throne with limited power.
- **1665–66** Great Plague and Great Fire decimate London.
- **1688** James II, a Catholic, is deposed, and William and Mary come to the throne, signing a bill of rights.

- **1727** George I, the first of the Hanoverians, assumes the throne.
- **1756–63** In the Seven Years' War, Britain wins Canada from France.
- **1775–83** Britain loses its American colonies.
- **1795–1815** The Napoleonic Wars lead, finally, to the Battle of Waterloo and the defeat of Napoleon.
continues

When his first wife, Catherine of Aragon, failed to produce an heir, and his ambitious mistress, Anne Boleyn, became pregnant, he tried to annul his marriage but the pope refused, and Catherine contested the action. Defying the power of Rome, Henry had his marriage with Catherine declared invalid and secretly married Anne Boleyn in 1533.

The events that followed had profound consequences and introduced the religious controversy that was to dominate English politics for the next 4 centuries. Henry's break with the Roman Catholic Church and the formation of the Church of England, with himself as supreme head, was a turning point in English history. It led eventually to the Dissolution of the Monasteries, civil unrest, and much social dislocation. The confiscation of the church's land and possessions brought untold wealth into the king's coffers, wealth that was distributed to a new aristocracy that supported the monarch. In one sweeping gesture, Henry destroyed the ecclesiastical culture of the Middle Ages. Among those executed for refusing to cooperate with Henry's changes was Sir Thomas More, humanist, international man of letters, and author of *Utopia*.

Anne Boleyn bore Henry a daughter, the future Elizabeth I, but failed to produce a male heir. She was brought to trial on a trumped-up charge of adultery and

beheaded; in 1536, Henry married Jane Seymour, who died giving birth to Edward VI. For his next wife, Henry looked farther afield and chose Anne of Cleves from a flattering portrait, but she proved disappointing—he called her "The Great Flanders Mare." He divorced her the same year and next picked a pretty young woman from his court, Catherine Howard. She was also beheaded on a charge of adultery but, unlike Anne Boleyn, was probably guilty. Finally, he married an older woman, Catherine Parr, in 1543. She survived him.

Henry's heir, sickly Edward VI (reigned 1547–53), did not live long. He died of consumption—or, as rumor has it, overmedication. He was succeeded by his sister, Mary I (reigned 1553–58), and the trouble Henry had stirred up with the break with Rome came home to roost for the first time. Mary restored the Roman Catholic faith, and her persecution of the adherents of the Church of England earned her the name "Bloody Mary." Some 300 Protestants were executed, many burned alive at the stake. She made an unpopular and unhappy marriage to Philip of Spain; despite her bloody reputation, her life was a sad one.

Elizabeth I (reigned 1558–1603) came next to the throne, ushering in an era of peace and prosperity, exploration, and a renaissance in science and learning. An

- **1837** Queen Victoria begins her reign as Britain reaches the zenith of its empire.
- **1901** Victoria dies, and Edward VII becomes king.
- **1914–18** England enters World War I and emerges victorious on the Allied side.
- **1936** Edward VIII abdicates to marry an American divorcée.
- **1939–45** In World War II, Britain stands alone against Hitler from the fall of France

in 1940 until America enters the war in 1941. Dunkirk is evacuated in 1940; bombs rattle London during the blitz.
- **1945** Germany surrenders. Churchill is defeated; the Labour government introduces the welfare state and begins to dismantle the empire.
- **1952** Queen Elizabeth II ascends the throne.

- **1973** Britain joins the European Union.
- **1979** Margaret Thatcher becomes prime minister.
- **1982** Britain defeats Argentina in the Falklands War.
- **1990** Thatcher is ousted; John Major becomes prime minister.
- **1991** Britain fights with Allies to defeat Iraq.

entire age was named after her: the Elizabethan age. She was the last great and grand monarch to rule England, and her passion and magnetism were said to match her father's. Through her era marched Drake, Raleigh, Frobisher, Grenville, Shakespeare, Spenser, Byrd, and Hilliard. During her reign, she had to face the appalling precedent of ordering the execution of a fellow sovereign, Mary, Queen of Scots. Her diplomatic skills kept war at bay until 1588, when at the apogee of her reign, the Spanish Armada was defeated. She will be forever remembered as "Good Queen Bess."

FROM THE RESTORATION TO THE NAPOLEONIC WARS

The reign of Charles II was the beginning of a dreadful decade that saw London decimated by the Great Plague and destroyed by the Great Fire.

Charles's successor, James II, attempted to return the country to Catholicism, an effort that so frightened the powers-that-be that Catholics were for a long time deprived of their civil rights. James was deposed in the "Glorious Revolution" of 1688 and succeeded by his daughter Mary (1662–94) and William of Orange (1650–1702). (William of Orange was the grandson of Charles I, the tyrannical king whom Cromwell helped depose.) This secured a Protestant succession that has continued to this day. These tolerant and levelheaded monarchs signed a bill of rights, establishing the principle that the monarch reigns not by divine right but by the will of Parliament. William outlived his wife, reigning until 1702.

Queen Anne then came to the throne, ruling from 1702 until her own death in 1714. She was the sister of Mary of Orange and was another daughter of James II. The last of the Stuarts, Anne marked her reign with the most significant event, the 1707 Act of Union with Scotland. She outlived all her children, leaving her throne without an heir.

Upon the death of Anne, England looked for a Protestant prince to succeed her and chose George of Hanover, who reigned from 1714 to 1727. Though he spoke only German and spent as little time in England as possible, he was chosen because he was the great-grandson of James I. Beginning with this "distant cousin" to the throne, the reign of George I marked the beginning of the 174-year rule of the Hanoverians who preceded Victoria.

George I left the running of the government to the English politicians and created the office of prime minister. Under the Hanoverians, the powers of Parliament were extended, and the constitutional monarchy developed into what it is today.

- **1992** Royals jolted by fire at Windsor Castle and by marital troubles of two of their sons. Britain joins the European Single Market. Deep recession signals the end of the booming 1980s.
- **1994** England is linked to the Continent by rail via the Channel Tunnel, or Chunnel. Tony Blair elected Labour party leader.

- **1996** The IRA breaks a 17-month cease-fire with a truck bomb at the Docklands that claims two lives. Charles and Di divorce. The government concedes a possible link between mad cow disease and a fatal brain ailment afflicting humans; British beef imports face banishment globally.
- **1997** London swings again. The Labour party ends 18

years of Conservative rule with a landslide election victory. The tragic death of Diana, princess of Wales, prompts worldwide outpouring of grief.
- **1998** Prime Minister Tony Blair launches "New Britain"—young, stylish, and informal.
- **1999** England rushes toward the 21st century with the Millennium Dome at Greenwich.

continues

The American colonies were lost under the Hanoverian George III, but other British possessions were expanded: Canada was won from the French in the Seven Years' War (1756–63), British control over India was affirmed, and Captain Cook claimed Australia and New Zealand for England. The British became embroiled in the Napoleonic Wars (1795–1815), achieving two of their greatest victories and acquiring two of their greatest heroes: Nelson at Trafalgar and Wellington at Waterloo.

THE INDUSTRIAL REVOLUTION & THE REIGN OF VICTORIA

The mid– to late 18th century saw the beginnings of the Industrial Revolution. This event changed the lives of the laboring class, created a wealthy middle class, and transformed England from a rural, agricultural society into an urban, industrial economy. England was now a world-class financial and military power. Male suffrage was extended, though women were to continue under a series of civil disadvantages for the rest of the century.

Queen Victoria's reign (1837–1901) coincided with the height of the Industrial Revolution. When she ascended the throne, the monarchy as an institution was in considerable doubt, but her 64-year reign, the longest tenure in English history, was an incomparable success.

The Victorian era was shaped by the growing power of the bourgeoisie, the queen and her consort's personal moral stance, and the perceived moral responsibilities of managing a vast empire. During this time, the first trade unions were formed, a public (state) school system was developed, and railroads were built.

Victoria never recovered from the death of her German husband, Albert. He died of typhoid fever in 1861, and the queen never remarried. Though she had many children, she found them tiresome; nonetheless, she was a pillar of family values. One historian said her greatest asset was her relative ordinariness.

Middle-class values ruled Victorian England and were embodied by the queen. The racy England of the past went underground. Our present-day view of England is still influenced by the attitudes of the Victorian era, and we tend to forget that English society in earlier centuries was famous for its rowdiness, sexual license, and spicy scandal.

Victoria's son Edward VII (reigned 1901–10) was a playboy who had waited too long in the wings. He is famous for mistresses, especially Lillie Langtry, and his love of elaborate dinners. During his brief reign, he, too, had an era named after him: the Edwardian age. Under Edward, the country entered the 20th

- **2000** London presides over millennium celebration. Gays allowed to serve openly in the military.
- **2001** Foot-and-mouth disease epidemic affects cattle, pigs, and sheep, and brings hard times to the British economy.

- **2002** Queen Elizabeth, the Queen Mother, dies at age 101.
- **2003** Britain backs the U.S. and sends troops to help fight the war in Iraq.

- **2005** Terrorists detonate bombs on London's Underground and on the city's famous double-decker buses, prompting worldwide outrage. Prince Charles marries Camilla Parker-Bowles.
- **2007** Gordon Brown replaces Tony Blair as prime minister.

century at the height of its imperial power. At home, the advent of the motorcar and the telephone radically changed social life, and the women's suffrage movement began.

World War I marked the end of an era. It had been assumed that peace, progress, prosperity, empire, and even social improvement would continue indefinitely. World War I and the troubled decades of social unrest, political uncertainty, and the rise of Nazism and fascism put an end to these expectations.

THE WINDS OF WAR   World War II began in 1939, and soon thereafter Britain found a new and inspiring leader, Winston Churchill. Churchill led the nation during its "finest hour." From the time the Germans took France, Britain stood alone against Hitler. The evacuation of Dunkirk in 1940, the blitz of London, and the Battle of Britain were dark hours for the British people, and Churchill is remembered for urging them to hold onto their courage. Once the British forces were joined by their American allies, the tide finally turned, culminating in the D-day invasion of German-occupied Normandy. These bloody events are still remembered by many with pride, and with nostalgia for the era when Britain was still a great world power.

The years following World War II brought many changes to England. Britain began to lose its grip on an empire (India became independent in 1947), and the Labour government, which came into power in 1945, established the welfare state and brought profound social change to Britain.

QUEEN ELIZABETH RULES TO THE PRESENT DAY   Upon the death of the "wartime king," George VI, Elizabeth II ascended the throne in 1953. Her reign has seen the erosion of Britain's once-mighty industrial power and, in recent years, a severe recession.

Political power has seesawed back and forth between the Conservative and Labour parties. Margaret Thatcher, who became prime minister in 1979, seriously eroded the welfare state and was ambivalent toward the European Union. Her popularity soared during the successful Falklands War, when Britain seemed to recover some of its military glory for a brief time.

Though the queen has remained steadfast and punctiliously has performed her ceremonial duties, rumors about the royal family abounded, and in the year 1992, which Queen Elizabeth labeled an *annus horribilis,* a devastating fire swept through Windsor Castle, the marriages of several of her children crumbled, and the queen agreed to pay taxes for the first time. Prince Charles and Princess Diana agreed to a separation, and there were ominous rumblings about the future of the House of Windsor. By 1994 and 1995, Britain's economy was improving after several glum years, but Conservative prime minister John Major, heir to Margaret Thatcher's legacy, was coming under increasing criticism.

The IRA, reputedly enraged at the slow pace of peace talks, relaunched its reign of terror across London in February 1996, planting a massive bomb that ripped through a building in London's Docklands, injuring more than 100 people and killing two. Shattered, too, was the 17-month cease-fire by the IRA, which brought hope that peace was at least possible. Another bomb went off in Manchester in June.

Headlines about the IRA bombing gave way to another big bomb: the end of the marriage of Princess Diana and Prince Charles. The Wedding of the Century had become the Divorce of the Century. The lurid tabloids had been right all along about this unhappy pair. But details of the $26-million divorce settlement didn't satisfy the curious: Scrutiny of

Prince Charles's relationship with Camilla Parker-Bowles, as well as gossip about Princess Diana's love life, continued in the press.

In 1997, the political limelight came to rest on the young Labour leader Tony Blair. From his rock-star acquaintances to his "New Labour" rhetoric, which is chock-full of pop-culture buzzwords, he is a stark contrast to the more staid Major. His media-savvy personality obviously registered with the British electorate. On May 1, 1997, the Labour Party ended 18 years of Conservative rule with a landslide election victory. At age 44, Blair became Britain's youngest prime minister in 185 years, following in the wake of the largest Labour triumph since Winston Churchill was swept out of office at the end of World War II.

Blair's election—which came just at the moment when London was being touted by the international press for its renaissance in art, music, fashion, and dining—had many British entrepreneurs poised and ready to take advantage of what they perceived as enthusiasm for new ideas and ventures. Comparisons to Harold Macmillan and his reign over the Swinging Sixties were inevitable, and insiders agreed that something was in the air.

However, events took a shocking turn in August 1997 when Princess Diana was killed—along with her companion, Harrods heir Dodi al-Fayed—in a high-speed car crash in Paris.

"The People's Princess" continued to dominate many headlines with bizarre conspiracy theories about her death.

Of course, the future of the monarchy still remains a hot topic of discussion in Britain. There is little support for doing away with the monarchy in Britain today in spite of wide criticism of the royal family's behavior in the wake of Diana's death. Apparently, if polls are to be believed, some three-quarters of the British populace want the monarchy to continue. Prince Charles is even making a

comeback with the British public, as has his once-reviled wife, Camilla Parker-Bowles. At the very least, the monarchy is good for the tourist trade, on which Britain is increasingly dependent. And what would the tabloids do without it?

The big news among royal watchers in Britain early in 2002 was the death of Princess Margaret at age 71, followed 7 weeks later by the death of Queen Mother Elizabeth at the age of 101. The most popular royal, the Queen "Mum" was a symbol of courage and dignity, especially during the tumultuous World War II years when London was under bombardment by Nazi Germany. The remains of the Queen Mother were laid to rest alongside her husband's in the George VI Memorial Chapel at St. George's at Windsor Castle. The ashes of Princess Margaret were interred with those of her parents in the same chapel.

At the dawn of the millennium, major social changes occurred in Britain. No sooner had the year 2000 begun than Britain announced a change of its code of conduct for the military, allowing openly gay men and women to serve in the armed forces. The action followed a European court ruling in the fall of 1999 that forbade Britain to discriminate against homosexuals. This change brings Britain in line with almost all other NATO countries, including France, Canada, and Germany. The United States remains at variance with the trend.

After promising beginnings, the 21st century got off to a bad start in Britain. In the wake of mad cow disease flare-ups, the country was swept by a foot-and-mouth disease epidemic that disrupted the country's agriculture and threatened one of the major sources of British livelihoods, its burgeoning tourist industry. After billions of pounds in tourism were lost, the panic has now subsided. The government has intervened to take whatever preventive measures it can.

Following the September 11, 2001, terrorist attacks on New York City and Washington, D.C., Tony Blair and his government joined in a show of support for the U.S. by condemning the aerial bombardments and loss of lives. Not only that, the British joined the war in Afghanistan against the dreaded Taliban. However, by 2003 Blair's backing of George Bush's stance against President Saddam Hussein of Iraq had brought his popularity to an all-time low.

England's equanimity took a further blow on the morning of July 7, 2005, when three Underground bomb blasts, later followed by an explosion on one of the famous double-decker buses, rocked London. More than 50 were killed and some 700 passengers wounded. London was momentarily paralyzed. Following the attacks, Queen Elizabeth II made the rounds of hospitals, vowing that her people would not change "our way of life."

She was right. Within hours after the explosions, London was back at work and play. Buses were running on time, as was the Underground, carrying millions of people to work. No theatre went dark, and the pubs were full, even on the night of the bombings. As one elderly woman in a pub said, "What can we do? Perhaps bond together like we did during the war, hold hands and sing about bluebirds flying once again over the White Cliffs of Dover. Our stiff upper lip has never been stiffer."

A memorial area has been established at **Victoria Embankment Gardens**, a narrow park next to the Embankment tube station. You may also see flowers placed near the bomb sites: between Russell Square and King's Cross tube stations, between Aldgate East and Liverpool Street tube stations, at the Edgware Road tube, and in Tavistock Square.

2 Pies, Pudding & Pints: The Lowdown on British Cuisine

The late British humorist George Mikes wrote that "the Continentals have good food; the English have good table manners." But the British no longer deserve their reputation for soggy cabbage and tasteless dishes. Contemporary London—and the country as a whole—boasts many fine restaurants and sophisticated cuisine.

If you want to see what Britain is eating today, just drop in at Harvey Nichol's Fifth Floor in London's Knightsbridge for its dazzling display of produce from all over the globe.

The new buzzword for British cuisine is *magpie*, meaning borrowing ideas from global travels, taking them home, and improving on the original.

WHAT YOU'LL FIND ON THE MENU   On any pub menu, you're likely to encounter such dishes as the **Cornish pasty** and **shepherd's pie.** The first, traditionally made from Sunday-meal leftovers

and taken by West Country fishers for Monday lunch, consists of chopped potatoes, carrots, and onions mixed together with seasoning and put into a pastry envelope. The second is a deep dish of chopped cooked lamb mixed with onions and seasoning, covered with a layer of mashed potatoes, and served hot. Another version is **cottage pie,** which is minced beef covered with potatoes and also served hot. Of course, these beef dishes are subject to availability. In addition to a pasty, Cornwall also gives us **Stargazy Pie**—a deep-dish fish pie with a crisp crust covering a creamy concoction of freshly caught herring and vegetables.

The most common pub meal, though, is the **ploughman's lunch,** traditional farmworker's fare, consisting of a good chunk of local cheese, a hunk of homemade crusty white or brown bread, some butter, and a pickled onion or two, washed down with ale. You'll now find such variations as pâté and chutney occasionally replacing the onions and cheese. Or you might find **Lancashire hot pot,** a stew of mutton, potatoes, kidneys, and onions (sometimes carrots). This concoction was originally put into a deep dish and set on the edge of the stove to cook slowly while the workers spent the day at the local mill.

Among appetizers, called **starters** in England, the most typical are potted shrimp (small buttered shrimp preserved in a jar), prawn cocktail, and smoked salmon. You might also be served pâté or fish pie, which is very light fish pâté. Most menus will feature a variety of soups, including cock-a-leekie (chicken soup flavored with leeks), and perhaps a game soup that has been doused with sherry.

Among the best-known traditional English meals is **roast beef and Yorkshire pudding.** (The pudding is made with a flour base and cooked under the roast, allowing the fat from the meat to drop onto it.) The beef could easily be a large sirloin (rolled loin), which, so the story goes, was named by James I when he was a guest at Houghton Tower, Lancashire. "Arise, Sir Loin," he cried, as he knighted the leg of beef before him with his dagger. Another dish that makes use of a flour base is toad-in-the-hole, in which sausages are cooked in batter. Game, especially pheasant and grouse, is also a staple on British tables.

On any menu, you'll find **fresh seafood:** cod, haddock, herring, plaice, and Dover sole, the aristocrat of flatfish. Cod and haddock are used in making British **fish and chips** (chips are fried potatoes or thick french fries), which the true Briton covers with salt and vinegar. If you like **oysters,** try some of the famous Colchester variety.

The British call desserts **sweets,** though some people still refer to any dessert as **pudding. Trifle** is the most famous English dessert, consisting of sponge cake soaked in brandy or sherry, coated with fruit or jam, and topped with cream custard. A **fool,** such as gooseberry fool, is a light cream dessert whipped up from seasonal fruits. Regional sweets include **northern flitting dumpling** (dates, walnuts, and syrup mixed with other ingredients and made into a pudding that is easily sliced and carried along when you're "flitting" from place to place). Similarly, **hasty pudding,** a Newcastle dish, is supposed to have been invented by people in a hurry to avoid the bailiff. It consists of stale bread, to which dried fruit and milk are added before it is put into the oven.

Cheese is traditionally served after dessert as a savory. There are many regional cheeses, the best known being cheddar, a good, solid, mature cheese. Others are the semi-smooth Caerphilly, from a beautiful part of Wales, and Stilton, a blue-veined, crumbly cheese that's often enjoyed with a glass of port.

ENGLISH BREAKFASTS & AFTERNOON TEA

Britain is famous for its enormous breakfast of bacon, eggs, grilled tomato, and fried bread. Some places have replaced this cholesterol festival with a continental breakfast, but you'll still find the traditional morning meal available.

Kipper, or smoked herring, is also a popular breakfast dish. The finest come from the Isle of Man, Whitby, or Loch Fyne, in Scotland. The herrings are split open, placed over oak chips, and slowly cooked to produce a nice pale-brown smoked fish.

Many people still enjoy afternoon tea, which may consist of a simple cup of tea. A formal tea starts with tiny crustless sandwiches filled with cucumber or watercress and proceeds through scones, crumpets with jam or clotted cream, and cakes and tarts—all accompanied by a proper pot of tea.

WHAT TO WASH IT ALL DOWN WITH English pubs serve a variety of cocktails, but their stock in trade is beer: brown beer, or bitter; blond beer, or lager; and very dark beer, or stout. The standard English draft beer is much stronger than American beer and is served "with the chill off," because it doesn't taste good cold. Lager is always chilled, whereas stout can be served either way. Beer is always served straight from the tap, in two sizes: half-pint (10 oz.) and pint (20 oz.).

One of the most significant changes in English drinking habits has been the popularity of wine bars, and you will find many to try, including some that turn into discos late at night. Britain isn't known for its wine, though it does produce some medium-sweet fruity whites. Its cider, though, is famous—and mighty potent in contrast to the American variety.

Whisky (spelled without the *e*) refers to scotch. Canadian and Irish whiskey (spelled with the *e*) are also available, but only the very best stocked bars have American bourbon and rye.

While you're in England, you may want to try the very English drink called **Pimm's,** a mixture developed by James Pimm, owner of a popular London oyster house in the 1840s. Though it can be consumed on the rocks, it's usually served as a Pimm's Cup—a drink that will have any number and variety of ingredients, depending on which part of the world (or empire) you're in. Here, just for fun, is a typical recipe: Take a very tall glass and fill it with ice. Add a thin slice of lemon (or orange), a cucumber spike (or a curl of cucumber rind), and 2 ounces of Pimm's liquor. Then finish with a splash of either lemon or club soda, 7-Up, or Tom Collins mix.

The English tend to drink everything at a warmer temperature than Americans are used to. So if you like ice in your soda, be sure to ask for lots of it, or you're likely to end up with a measly, quickly melting cube or two.

Appendix B: England's Art & Architecture

by Reid Bramblett

No one artist, period, or museum defines England's art and architecture. You can see the country's art in medieval illuminated manuscripts, Thomas Gainsborough portraits, and Damien Hirst's pickled cows. Its architecture ranges from Roman walls and Norman castles to baroque St. Paul's Cathedral and towering postmodern skyscrapers. This chapter will help you make sense of it all.

1 Art 101

CELTIC & MEDIEVAL (CA. 800 B.C.–16TH C.)

The Celts, mixed with plenty of Scandinavian and Dutch tribes of varying origins, ruled England until the Romans established rule there in A.D. 43. **Celtic art** survived the Roman conquest and medieval Christianity mainly as carved swirls and decorations on the "Celtic Crosses" peppering cemeteries. During the medieval period, colorful Celtic images and illustrations decorated the margins of Bibles and Gospels, giving the books their moniker **"illuminated manuscripts."**

Important examples and artists of this period include:

- **Wilton Diptych, National Gallery, London.** The first truly important, truly British painting, this diptych (a painting on two hinged panels) was crafted in the late 1390s for Richard II by an unknown artist who combined Italian and northern European influences.
- **Lindisfarne Gospels, British Library, London.** One of Europe's greatest illuminated manuscripts from the 7th century, this work is particularly well crafted and well preserved.
- **Matthew Paris (d. 1259).** A Benedictine monk who illuminated his own writings, Paris put his significant artistic gifts to good use as the official St. Albans Abbey chronicler. Examples of his work are now in London's **British Library** and Cambridge's **Corpus Christi College.**

RENAISSANCE & BAROQUE (16TH–18TH C.)

The **Renaissance** hit England late, but its museums contain many important Old Master paintings from Italy and Germany. Renaissance means "rebirth"; in this case, it means the renewed use of classical styles and forms originating in ancient Greece and Rome. Artists strove for greater naturalism, using newly developed techniques such as linear perspective. A few foreign Renaissance masters did come to work at the English courts and had an influence on some local artists, but significant Brits didn't emerge until the baroque period.

The **baroque,** a more decorative version of the Renaissance approach, mixes compositional complexity and explosions of dynamic fury, movement, color, and figures with an exaggeration of light and dark, called *chiaroscuro,* and a kind of super-realism based on using peasants as models. The **rococo** period is baroque art gone awry, frothy, and chaotic.

Significant artists of this period include:

- **Pietro Torrigiano (1472–1528).** An Italian Renaissance sculptor, Torrigiano had to flee Florence after breaking the nose of classmate Michelangelo. He ended up in London crafting elaborate tombs for the Tudors in **Westminster Abbey,** including Lady Margaret Beaufort, and Henry VII and Elizabeth of York. London's **Victoria and Albert Museum** preserves Torrigiano's terra-cotta bust of Henry VII.

- **Hans Holbein the Younger (1497–1543).** A German Renaissance master of penetrating portraits, Holbein the Younger cataloged many significant figures in 16th-century Europe: Sir Thomas More's family (**Nostel Priory** outside Wakefield in West Yorkshire; this may be a copy); Henry VIII and the duke of Norfolk (**Castle Howard** outside York); and Erasmus (whom Holbein knew; **Longford Castle,** Wiltshire). More portraits are in London's **National Gallery** and **National Portrait Gallery** and in **Windsor Castle.**

- **Anthony van Dyck (1599–1641).** This Belgian artist painted passels of portraits in the baroque style for the Stuart court, setting the tone for British portraiture for the next few centuries. You'll find his works in London's **National Portrait Gallery, National Gallery, Wallace Collection,** and **Wilton House,** with more in Oxford's **Ashmolean Museum** and Liverpool's **Walker Art Gallery.**

- **Joshua Reynolds (1723–92).** A fussy baroque painter and first president of the Royal Academy of Arts, Reynolds was a firm believer in a painter's duty to celebrate history. Reynolds spent much of his career casting his noble patrons as ancient gods in portrait compositions cribbed from Old Masters. Many of his works are in London's **National Gallery, Tate Britain, Wallace Collection,** and **Dulwich Picture Gallery;** Oxford's **Cathedral Hall;** Liverpool's **Walker Art Gallery;** and Birmingham's **Museum and Art Gallery** and **Barber Institute of Fine Arts.**

- **Thomas Gainsborough (1727–88).** Although he was a classical/baroque portraitist like his rival Reynolds, at least Gainsborough could be original. Too bad his tastes ran to rococo pastels, frothy feathered brushwork, and busy compositions. When not immortalizing noble patrons such as Jonathan Buttell (better known as "Blue Boy"), he painted a collection of landscapes just for himself. His works grace the **Victoria Art Gallery** in Bath (where he first came to fame), London's **National Gallery** and **National Portrait Gallery,** Cambridge's **Fitzwilliam Museum,** Oxford's **Cathedral Hall** and **Ashmolean Museum,** Liverpool's **Walker Art Gallery,** and Birmingham's **Museum and Art Gallery** and **Barber Institute of Fine Arts.**

THE ROMANTICS (LATE 18TH TO 19TH C.)

The romantics felt that the classically minded Renaissance and baroque artists had gotten it wrong; the Gothic Middle Ages was the place to be. They idealized the romantic tales of chivalry; had a deep respect for nature, human rights, and the nobility of peasantry; and were suspicious of progress. Their paintings tended to be heroic, historic, dramatic, and beautiful. They were inspired by critic and art theorist **John Ruskin** (1819–1900), who traveled throughout northern Italy and was among the first to sing the praises of pre-Renaissance painting and Gothic architecture.

Significant artists of this period include:

- **William Blake (1757–1827).** Romantic archetype, Blake snubbed the stuffy Royal Academy of Arts to do his own engraving, prints, illustrations, poetry, and painting. His works were filled with melodrama, muscular figures, and sweeping lines; modern, angst-ridden, "Goth" teens really dig his stuff. Judge for yourself at London's **Tate Britain** and Manchester's **Whitworth Art Gallery.**
- **John Constable (1776–1837).** Constable was a great British landscapist, whose scenes (especially those of happy, agricultural peasants) became more idealized with each passing year—while his compositions and brushwork became freer. You'll find his best works in London's **National Gallery** and **Victoria and Albert Museum,** and in Liverpool's **Walker Art Gallery.**
- **J. M. W. Turner (1775–1851).** Turner, called by some "The First Impressionist," was a prolific and multitalented artist whose mood-laden, freely brushed, watercolor landscapes influenced Monet. The River Thames and London, where he lived and died, were frequent subjects. He bequeathed his collection of some 19,000 watercolors and 300 paintings to the people of Britain with the request that they be kept in one place. London's **Tate Britain** displays the largest number of Turner's works, while others grace London's **National Gallery,** Cambridge's **Fitzwilliam Museum,** Liverpool's **Walker Art Gallery,** Birmingham's **Museum and Art Gallery** and **Barber Institute of Fine Arts,** and Manchester's **Whitworth Art Gallery.**
- **Pre-Raphaelites (1848–1870s).** This "brotherhood" of painters declared that art had gone all wrong with Italian Renaissance painter Raphael (1483–1520) and set about to emulate the Italian painters who preceded him—though they were not actually looking at specific examples. Their symbolically imbued, sweetly idealized, hyper-realistic work depicts scenes from romantic poetry and Shakespeare as much as from the Bible. There were seven founders and many followers, but the most important were Dante Gabriel Rossetti, William Hunt, and John Millais; you can see work by all three at London's **Tate Britain,** Oxford's **Ashmolean Museum,** Liverpool's **Walker Art Gallery,** and Manchester's **City Art Gallery.**

THE 20TH CENTURY

The only artistic movement or era in which the Brits can claim a major stake is contemporary art, with many young British artists bursting onto the international gallery scene just before and after World War II. Art of the last century often followed international schools or styles—no major ones truly originated in Britain—and artists tended to move in and out of styles over their careers. If anything, the greatest artists of this period strove for unique and individual expression rather than adherence to a particular school.

In the examples below, a city name refers to the major modern art gallery in that location; "London" stands for the **Tate Modern,** "Birmingham" for the **Museum and Art Gallery,** and "Liverpool" for the **Walker Art Gallery.** Important British artists of the 20th century include:

- **Henry Moore (1898–1986).** A sculptor, Moore saw himself as a sort of reincarnation of Michelangelo. He mined his marbles from the same quarries as the Renaissance master and let the stone itself dictate the flowing, abstract, surrealistic figures carved from it. The **Henry Moore Institute** in Leeds, where he studied, preserves his drawings and sculpture. You'll also find his work in London, Liverpool, Birmingham, and Cambridge's **Fitzwilliam Museum** and **Clare College.**

- **Francis Bacon (1909–92).** A dark and brooding expressionist (a style that expresses an artist's inner thoughts and feelings), Bacon presented man's foibles in formats usually reserved for religious subjects (such as the triptych, a set of three panels, often hinged and used as an altarpiece). His works may be found in London, Birmingham, and Manchester's **Whitworth Art Gallery.**

- **Lucien Freud (b. 1922).** Freud's portraits and marvelous nudes live in a depressing world of thick paint, fluid lines, and harsh light. The grandson of psychiatrist Sigmund Freud, the artist has pieces in London, Liverpool, and Manchester's **Whitworth Art Gallery.**

- **David Hockney (b. 1937).** The closest thing to a British Andy Warhol, Hockney employs a less pop-arty style than the famous American—though Hockney does reference modern technologies and culture—and is much more playful with artistic traditions. His work resides in London and Liverpool.

- **Damien Hirst (b. 1965).** The guy who pickles cows, Hirst is a celebrity/artist whose work sets out to shock. He's a winner of Britain's Turner Prize, and his work is prominent in the collection of Charles Saatchi, whose Saatchi Gallery in London displays his holdings.

2 Architecture 101

While each architectural era has its distinctive features, there are some elements, floor plans, and terms common to many. This is particularly true of churches, large numbers of which were built in Europe from the Middle Ages through the 18th century.

From the Norman period on, most **churches** consist either of a single wide **aisle** or a wide central **nave** flanked by two narrower aisles. The aisles are separated from the nave by a row of **columns,** or square stacks of masonry called **piers,** connected by **arches.** Sometimes—especially in the medieval Norman and Gothic eras—there is a second level to the nave, above these arches (and hence above the low roof over the aisles) punctuated by windows called a **clerestory.**

This main nave/aisle assemblage is usually crossed by a perpendicular corridor called a **transept** near the far, east end of the church so that the floor plan looks like a **Latin Cross** (shaped like a crucifix). The shorter, east arm of the nave is called the **chancel;** it often houses the **altar** and stalls of the

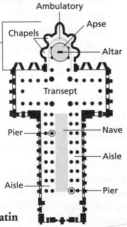

Church Floor Plan

choir. Some churches use a **rood screen** (so called because it supports a *rood*, the Saxon word for *crucifixion*) to separate the nave from the chancel. If the far end of the chancel is rounded off, it is called an **apse.** An **ambulatory** is a curving corridor outside the altar and choir area, separating it from the ring of smaller chapels radiating off the chancel and apse.

Some churches, especially after the Renaissance when mathematical proportion became important, were built on a **Greek Cross** plan, with each axis the same length like a giant plus sign (+).

It's worth pointing out that very few buildings (especially churches) were built in only one particular style. Massive, expensive structures often took centuries to complete, during which time tastes would change and plans would be altered.

NORMAN (1066–1200)

Aside from a smattering of ancient sights—**pre-classical** stone circles as at Stonehenge and Avebury and **Roman** ruins such as the Bath spa and Hadrian's Wall—the oldest surviving architectural style in England dates to when the 1066 Norman Conquest brought the Romanesque era to Britain, where it flourished as the **Norman** style.

Churches in this style were large, with wide naves and aisles to accommodate the masses who came to hear Mass and worship at the altars of various saints. But to support the weight of all that masonry, the walls had to be thick and solid (meaning they could be pierced only by few and small windows) and rest on huge piers, giving Norman churches a dark, somber, mysterious, and often oppressive feeling.

IDENTIFIABLE FEATURES
- **Rounded arches.** These load-bearing architectural devices allowed the architects to open up wide naves and spaces, channeling all the weight of the stone walls and ceilings across the curves of the arches and down into the ground via the columns or pilasters.
- **Thick walls.**
- **Infrequent and small windows.**
- **Huge piers.** These load-bearing, vertical features resemble square stacks of masonry.
- **Chevrons.** These zigzagging decorations often surround a doorway or wrap around a column.

BEST EXAMPLES
- **White Tower, London (1078).** William the Conqueror's first building in Britain, White Tower is the central keep of the Tower of London. The fortress-thick walls and rounded archways are textbook Norman.
- **Durham Cathedral (1093–1488).** The layout is Norman, save for the proto-Gothic, pointy rib vaulting along the nave. The massive piers are incised with chevrons.

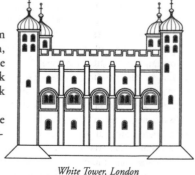

White Tower, London

- **Ely Cathedral (1083–1189).** The nave and south transept are perfectly Norman, though much of the rest of the interior is as Gothic as the exterior.

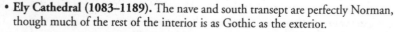

GOTHIC (1150–1550)

The French Gothic style invaded England in the late 12th century, trading rounded arches for pointy ones—an engineering discovery that freed church architecture from the heavy, thick walls of Norman structures and allowed ceilings to soar, walls to thin, and windows to proliferate.

Instead of dark, somber, relatively unadorned Norman interiors that forced the eyes of the faithful toward the altar where the priest stood droning on in unintelligible Latin, the Gothic interior enticed the churchgoers' gaze upward to high ceilings filled with light. While the priests conducted Mass in Latin, the peasants could "read" the Gothic comic books of stained-glass windows.

The squat, brooding exteriors of the Norman fortresses of God were replaced by graceful buttresses and soaring spires, which rose from town centers like beacons of religion.

The Gothic proper in Britain can be divided into three overlapping periods or styles: **Early English** (1150–1300), **Decorated** (1250–1370), and **Perpendicular** (1350–1550). While they all share some identifiable features (see the next section), others are characteristic of the individual periods.

Gothic style proved hard to kill in Britain. It would make comebacks in the 17th century as **Laudian Gothic** in some Oxford and Cambridge buildings, in the late 18th century as **rococo** or **Strawberry Hill Gotick** at Lacock Abbey, and in the 19th-century **Victorian Gothic revival,** discussed later.

IDENTIFIABLE FEATURES

- **Pointed arches (all periods).** The most significant development of the Gothic era was the discovery that pointed arches could carry far more weight than rounded ones.
- **Cross vaults (all periods).** Instead of being flat, the square patch of ceiling between four columns arches up to a point in the center, creating four sail shapes, sort of like the underside of a pyramid. The "X" separating these four sails is often reinforced with ridges called **ribbing.** As the Gothic era progressed, four-sided cross vaults became **fan vaults** (see below), and the spaces between the structural ribbing were spanned with decorative **tracery** (see below).

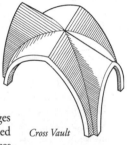

Cross Vault

- **Flying buttresses (all periods).** These free-standing exterior pillars connected by graceful, thin arms of stone help channel the weight of the building and its roof out and down into the ground. Not every Gothic church has evident buttresses.
- **Dogtooth molding (Early English).** Bands of a repeated decoration of four triangle-shaped petals are placed around a raised center.
- **Lancet windows (Early English).** Tall, thin, pointy windows, often in pairs or multiples, are all set into a larger, elliptical pointy arch.
- **Tracery (Decorated and Perpendicular).** These delicate, lacy spider webs of carved stone grace the pointy ends of windows and the acute lower intersections of **cross vaults** (see above).
- **Fan vaults (Perpendicular).** Lots of side-by-side, cone-shaped, concave vaults springing from the same point, fan vaults are usually covered in tracery (see above).

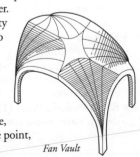

Fan Vault

- **An emphasis on horizontal and vertical lines (Perpendicular).** What defines the Perpendicular is its broad and rectilinear fashion, especially in the windows.
- **Mullioned, transomed windows (Perpendicular).** Perpendicular windows tend to be wide, under flattened arches, with their bulk divided into dozens of tiny pointed panes by **mullions** (vertical bars) and **transoms** (horizontal bars). This cage-like motif often carries over to the decoration on the walls as well.
- **Stained glass (all periods but more common later).** The multitude and size of Gothic windows allowed them to be filled with Bible stories and symbolism writ in the colorful patterns of stained glass. The use of stained glass was more common in the later Gothic periods.
- **Rose windows (all periods).** These huge circular windows, often appearing as the centerpieces of facades, are filled with elegant **tracery** (see above) and "petals" of stained glass.
- **Spires (all periods).** These pinnacles of masonry seem to defy gravity and reach toward heaven itself.
- **Gargoyles (all periods).** Disguised as wide-mouthed creatures or human heads, gargoyles are actually drain spouts.
- **Choir screen (all periods).** Serving as the inner wall of the ambulatory and outer wall of the choir section, the choir screen is often decorated with carvings or tombs.

BEST EXAMPLES

- **Early English: Salisbury Cathedral** (1220–65) is unique in Europe for the speed with which it was built and the uniformity of its architecture. (Even if the spire was added 100 years later, it was kept Early English.) The first to use pointy arches was **Wells Cathedral** (1180–1321), which has 300 statues on its original facade and some early stained glass.
- **Decorated:** The facade, nave, and chapter house of **York Minster** (1220–1480), which preserves the most medieval stained glass in Britain, are Decorated, though the chancel is Perpendicular and the transepts are Early English. **Exeter Cathedral** (1112–1206) has an elaborate Decorated facade and fantastic nave vaulting.
- **Perpendicular: King's College Chapel at Cambridge** (1446–1515) has England's most magnificent fan vaulting, along with some fine stained glass. **Henry VII's Chapel** (1503–19) in London's Westminster Abbey is textbook Perpendicular.

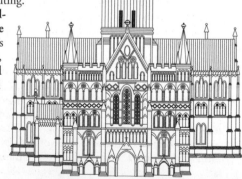

Salisbury Cathedral

RENAISSANCE (1550–1650)

While the Continent was experimenting with the Renaissance ideals of proportion, order, classical inspiration, and mathematical precision to create unified and balanced structures, England was still trundling along with the late **Tudor Gothic** Perpendicular style (the Tudor use of redbrick became a major feature of later Gothic revivals) in places such as Hampton Court Palace and Bath Abbey (great fan vaulting).

It wasn't until the Elizabethan era that the Brits turned to the **Renaissance** style sweeping the Continent. England's greatest Renaissance architect, **Inigo Jones** (1573–1652), brought back from his Italian travels a fevered imagination full of the exactingly classical theories of **Palladianism,** a style derived from the buildings and publications of **Andrea Palladio** (1508–80). However, most English architects of this time tempered the Renaissance style with a heavy dose of Gothic-like elements.

IDENTIFIABLE FEATURES

- **Sense of proportion.**
- **Reliance on symmetry.**
- **Use of classical orders.** This specifies three different column capitals: Corinthian, Ionic, and Doric.

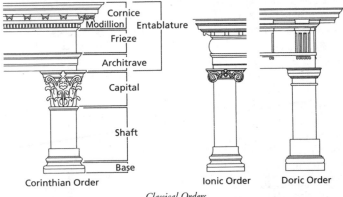

Classical Orders

BEST EXAMPLES

- **Robert Smythson (1535–1614).** This early Elizabethan architect was responsible for two of the greatest mansions of the period: **Hardwick Hall** (1590–97) in Derbyshire, virtually abandoned and therefore wonderfully preserved (if a bit dilapidated) in its 16th-century condition; and **Longleat House** (1559–80), an elegant Wiltshire manse with a park designed by Renaissance landscape architect and garden designer **Capability Brown.**
- **Inigo Jones (1573–1652).** Jones applied his theories of Palladianism to such edifices as **Queen's House** (1616–18 and 1629–35) in Greenwich; the **Queen's Chapel** (1623–25) in St. James's Palace and the **Banqueting House** (1619–22) in Whitehall, both in London; and the staterooms of Wiltshire's **Wilton House** (1603), where Shakespeare performed and D-day was planned. Recently, London's **Shakespeare's Globe Theatre** dusted off one of his never-realized plans and used it to construct their new indoor theatre annex.

BAROQUE (1650–1750)

England's greatest architect was **Christopher Wren** (1632–1723), a scientist and member of Parliament who got the job of rebuilding London after the Great Fire of 1666. He designed 53 replacement churches alone, plus the new St. Paul's Cathedral and numerous other projects. Other proponents of baroque architecture were **John Vanbrugh** (1664–1726) and his mentor and oft collaborator, **Nicholas Hawksmoor** (1661–1736), who sometimes worked in a more Palladian idiom.

IDENTIFIABLE FEATURES

- **Classical architecture rewritten with curves.** The baroque is similar to the Renaissance style, but many of the right angles and ruler-straight lines are exchanged for curves of complex geometry and an interplay of concave and convex surfaces. The overall effect is to lighten the appearance of structures and to add some movement of line.
- **Complex decoration.** Unlike the sometimes severe designs of the Renaissance and other classically inspired styles, the baroque was often playful and apt to festoon structures with decorations intended to liven things up.

BEST EXAMPLES

- **St. Paul's Cathedral, London (1676–1710).** This cathedral is the crowning achievement of both English baroque and of Christopher Wren himself. London's other main Wren attraction is the **Royal Naval College,** Greenwich (1696).
- **Queen's College, Sheldonian Theatre, and Radcliffe Camera, Oxford. Queen's College** is the only campus of Oxford constructed entirely in one style, and it includes a library by Hawksmoor. The **Sheldonian Theatre** (1664–69), an almost classically subdued rotunda showing little of later baroque exuberance, was Wren's first crack at architecture. Compare this to the more baroque **Radcliffe Camera** (1737–49), designed by James Gibbs (1662–1754), who influenced Thomas Jefferson.
- **Blenheim Palace, Woodstock (early 1700s).** John Vanbrugh's crowning achievement, Blenheim Palace is a British Versailles surrounded by perhaps the best of Capability Brown's gardens.
- **Castle Howard, Yorkshire (1699–1726).** Another masterpiece by the team of Nicholas Hawksmoor and then-neophyte John Vanbrugh, Castle Howard became famous as a backdrop to *Brideshead Revisited.*

NEOCLASSICAL & GREEK REVIVAL (1714–1837)

Many 18th-century architects cared little for the baroque period, and during the Georgian era (1714–1830) a restrained, simple **neoclassicism** reigned. It was balanced between a resurgence of the precepts of Palladianism (see "Renaissance [1550–1650]," above) and an even more distilled vision of classical theory called **Greek revival.** This latter style was practiced by architects such as **James "Athenian" Stuart** (1713–88), who wrote a book on antiquities after a trip to Greece, and the somewhat less strict **John Soane** (1773–1837).

IDENTIFIABLE FEATURES

- **Mathematical proportion, symmetry, classical orders.** These classical ideals first rediscovered during the Renaissance are the hallmark of every classically styled era.

- **Crescents and circuses.** The Georgians were famous for these seamless curving rows of identical stone town houses with tall windows, each one simple yet elegant inside.
- **Open double-arm staircases.** This feature was a favorite of the neo-Palladians.

BEST EXAMPLES
- **Bath (1727–75).** Much of the city of Bath was made over in the 18th century, most famously by the father-and-son team of **John Woods, Sr., and Jr.** (1704–54 and 1728–81, respectively). They were responsible, among others, for the **Royal Crescent** (1767–75), where you can visit one house's interior and even lodge in another.

Royal Crescent, Bath

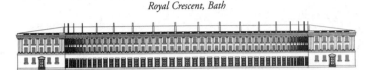

- **John Soane's London sights.** The best Greek revival building by Soane in London is his own idiosyncratic house (1812–13), now **Sir John Soane's Museum.** Of his most famous commission, the **Bank of England** (1732–34) in Bartholomew Lane, only the facade survived a 20th-century restructuring.
- **British Museum, London (1823).** Not the most important example of Greek revival, the British Museum, by Robert and Sidney Smirke, is nevertheless one that just about every visitor to England is bound to see.

VICTORIAN GOTHIC REVIVAL (1750–1900)
While neoclassicists were sticking to their guns in Bath, the early romantic movement swept up others with rosy visions of the past. This imaginary and fairy-tale version of the Middle Ages led to such creative developments as the pre-Raphaelite painters (see "The Romantics," earlier in this chapter) and Gothic revival architects, who really got a head of steam under their movement during the eclectic Victorian era.

Gothic "revival" is a bit misleading, as its practitioners usually applied their favorite Gothic features at random rather than faithfully re-created a whole structure. Aside from this eclecticism, you can separate the revivals from the originals by age (Victorian buildings are several hundred years younger and tend to be in considerably better shape) and size (the revivals are often much larger).

IDENTIFIABLE FEATURES
- **Mishmash of Gothic features.** Look at the features described under "Gothic," earlier in this chapter, and then imagine going on a shopping spree through them at random.
- **Eclecticism.** Few Victorians bothered with correctly rendering all the formal details of a particular Gothic era. They just wanted the overall effect to be pointy, busy with decorations, and terribly medieval.
- **Grand scale.** These buildings tend to be very, very large. This was usually accomplished by using Gothic style only on the surface, with newfangled industrial-age engineering underneath.

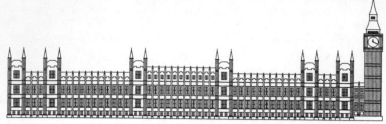

Palace of Westminster, LondonPalace of Westminster, London

BEST EXAMPLES

- **Palace of Westminster (Houses of Parliament), London (1835–52).** Charles Barry (1795–1860) designed the wonderful British seat of government in a Gothic idiom that, more than most, sticks pretty faithfully to the old Perpendicular period's style. His clock tower, usually called "Big Ben" after its biggest bell, has become an icon of London itself.
- **Albert Memorial, London (1863–72).** In 1861, Queen Victoria commissioned George Gilbert Scott (1811–78) to build this massive (and outlandish) Gothic canopy to memorialize her beloved husband.
- **Natural History Museum, London (1873–81).** The Natural History Museum is a delightful marriage of imposing neo-Gothic clothing hiding an industrial-age steel-and-iron framework, courtesy of architect Alfred Waterhouse (1830–1905).

THE 20TH CENTURY

For the first half of the 20th century, England was too busy expanding into suburbs (in an architecturally uninteresting way) and fighting World Wars to pay much attention to architecture. After the Blitz during World War II, much of central London had to be rebuilt. Most of the new commercial buildings in the city held to a functional school of architecture aptly named Brutalism. It wasn't until the boom of the late 1970s and 1980s that **postmodern** architecture gave British architects a bold, new direction.

IDENTIFIABLE FEATURES

- **Skyscraper motif.** Glass and steel as high as you can stack it.
- **Reliance on historical details.** Like the Victorians, postmodernists recycled elements from architectural history, from classical to exotic.

BEST EXAMPLES

- **Lloyd's Building, London (1978–86).** Lloyd's is *the* British postmodern masterpiece by Richard Rogers (b. 1933), who had a hand in Paris's funky Centre Pompidou.
- **Canary Wharf Tower, London (1986).** Britain's tallest building, by César Pelli (b. 1926), is the postmodern centerpiece of the Canary Wharf office complex and commercial development.
- **Charing Cross, London (1991).** Whimsical designer Terry Farrell (b. 1938) capped the famous old train station with an enormous postmodern office-and-shopping complex in glass and pale stone.

Canary Wharf Tower, London

Appendix C: Useful Toll-Free Numbers & Websites

U.S. AIRLINES
Note: Asterisk (*) denotes airlines with international flights.

Alaska Airlines/Horizon Air
℗ 800/252-7522
www.alaskaair.com

American Airlines *
℗ 800/433-7300 (in U.S. and Canada)
℗ 020/7365-0777 (in U.K.)
www.aa.com

ATA Airlines
℗ 800/435-9282
www.ata.com

Cape Air
℗ 800/352-0714
www.flycapeair.com

Continental Airlines *
℗ 800/523-3273 (in U.S. and Canada)
℗ 084/5607-6760 (in U.K.)
www.continental.com

Delta Air Lines *
℗ 800/221-1212 (in U.S. and Canada)
℗ 084/5600-0950 (in U.K.)
www.delta.com

Frontier Airlines
℗ 800/432-1359
www.frontierairlines.com

Hawaiian Airlines *
℗ 800/367-5320 (in U.S. and Canada)
www.hawaiianair.com

JetBlue Airways
℗ 800/538-2583 (in U.S.)
℗ 080/1365-2525 (in U.K. and Canada)
www.jetblue.com

Midwest Airlines
℗ 800/452-2022
www.midwestairlines.com

North American Airlines *
℗ 800/371-6297
www.flynaa.com

Nantucket Airlines
℗ 800/635-8787
www.nantucketairlines.com

Northwest Airlines
℗ 800/225-2525 (in U.S.)
℗ 870/0507-4074 (in U.K.)
www.flynaa.com

Pan Am Clipper Connection
© 800/359-7262
www.flypanam.com

PenAir (The Spirit of Alaska)
© 800/448-4226 (in U.S.)
www.penair.com

Skybus
© no phone
www.skybus.com

INTERNATIONAL AIRLINES

Aeroméxico
© 800/237-6639 (in U.S.)
© 020/7801-6234 (in U.K., information only)
www.aeromexico.com

Air France
© 800/237-2747 (in U.S.)
© 800/375-8723 (U.S. and Canada)
© 087/0142-4343 (in U.K.)
www.airfrance.com

Air India
© 212/407-1371 (in U.S.)
© 91 22 2279 6666 (in India)
© 020/8745-1000 (in U.K.)
www.airindia.com

Air Jamaica
© 800/523-5585 (in U.S. and Canada)
© 208/570-7999 (in Jamaica)
www.airjamaica.com

Air New Zealand
© 800/262-1234 (in U.S.)
© 800/663-5494 (in Canada)
© 0800/028-4149 (in U.K.)
www.airnewzealand.com

Air Tahiti Nui
© 877/824-4846 (in U.S. and Canada)
www.airtahitinui-usa.com

Alitalia
© 800/223-5730 (in U.S.)
© 800/361-8336 (in Canada)
© 087/0608-6003 (in U.K.)
www.alitalia.com

United Airlines *
© 800/864-8331 (in U.S. and Canada)
© 084/5844-4777 in U.K.
www.united.com

US Airways *
© 800/428-4322 (in U.S. and Canada)
© 084/5600-3300 (in U.K.)
www.usairways.com

Virgin America *
© 877/359-8474
www.virginamerica.com

American Airlines
© 800/433-7300 (in U.S. and Canada)
© 020/7365-0777 (in U.K.)
www.aa.com

Aviacsa (Mexico and southern U.S.)
www.aviacsa.com.mx

Bahamasair
© 800/222-4262 (in U.S.)
© 242/300-8359 (in Family Islands)
© 242/377-5505 (in Nassau)
www.bahamasair.com

British Airways
© 800/247-9297 (in U.S. and Canada)
© 087/0850-9850 (in U.K.)
www.british-airways.com

Caribbean Airlines (formerly BWIA)
© 800/920-4225 (in U.S. and Canada)
© 084/5362 4225 (in U.K.)
www.caribbean-airlines.com

China Airlines
© 800/227-5118 (in U.S.)
© 022/715-1212 (in Taiwan)
www.china-airlines.com

Continental Airlines
© 800/523-3273 (in U.S. and Canada)
© 084/5607-6760 (in U.K.)
www.continental.com

Cubana
© 888/667-1222 (in Canada)
© 020/7538-5933 (in U.K.)
www.cubana.cu

Delta Air Lines
☎ 800/221-1212 (in U.S. and Canada)
☎ 084/5600-0950 (in U.K.)
www.delta.com

EgyptAir
☎ 212/581-5600 (in U.S.)
☎ 020/7734-2343 (in U.K.)
☎ 09/007-0000 (in Egypt)
www.egyptair.com

El Al Airlines
☎ 972/3977-1111 (outside Israel)
☎ *2250 (from any phone in Israel)
www.elal.co.il

Emirates Airlines
☎ 800/777-3999 (in U.S.)
☎ 087/0243-2222 (in U.K.)
www.emirates.com

Finnair
☎ 800/950-5000 (in U.S. and Canada)
☎ 087/0241-4411 (in U.K.)
www.finnair.com

Hawaiian Airlines
☎ 800/367-5320 (in U.S. and Canada)
www.hawaiianair.com

Iberia Airlines
☎ 800/722-4642 (in U.S. and Canada)
☎ 087/0609-0500 (in U.K.)
www.iberia.com

Icelandair
☎ 800/223-5500, ext. 2, prompt 1
(in U.S. and Canada)
☎ 084/5758-1111 (in U.K.)
www.icelandair.com
www.icelandair.co.uk (in U.K.)

Israir Airlines
☎ 877/477-2471 (in U.S. and Canada)
☎ 700/505-777 (in Israel)
www.israirairlines.com

Japan Airlines
☎ 012/025-5931 (international)
www.jal.co.jp

Korean Air
☎ 800/438-5000 (in U.S. and Canada)
☎ 0800/413-000 (in U.K.)
www.koreanair.com

Lan Airlines
☎ 866/435-9526 (in U.S.)
☎ 305/670-9999 (in other countries)
www.lanchile.com

Lufthansa
☎ 800/399-5838 (in U.S.)
☎ 800/563-5954 (in Canada)
☎ 087/0837-7747 (in U.K.)
www.lufthansa.com

North American Airlines
☎ 800/359-6222
www.flynaa.com

Olympic Airlines
☎ 800/223-1226 (in U.S.)
☎ 514/878-9691 (in Canada)
☎ 087/0606-0460 (in U.K.)
www.olympicairlines.com

Qantas Airways
☎ 800/227-4500 (in U.S.)
☎ 084/5774-7767 (in U.K. and Canada)
☎ 13 13 13 (in Australia)
www.qantas.com

Philippine Airlines
☎ 800/I-Fly-Pal (800/435-9725)
(in U.S. and Canada)
☎ 632/855-8888 (in Philippines)
www.philippineairlines.com

South African Airways
☎ 271/1978-5313 (international)
☎ 0861 FLYSAA (086/135-9122)
(in South Africa)
www.flysaa.com

Swiss Air
☎ 877/359-7947 (in U.S. and Canada)
☎ 084/5601-0956 (in U.K.)
www.swiss.com

TACA
☎ 800/535-8780 (in U.S.)
☎ 800/722-TACA (8222) (in Canada)
☎ 087/0241-0340 (in U.K.)
☎ 503/2267-8222 (in El Salvador)

Thai Airways International
☎ 212/949-8424 (in U.S.)
☎ 020/7491-7953 (in U.K.)
www.thaiair.com

Turkish Airlines
© 90 212 444 0 849
www.thy.com

United Airlines *
© 800/864-8331 (in U.S. and Canada)
© 084/5844-4777 (in U.K.)
www.united.com

BUDGET AIRLINES

Aegean Airlines
© 210/626-1000 (in U.S., Canada and U.K.)
www.aegeanair.com

Aer Lingus
© 800/474-7424 (in U.S. and Canada)
© 087/0876-5000 (in U.K.)
www.aerlingus.com

Aero California
© 800/237-6225 (in U.S. and Mexico)
www.aerocalifornia.com.mx

AirTran Airways
© 800/247-8726
www.airtran.com

Air Berlin
© 087/1500-0737 (in U.K.)
© 018/0573-7800 (in Germany)
© 180/573-7800 (all others)
www.airberlin.com

ATA Airlines
© 800/435-9282
www.ata.com

Avolar
© 888/3-AVOLAR (800/326-8527) (in U.S.)
© 800/21-AVOLAR (800/326-8527) (in Mexico)
© 086/6370-4065 (in U.K.)
www.avolar.com.mx

BMI Baby
© 087/1224-0224 (in U.K.)
© 870/126-6726 (in U.S.)
www.bmibaby.com

US Airways *
© 800/428-4322 (in U.S. and Canada)
© 084/5600-3300 (in U.K.)
www.usairways.com

Virgin Atlantic Airways
© 800/821-5438 (in U.S. and Canada)
© 087/0574-7747 (in U.K.)
www.virgin-atlantic.com

Click Mexicana
© 800/11-click (800/112-5425) (international)
© 800/112-5425 (in Mexico)
www.clickmx.com

easyJet
© 870/600-0000 (in U.S.)
© 090/5560-7777 (in U.K.)
www.easyjet.com

Frontier Airlines
© 800/432-1359
www.frontierairlines.com

go!
© 888/435-9462
www.iflygo.com
(Hawaii based)

Interjet
© 800/101-2345
www.interjet.com.mx

JetBlue Airways
© 800/538-2583 (in U.S.)
© 801/365-2525 (in U.K. and Canada)
www.jetblue.com

Jetstar (Australia)
© 866/397-8170
www.jetstar.com

Ryanair
© 1 353 1 249 7700 (in U.S.)
© 081/830-3030 (in Ireland)
© 087/1246-0000 (in U.K.)
www.ryanair.com

Southwest Airlines
© 800/435-9792 (in U.S., U.K., and Canada)
www.southwest.com

Skybus
ⓒ no phone
www.skybus.com

Spirit Airlines
ⓒ 800/772-7117
www.spiritair.com

Ted (part of United Airlines)
ⓒ 800/225-5561
www.flyted.com

CAR RENTAL AGENCIES

Advantage
ⓒ 800/777-5500 (in U.S.)
ⓒ 021/0344-4712 (outside of U.S.)
www.advantagerentacar.com

Alamo
ⓒ 800/GO-ALAMO (800/462-5266)
www.alamo.com

Auto Europe
ⓒ 888/223-5555 (in U.S. and Canada)
ⓒ 0800/2235-5555 (in U.K.)
www.autoeurope.com

Avis
ⓒ 800/331-1212 (in U.S. and Canada)
ⓒ 084/4581-8181 (in U.K.)
www.avis.com

Budget
ⓒ 800/527-0700 (in U.S.)
ⓒ 087/0156-5656 (in U.K.)
ⓒ 800/268-8900 (in Canada)
www.budget.com

Dollar
ⓒ 800/800-4000 (in U.S.)
ⓒ 800/848-8268 (in Canada)
ⓒ 080/8234-7524 (in U.K.)
www.dollar.com

Enterprise
ⓒ 800/261-7331 (in U.S.)
ⓒ 514/355-4028 (in Canada)
ⓒ 012/9360-9090 (in U.K.)
www.enterprise.com

Volaris
ⓒ 866/988-3527
ⓒ 800/7-VOLARIS (800/786-5274) (in Mexico)
www.volaris.com.mx

WestJet
ⓒ 800/538-5696 (in U.S. and Canada)
www.westjet.com

Hertz
ⓒ 800/645-3131
ⓒ 800/654-3001 (for international reservations)
www.hertz.com

Kemwel (KHA)
ⓒ 877/820-0668
www.kemwel.com

National
ⓒ 800/CAR-RENT (800/227-7368)
www.nationalcar.com

Payless
ⓒ 800/PAYLESS (800/729-5377)
www.paylesscarrental.com

Rent-A-Wreck
ⓒ 800/535-1391
www.rentawreck.com

Thrifty
ⓒ 800/367-2277
ⓒ 918/669-2168 (international)
www.thrifty.com

Index

See also Accommodations and Restaurant indexes, below.

FROMMER'S® COMPLETE TRAVEL GUIDES

Alaska
Amalfi Coast
American Southwest
Amsterdam
Argentina
Arizona
Atlanta
Australia
Austria
Bahamas
Barcelona
Beijing
Belgium, Holland & Luxembourg
Belize
Bermuda
Boston
Brazil
British Columbia & the Canadian
  Rockies
Brussels & Bruges
Budapest & the Best of Hungary
Buenos Aires
Calgary
California
Canada
Cancún, Cozumel & the Yucatán
Cape Cod, Nantucket & Martha's
  Vineyard
Caribbean
Caribbean Ports of Call
Carolinas & Georgia
Chicago
Chile & Easter Island
China
Colorado
Costa Rica
Croatia
Cuba
Denmark
Denver, Boulder & Colorado Springs
Eastern Europe
Ecuador & the Galapagos Islands
Edinburgh & Glasgow
England
Europe
Europe by Rail

Florence, Tuscany & Umbria
Florida
France
Germany
Greece
Greek Islands
Guatemala
Hawaii
Hong Kong
Honolulu, Waikiki & Oahu
India
Ireland
Israel
Italy
Jamaica
Japan
Kauai
Las Vegas
London
Los Angeles
Los Cabos & Baja
Madrid
Maine Coast
Maryland & Delaware
Maui
Mexico
Montana & Wyoming
Montréal & Québec City
Morocco
Moscow & St. Petersburg
Munich & the Bavarian Alps
Nashville & Memphis
New England
Newfoundland & Labrador
New Mexico
New Orleans
New York City
New York State
New Zealand
Northern Italy
Norway
Nova Scotia, New Brunswick &
  Prince Edward Island
Oregon
Paris
Peru

Philadelphia & the Amish Country
Portugal
Prague & the Best of the Czech
  Republic
Provence & the Riviera
Puerto Rico
Rome
San Antonio & Austin
San Diego
San Francisco
Santa Fe, Taos & Albuquerque
Scandinavia
Scotland
Seattle
Seville, Granada & the Best of
  Andalusia
Shanghai
Sicily
Singapore & Malaysia
South Africa
South America
South Florida
South Korea
South Pacific
Southeast Asia
Spain
Sweden
Switzerland
Tahiti & French Polynesia
Texas
Thailand
Tokyo
Toronto
Turkey
USA
Utah
Vancouver & Victoria
Vermont, New Hampshire & Maine
Vienna & the Danube Valley
Vietnam
Virgin Islands
Virginia
Walt Disney World® & Orlando
Washington, D.C.
Washington State

FROMMER'S® DAY BY DAY GUIDES

Amsterdam
Barcelona
Beijing
Boston
Cancun & the Yucatan
Chicago
Florence & Tuscany

Hong Kong
Honolulu & Oahu
London
Maui
Montréal
Napa & Sonoma
New York City

Paris
Provence & the Riviera
Rome
San Francisco
Venice
Washington D.C.

PAULINE FROMMER'S GUIDES: SEE MORE. SPEND LESS.

Alaska
Hawaii
Italy

Las Vegas
London
New York City

Paris
Walt Disney World®
Washington D.C.

FROMMER'S® PORTABLE GUIDES

Acapulco, Ixtapa & Zihuatanejo
Amsterdam
Aruba, Bonaire & Curacao
Australia's Great Barrier Reef
Bahamas
Big Island of Hawaii
Boston
California Wine Country
Cancún
Cayman Islands
Charleston
Chicago
Dominican Republic

Florence
Las Vegas
Las Vegas for Non-Gamblers
London
Maui
Nantucket & Martha's Vineyard
New Orleans
New York City
Paris
Portland
Puerto Rico
Puerto Vallarta, Manzanillo &
  Guadalajara

Rio de Janeiro
San Diego
San Francisco
Savannah
St. Martin, Sint Maarten, Anguila &
  St. Bart's
Turks & Caicos
Vancouver
Venice
Virgin Islands
Washington, D.C.
Whistler

FROMMER'S® CRUISE GUIDES

Alaska Cruises & Ports of Call

Cruises & Ports of Call

European Cruises & Ports of Call

FROMMER'S® NATIONAL PARK GUIDES

Algonquin Provincial Park
Banff & Jasper
Grand Canyon

National Parks of the American West
Rocky Mountain
Yellowstone & Grand Teton

Yosemite and Sequoia & Kings
  Canyon
Zion & Bryce Canyon

FROMMER'S® WITH KIDS GUIDES

Chicago
Hawaii
Las Vegas
London

National Parks
New York City
San Francisco

Toronto
Walt Disney World® & Orlando
Washington, D.C.

FROMMER'S® PHRASEFINDER DICTIONARY GUIDES

Chinese
French

German
Italian

Japanese
Spanish

SUZY GERSHMAN'S BORN TO SHOP GUIDES

France
Hong Kong, Shanghai & Beijing
Italy

London
New York
Paris

San Francisco
Where to Buy the Best of Everything.

FROMMER'S® BEST-LOVED DRIVING TOURS

Britain
California
France
Germany

Ireland
Italy
New England
Northern Italy

Scotland
Spain
Tuscany & Umbria

THE UNOFFICIAL GUIDES®

Adventure Travel in Alaska
Beyond Disney
California with Kids
Central Italy
Chicago
Cruises
Disneyland®
England
Hawaii

Ireland
Las Vegas
London
Maui
Mexico's Best Beach Resorts
Mini Mickey
New Orleans
New York City
Paris

San Francisco
South Florida including Miami &
  the Keys
Walt Disney World®
Walt Disney World® for
  Grown-ups
Walt Disney World® with Kids
Washington, D.C.

SPECIAL-INTEREST TITLES

Athens Past & Present
Best Places to Raise Your Family
Cities Ranked & Rated
500 Places to Take Your Kids Before They Grow Up
Frommer's Best Day Trips from London
Frommer's Best RV & Tent Campgrounds in the U.S.A.

Frommer's Exploring America by RV
Frommer's NYC Free & Dirt Cheap
Frommer's Road Atlas Europe
Frommer's Road Atlas Ireland
Retirement Places Rated

CLOSED
due to
accidental demolition

WEGEN BISSIGEN
EICHHÖRNCHEN GESCHLOSSEN

CERRADO

CABRAS

Κλειστό
Μετεωρίτες

POOL CLOSED

プール も, ELECTRIC EELS 閉
鎖
中

Hotel
closed for
facelifting

FERMÉ POUR
RAISON
DE GRÈVE
DES BONNES

FECHADO!
POR CAUSA DE
ATAQUES DOS CROCODILOS

— I don't speak
sign language.

A hotel can close for all kinds of reasons.
Our Guarantee ensures that if your hotel's undergoing construction, we'll
let you know in advance. In fact, we cover your entire travel experience.
See www.travelocity.com/guarantee for details.

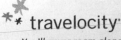

***** travelocity*

You'll never roam alone.

There's a parking lot where my ocean view should be.

 À la place de la vue sur l'océan, me voilà avec une vue sur un parking.

 Anstatt Meerblick habe ich Sicht auf einen Parkplatz.

 Al posto della vista sull'oceano c'è un parcheggio.

 No tengo vista al mar porque hay un parque de estacionamiento.

 Há um parque de estacionamento onde deveria estar a minha vista do oceano.

 Ett parkeringsområde har byggts på den plats där min utsikt över oceanen borde vara.

 Er ligt een parkeerterrein waar mijn zee-uitzicht zou moeten zijn.

 هنالك موقف للسيارات مكان ما وجب ان يكون المنظر الخلاب المطل على المحيط .

 眼前に広がる紺碧の海・・・じゃない。窓の外は駐車場！

 停车场的位置应该是我的海景所在。

— I'm fluent in pig latin.

Hotel mishaps aren't bound by geography.
Neither is our Guarantee. It covers your entire travel experience, including the price. So if you don't get the ocean view you booked, we'll work with our travel partners to make it right, right away. See www.travelocity.com/guarantee for details.

travelocity
You'll never roam alone.